Trends that will determine the nature of the education of our grandchildren are already present in the 1970s. The purpose of this book is to examine them, so that parents and educators can more appropriately harness the growing technology of the classroom to the development of human potential. *Modern Trends in Education* was conceived as a series of key expositions by educational specialists who had been personally concerned with the promotion of new ideas and techniques. As it was developed, the book took on an international appearance until, at publication, its contributors had been drawn from America, Europe and Africa. In its present form it represents a fair canvas of the contemporary growing-points of educational endeavor.

The educational technology of the 1970s is an inevitable offshoot of the current revolution in electronics. But while careful attention has been paid to significant material of this sort, the editor has been concerned with the theoretical implications as well, since they provide the criteria which help us to differentiate fads from genuine developments. Recent research, for instance, has led to a fundamental reconsideration of the significance and use of intelligence measurements in our schools — a matter that must eventually lead to a reassessment of our present notions of streaming. Or again, the increased pressure for universal literacy in

ALSO BY BRIAN ROSE

The Broken Link
Education in Southern Africa
Lines of Action (co-author)
Modern Narrative Poetry (co-author)

MODERN TRENDS
IN EDUCATION

edited by

BRIAN ROSE

Ph.D., M.A., B.Ed., B.A. (Soc. Sc.)
Head, Department of Education,
Johannesburg College of Education

MACMILLAN

ST MARTIN'S PRESS

First published 1971 by
THE MACMILLAN PRESS LTD
London and Basingstoke
Associated companies in New York Toronto
Dublin Melbourne Johannesburg and Madras

SBN 333 01089 2

Library of Congress Catalogue Card Number 79–174706

Printed in Great Britain by
R. & R. CLARK LTD
Edinburgh

Contents

Introduction   vii

PART ONE:
MODERN TRENDS IN THE PRIMARY SCHOOL   1

1   The Purpose, Meaning and Future of i.t.a.
    Sir James Pitman   7
2   Reading Retardation
    Ernest W. Rayner   32
3   The Teaching of Elementary Mathematics
    Leonard Sealey   60
4   The Culturally Deprived Child
    Brian Rose   77

PART TWO:
MODERN TRENDS IN SECONDARY SCHOOL TEACHING   95

5   New Trends in Science Education
    John L. Lewis   101
6   Recent Developments in Second Language Teaching
    J. Donald Bowen   122
7   Programmed Instruction
    G. O. M. Leith   138

PART THREE:
MODERN TRENDS IN SUPPORT DISCIPLINES   173

8   The Meaning and Use of Intelligence in Modern
    Education
    John F. Lavach   179
9   The Influence of Group Research on Educational
    Practice
    R. K. Muir   196

10 Teaching Machines
   Gordon Pask 216

Bibliography 260
Notes on the Contributors 283
Index 287

Introduction

This book describes some of the new approaches to teaching that, during the 1960s, laid the foundations for further developments in the 1970s. It is concerned not only with what has come to be called the *hardware* of the technological revolution in teaching, but with the evidence that justifies our use of a variety of electronic equipment. It would, we contend, be inadvisable to accept any teaching machine without understanding something of the theory of programmed instruction that underlies its use. We have therefore not only surveyed the several contributions made to education through the electronic innovations but we have considered the valuable intellectual investment of men such as Piaget, Pask and Skinner, which made them possible.

Education itself is a strange compound of careful blueprinting and undirected growth that is at times completely adventitious. Throughout history its function to conserve values and skills from one generation to another has been counterpointed by the realisation of statesmen that a careful manipulation of the content and method of education can influence the future both ideologically and economically. Some communities have developed this teleological function by a completely centralised, authoritarian control of education. But the general tendency in Western Europe would seem to be towards an uneasy and sometimes inefficient balance between a central control justified by the provision of funds and the latent political power of parents that can be expressed through the local authority.

Inevitably, without a sort of Educational High Command, research in education is only minimally co-ordinated, and the pattern of new thinking is seldom either neat or orderly. This was noticeable when we came to report in this book the *growing points of contemporary education*. We found significant developments in mathematics and science but very little progress in our treatment of mother-tongue teaching. The impact of *communications studies* on the literary stagnation of mother-tongue teaching is – as yet – negligible. This sort of raggedness of format, whilst trying for the tidy-minded, is part of the reality of the educational scene.

In so far as the trends of the 1960s can be patterned, they achieve the following format:

1. *Trends evident in the primary school:*
   Studies in the causes and educational treatment of reading retardation.
   New approaches to the teaching of elementary mathematics.
   i.t.a.* as a solution of some of our problems of reading.
   Cultural deprivation as a source of educational retardation.

2. *Trends evident in the secondary school:*
   Increased pupil participation in the work of science.
   New strategies in second language teaching.
   Programmed instruction as an experimentally derived methodology.

3. *Trends in thinking closely related to education include:*
   Much new thought about the nature of intelligence.
   The application of small group theory to the ordinary classroom situation.
   Some important contributions from cybernetics – teaching machines, among others.

In retrospect, the 1960s showed our concern with cognitive skills and strategies. Except for work developed in *small group* research, little attention was devoted to urgent problems of emotional development and control. Although it is widely admitted that emotionally disturbed children are cognitively inefficient and neither learn easily nor retain their learning adequately, we have made little progress in helping them.

EDUCATION IN REVOLUTION

We may often be tempted to wonder whether our times are as revolutionary as we sometimes assert. Will our contemporary

---

* The Initial Teaching Alphabet, here referred to as i.t.a., is a recent innovation in education, having been designed by Sir James Pitman as an initial learning medium for the teaching of reading and writing to beginners of all ages.

teaching machines be relegated to history as a passing fad, of no greater general importance to the teachers of A.D. 2000 than Froebel's *First Building Box*'?

THE HUMAN EXPLOSION

1. All thinking people realise that our concept of *Man* must change if the population explosion continues. In a 'standing-room-only' world, the importance of the individual will diminish and his autonomy will be seriously threatened. One has to consider that in 1830 the world population stood at about 1000 million people. By the year A.D. 2000 – less than thirty years ahead – it will reach 6000 million. If it continues to double every thirty or forty years, our social problems will soon be alarming – and our educational problems almost insoluble. We find it difficult enough to provide adequate educational services in the 1970s, so our quandary with a doubled population in the lifetime of most readers of this book can be imagined.

THE EXPLOSION OF KNOWLEDGE

2. A second aspect of the contemporary social revolution is that knowledge is increasing at so fast a rate that few specialists can keep up with the progress in their own field. During the sixties a group of international scientists debated this problem, and the American physicist Robert Oppenheimer supported the view that most human knowledge could be expected to double itself every ten years. This would mean that if we took the world's total stock of knowledge up to 1960, *that stock* doubled itself by 1970. Recent discussions in America suggested that in fields such as electronics, a seven-year period might be more appropriate. These facts involve us in the problem of the obsolescence of human skills. Electronic theorists are often out of date by the age of 30. They must then submit themselves for retraining or move into the less specialised fields of administration.

YOUTH AS A WORLD POWER

But the population explosion is affecting our concepts of retraining. France has passed from being demographically one of the oldest countries in postwar Europe to being one of the youngest. François Nourissier in a recent survey of French society suggested that the only way to deal fairly with the *privilege of work* was to *limit* a person's working life to the ages between 20 and 40. With about 50 per cent of a population under 30 years of age, it will hardly be worthwhile retraining obsolescent human skills. At the same time it is clear that we shall during the 1970s begin to face the problem of tremendously increased numbers of pupils and students in secondary schools, colleges and universities, and our already extended teaching resources are likely to be strained beyond capacity altogether unless we reconsider the function of the teacher in education.

THE DEMAND FOR UNIVERSAL PRIMARY EDUCATION AS A BASIS FOR LITERACY

3. The third contribution to the revolution of our times is the demand for universal education. Only through a basic primary education can we provide that general literacy which is essential for a sophisticated industrial community. Even in advanced industrial countries such as Britain, the achievement of *effective* universal primary education imposes a very considerable strain on limited resources – and it is doubtful whether any experienced British educationist would claim that the degree of literacy (and hence of skill in communication) being achieved today is as satisfactory as one would wish. In underdeveloped countries where a universal primary education is seen as a panacea for many economic ills and where it has achieved considerable political implication as well, the problem is even more intransigent.

THE CHANGING IMAGE OF THE TEACHER

It would seem to be increasingly doubtful whether we can continue to accept the idea of the teacher as a sort of renaissance don, a modern

Commenius. The old idea of the teacher as *the giver of information*, the urbane scholar whose personal guidance provided something of the sort of discipleship of learning that was the basis of humanism – this no longer obtains in overcrowded popular education. We can no longer base a national educational policy on those elites that T. S. Eliot commended with such eloquence. We constitute a sophisticated industrial society, and if Servan Schreiber, the French economic commentator, is correct, one rapidly moving into a more complex phase. Such a society is based upon universal literacy as a minimum requirement for the exploitation of those human skills without which a nation would slowly stagnate. The concept of 'normal distribution' makes it clear that we are not *all* going to be scientists, managers, innovators or leaders of research. But recent developments in our understanding of the outcropping of superior mental skills in individuals should make us realise the unwisdom of assuming that such skills can always be forecast from previous parental performances. *Equality of educational opportunity*, then, is not merely demanded to satisfy our sense of moral justice, but it is essential if the full human resources of any community are to be developed. The stifling of such resources for whatever reason may result in critically detrimental economic and social consequences.

THE NEW TEACHER

There are a number of reasons why the urbane, scholarly information-giver was unlikely to survive in modern education, much though many of us may regret his passing. We have other ways of communicating information – books are in plentiful supply, library services are general and often efficient, there are films and other visual communication media available. In fact the old-fashioned lecturer who (as information-giver) reads his lecture to a group is usually being inefficient even in this function. Recent research has shown that most auditors can be expected to attend for between 20 and 40 per cent of the time. The need to organise pupil or student participation in the process of learning has been recognised over and over again in the course of educational history. But with the massive demands made on shrinking educational resources, we certainly cannot afford today to continue with methods that may contribute to 'drop-out' or to inefficiency. It is doubtful, for instance, whether many modern communities would claim that ten years' or more schooling makes the majority of *ordinary* pupils articulate. Indeed work done at the Welsh University at Cardiff has suggested that not only are graduates in the technologies often only *partially* literate, but arts students are frequently in not much better a state.

The growth of school populations in many parts of the world is forcing us to divide large groups of pupils into smaller groups, and to think out new ways of handling the learning situation. *Small group theory*, widely recognised in the United States, is contributing usefully here. But what is being changed is the function of the teacher. He becomes in the new dispensation more of a *manager of a learning situation* than a giver of information. He should be assessed not simply on his rhetoric or the theatrical skill of his presentation, but on his capacity to motivate pupils and so to control the situation which he has devised for them that maximum learning takes place. Much of his work takes place before and after any particular lesson. We can learn much about these implications from the underlying philosophy of programmed instruction, which is outlined succinctly later in this book. Of course one may never have occasion either to write or to use a programme. But a course in programmed instruction has one side-effect that is valuable – it provides the teacher with a methodological strategy, a useful working approach to lesson construction and assessment. As one wit remarked, 'Perhaps the "programmed teacher" is the most important result of this method.' In many ways teachers of mathematics and science have been able to accept the new educational format more easily than historians and language teachers. Science in particular is a subject that lends itself to small group work around laboratory benches, and active participation in scientific work is essential to learning.

Whether our current diagnoses are correct or not, it would seem that minimally 20 per cent of any school population in an urban industrial community do not benefit from current (and, perhaps, conservative) educational methods. To what extent these wastages are allied to deeper social stresses is another matter. But certainly the inefficiency and resultant sense of frustrated unhappiness that arises in schools because of a failure to achieve reading skills, together with a high degree of emotional blocking in the field of interpersonal relations, produces an appalling (if usually unrecognised) bill of wastage across the community. These two factors alone must contribute effectively to the costly tally of adolescent misfits who eventually retreat into drink or drugs – a sad commentary not only on educational failure in the schools, but in the broader context of a society unable to maintain direction in a period of violent change. Studies of the child with reading disabilities – of which dyslexia is merely a form – and of the deprived child have been included so that we can understand the nature and origin of some of the problems that teachers face later. It is only when the theoretical nature of such problems is correctly delineated that one can effectively consider new teaching approaches.

OUR CONTRIBUTORS

All the contributors to *Modern Trends in Education* are close to the growing-points of educational development. In these times hardly anyone can claim sole invention. Everyone recognises the unique role that Sir James Pitman has played in the promotion of i.t.a., for instance; but the development of i.t.a. as a widespread educational innovation was not accomplished single-handed, as Sir James would be the first to admit, although without his enthusiasm it would hardly have acquired the interest it enjoys today. The same could be said about the important contributions made by Dr Pask to cybernetics. In this field he is highly regarded far beyond his native Britain, and he is certainly one of a band of seminal thinkers. All contributors to this book are in much the same position: they have been closely associated with the early stages of a particular development which they have helped to some extent to influence in their particular community. Perhaps this is as close to the fountain-head as one should hope to get. It is because many of us feel that during the seventies the massive social stresses that are at present convulsing society all over the world will force each of us to review our methods and approaches in education, that the making of this book seemed important. It is an attempt to survey a body of developing skills and strategies which will increasingly be needed in the classrooms of the future.

B. W. R.

Part One

MODERN TRENDS IN THE PRIMARY SCHOOL

Western society has produced further strains on our primary school system and many of us feel that we must soon reconsider the effectiveness of our current primary school system and the relevancy of much that we are attempting to teach in it.

If there is one thing that a study of present-day trends show, it is that in these uncertain times all 'formula education' is of dubious value. To train tomorrow's men and women to think in yesterday's clichés — whether economic, political or social — is to betray them.

Dr Brian Rose is Head of the Department of Education at Johannesburg College of Education. He was awarded an Oppenheimer Grant to study technological advances in Britain in 1962, and the U.S.A.– South Africa Leader Exchange in 1964–5. He lectured in communications and programmed instruction in Massachusetts in 1968–9.

His publications include: *Education in Southern Africa, The Broken Link* (a study in drug addiction) and *Modern Narrative Poetry.*

In this section we examine important changes in educational strategy that concern the child's introduction to word and number. We consider the effects of his home and neighbourhood on his emotional health, and how (in its turn) this may affect his ability to learn.

Everyone would agree that the 3 R's continue to provide the educational basis from which primary and secondary school work is developed. Few would quarrel with the contention that today educators are uncomfortably aware that far too many children leave our schools only partially literate and, to a considerable extent, mathematically incompetent. This is not to say that they are unable to read, write or count, but it certainly does imply that as adults many people use both word and number inefficiently, thus reducing both their economic and social potential. As a failure in our educational system, it represents a multimillion wastage.

During the 1960s we began to focus educational attention on some of the key-points of our problem. The illogicalities of the English language as a tool for the thought of millions has long been recognised. Indeed, of all modern languages, English shows the least predictable correspondence of sign and sound and a number of earlier unsuccessful attempts to introduce a new orthography failed before Sir James Pitman won over sufficient support to make possible the widespread introduction of i.t.a. – no small achievement in a pedagogy that had, in this instance, shown very little change for centuries. Sir James presents the problem and his solution with acuity; but what is perhaps of even greater importance, he has intentionally stimulated research into the problems of learner readers and a by-product of spirited promotion of i.t.a. has been a series of independent research checks into the validity of his claims. Aware of the sign confusion so often experienced in English (as in the example of upper and lower case E and e), of the use of the same sign to carry different sounds (consider the a in rat and raw), can we ever again maintain that anything is 'as simple as learning the ABC'?

The reader will find many questions presenting themselves as Sir James outlines his case. Won't the child experience difficulty in converting to the conventional orthography, for instance? May not i.t.a. harm the child's ability to spell at a later stage? Sir James discusses a number of similar issues and points to current research findings.

The problem of reading retardation is not a simple one based on a confusing orthography. Certain children, conservatively estimated at 10 per cent of the school-going population, have particular difficulties with the written word. Educators have used a number of verbal labels to describe reading disability, including dyslexia and word blindness. Anyone who has studied the literature may well have wished that experts would settle their nomenclature and at the same time reach general agreement on the meaning of their terms. The problem of reading retardation in education is difficult enough without these procedural confusions. We are by no means agreed as to whether we are dealing basically with an inherited deficit, one that is primarily physiological (whether due to innate or environmental causes) or one that is largely environmentally induced. Possibly later research will reveal a multivariate causation. At present we seem to a considerable extent to apply a blanket educational therapy, despite the fact that we tend increasingly to reserve the term dyslexia for those reading disabilities that stem primarily from innate causes such as anoxia, brain damage due to physical trauma or certain diseases, as well as children suffering from some innate deficit of perceptual organisation. The problem of reasonably accurate diagnosis, because it involves costly and skilful specialist medical resources, is a major one.

The implications of serious reading disability are manifold: constant failure to acquire a 'tool' subject may have a disastrous emotional effect on the child's attitude both to school and to learning. Negatively conditioned from the start, he all too easily becomes a back-row dreamer, an occasional truant or an aggressive behaviour problem. He is caught in a network of personal inadequacies which offer him a series of dissatisfactions that result in a shrinkage of his personality and self-confidence. We know that strong emotional states may reduce the range of human perception, and there is evidence that the anxiety and guilt originating from continual learning failure set up a vicious circle that ends in school drop-out.

Dr Ernest Rayner is an authority on reading disabilities who commands international respect. Concerned initially with the emotional disturbances that these disabilities caused, he soon realised that his interests were moving into an interdisciplinary area in which medicine, psychology and education formed an essential partnership. His struggle to set up a professionally manned clinic in which to provide a multidisciplinary therapy has shown not only faith in his inner vision but a robust tenacity and concern for essentials. Dr Rayner at once forms a *mental partnership with his reader, with whom he allies himself to make a broad but sensitive analysis of an urgent educational problem. The great advantage that teachers and parents reap from increased knowledge of this topic is that much child behaviour that was dismissed as a 'phase', or which was seen as unmotivated naughtiness, now can be recognised as a cry for help. As teachers acquire professional know-how and move away from a sort of Bedlam philosophy of child behaviour, they acquire a status in no way inferior to that accorded to other professions. The need for well-based educational diagnostics is a growing one, and the Rayner study makes an important contribution to it.*

The third R, the traditional arithmetic, has largely been replaced by 'new mathematics' – which, since it starts in the primary school and is continued into secondary school syllabuses, may be taken as our bridge. To a widening circle of able teachers the conventional approach to number teaching left much to be desired. It had become formal, rigid; it was all too easily subject to the worst effects of rote teaching – and, what was worse, it incapacitated far too many people who, with a more modern approach, would have acquired a much higher level of mathematical skill. Professional concern was fortunately well supported by the research of Jean Piaget, whose theory of the cognitive development of the child understruts the classroom practice of new mathematics. Mr Leonard Sealey is one of the most experienced British protagonists of this important new trend, and his lucid account of what it means and why it has been developed is an important contribution to our understanding of current educational ferment.

The problem of what is politely termed cultural deprivation *has become a contentious issue recently, and it has forced educators to re-think conventional approaches, since deprivation at the preschool stage may demonstrably reduce the child's educational potenital. The issue has been dramatically demonstrated in the American Negro problem. Here one had a 22-million people minority group whose economic and social disadvantages were clearly linked to a low level of education. Throughout the 1960s, massive amounts of money, expertise and energy were devoted to improving the educational performance of Negro children. By the end of the decade there was a noticeable dissatisfaction in American society with the results. It was not so much a resentment of the price being paid, but a feeling that the returns on the huge investment were inadequate. There was considerable support for those who maintained that current educational methods, strategies and techniques were inefficient. Particularly in America, a growing dubiety was reflected in new* studies of the nature and implication of intelligence, of the relevant insights provided by Piaget's developmental concepts and more particularly by his concept of 'critical periods'. Work done on stimulus deprivation tended to support the idea that cultural deprivation involved in a similar way a reduction of the range of perception which, operating at critical or crucial periods of development, might well cripple cognitive function irreversibly. The consideration of cultural deprivation is included in this group of studies because it throws light on primary or elementary school problems.

One is very much aware of the close relationship between social and cultural factors on the one hand, and emotional behaviour on the other; between cognitive function on the one hand and emotional conditions on the other. Indeed, emotional disturbance frequently relates to a failure of interpersonal relationships and is expressed in reduced cognitive efficiency. To the ordinary parent this is often expressed as a matter of puzzlement over a suddenly disastrous school report. But to the parent struggling under slum conditions it may well be the problem of an intelligent youngster increasingly failing to maintain his level of performance. While we are not legislators, as contributors to this survey of educational problems and trends we can initiate an informed debate from which corrective social action is possible.

1 The Purpose, Meaning and Future of i.t.a.

Sir James Pitman

My friend Brian Rose told me last year of his intention to collect papers 'for students of education as an account of significant modern developments', and invited me to be the contributor on the Initial Teaching Alphabet and to cover particularly its 'purpose, meaning and future'.

There can thus be no better start than this specimen, which, with only insignificant variations, was the very first specimen to be widely distributed, having been printed as the first two paragraphs of an article which I submitted to the *Educational Supplement* of *The Times* published on 29 May 1959.

ſhis is printed in ſhe iniſhial teeᴄhiŋ alfabet, ſhe purpos ov whiᴄh is not, as miet bee suppœsd, too reform our spelliŋ, but too improov ſhe lerniŋ ov reediŋ. it is intended ſhat when ſhe beginner is flooent in ſhis meedium hee ſhood bee confiend too reediŋ in ſhe tradiſhonal alfabet.

if yoo hav red as far as ſhis, ſhe nue meedium will hav proovd too yoo several points, ſhe mœst important ov whiᴄh is ſhat yoo, at eny ræt, hav eesily mæd ſhe ᴄhænj from ſhe ordinary rœman alfabet wiſh convenſhonal spelliŋs too ſhe iniſhial teeᴄhiŋ alfabet wiſh systematic spelliŋ.

Two of the main purposes, the one negative (to have no truck with spelling reform) and the other positive (to accept the aim of teaching of reading and writing in the traditional way) were thus placed in the forefront from the very beginning. It was *not* to be even the thin end of a wedge for spelling reform. It was to be the means of more successful learning.

Let us emphasise the positive and return later to the negative.

The article in *The Times Educational Supplement* was a step in that positive direction taken after a meeting held in the House of Commons in 1958.*

---

* Present at t his meeting were Lionel Elvin and William Wall, respectivel the directors of the London University Institute of Education and of the Nationa Foundation for Educational Research in England and Wales; Sir William Alexander and Sir Ronald Gould, respectively the secretaries of the Association

We had long debated the proposition that the accident of history which had given to the English language more than two alphabets – e.g. the *upper-case* or capital A, the *lower-case* a, and the cursive *a* – and such an employment of the resulting sixty-six characters that it is impossible to deduce the pronunciation of any English word from its spelling or to induce the spelling from its pronunciation, might well be the cause of much of the existing failure, frustration and slowness in learning to read and write. We debated, too, the proposition that here for once educational *research* might precede decision on educational *change*, and that research comparing the results from two groups of children in their first years of school might not only settle the question but in so doing set a healthy precedent for the future. The results of the group using the traditional alphabets and the traditional spelling (I will refer to this combination as Traditional Orthography, or T.O.) could be compared with the other, using an alphabet (and spellings with it) designed to be alphabetic as far as might be desirable. We were attracted by this proposition that educational policy might be based upon ascertained fact rather than upon hunches.

We had also debated whether, if children were taught first with such a new medium, there would be any 'unlearning' in passing from successful reading and writing *with the designed alphabet and spellings*, and recognised that only trial would settle that too. We postulated that there could be as little unlearning as there is unlearning of the English language when learning French, and as there is in adding a knowledge of the other nine alternatives to that of the basic version of the single word BAG.

BAG	Bag	bag	bag
Bag	Bag	bag	bag
Bag		*bag*	

of Education Committees and of the National Union of Teachers; Walter James, the editor of *The Times Educational Supplement*; and myself. (See the introduction by Lionel Elvin to *The i.t.a. Symposium* by Dr John Downing, published in 1967 by the National Foundation for Educational Research, Slough.)

We had good *a priori* grounds for being thus optimistic. To begin with there was the ease with which we can all read at least the more legible but nevertheless essentially different handwritings of so many individual correspondents; also we found ourselves easily able to read the specimen and yet had not thereby lost our ability to read T.O. These and other considerations at least augured well for a comparable transition by the learner in the other direction.

The article in *The Times Educational Supplement* was thus a fly cast over the educational world of Britain and over headteachers in particular. Were any headteachers of the opinion that some at least of their children experienced difficulty in learning to read and write, and did they suppose that it would be worth trying an augmented alphabet used with rational spellings? Would a trial be likely to be supported practically?

Teachers responded in a number sufficient to indicate that a trial would be practicable and could be mounted. The alphabet was ready in printers' type and the spellings determined. In the spring of 1960 the post of research officer at London University Institute of Education was advertised, the necessary disclosure of the intended research was widely publicised by press and television conferences, John Downing was selected, the task of planning the details of the research undertaken, and the first steps taken for providing the necessary teachers' and learners' materials printed in i.t.a.

Teaching began in September 1961, but it was not until February 1967 that the report was published (*The i.t.a. Symposium* referred to above). The report aroused great interest and comment. Dr Wall, in his summary in the final pages of *The i.t.a. Symposium*, wrote:

'For the most part, innovations have escaped objective study and, if evaluated at all, have been assessed mainly on partisan opinion. Faith rather than science has been the guide. In the phase into which education seems now to be passing of large-scale innovation in method, curriculum and organisation, there are not wanting many and powerful voices to say that objective evaluation is unnecessary or impossible. The work carried out by Downing and his team gives the lie to both.'

What then have been the 'objective evaluations'? Clearly the most important question for determination was – how much easier is the new medium than the old? How much sooner do children who are 'ready for reading' learn to read effectively? Table 1 (which is derived from Table E1 in *The i.t.a. Symposium*) gives the findings of the research on this question. Since the two groups were selected from a population of 2500 in each group and most carefully matched to achieve comparability, the quantities of children in each group who were ready for reading may be assumed to have been equal, for all practical purposes. That being so, the figures in Table 1 may be so set out as to give the percentage distribution of 'reading readiness' of the total population among the four groups who succeeded and the

TABLE 1. Progress in Reading Basic Reader Series
Percentage frequency distribution of reading primer reached

Reading primer reached	1 After 1 yr i.t.a.	T.O.	2 After 1⅓ yrs i.t.a.	T.O.	3 After 2 yrs i.t.a.	T.O.	4 After 2⅓ yrs i.t.a.	T.O.
	%	%	%	%	%	%	%	%
Non-starters	6·6	5·2	2·2	0·3	2·1	0·3	0·7	0
In Books Intro, I or II	55·0	75·9	28·8	54·5	15·6	35·4	9·4	25·9
In Book III	17·8	15·7	12·8	17·2	7·8	17·1	5·0	19·1
In Book IV	10·9	2·8	14·5	13·3	5·1	12·0	4·3	11·2
In Book V	4·0	0·5	8·1	7·2	3·0	4·5	2·5	6·1
Beyond Book V	5·7	0	33·6	7·4	66·4	30·6	78·1	37·8
N	651	651	580	580	333	333	278	278
Median primer position	Intro, I, II	Intro, I, II	IV	Intro, I, II	Beyond V	III	Beyond V	IV

fifth group who failed; the four successful groups being differentiated by the four increases in the length of time taken to achieve success (1 year, 1⅓ years, 2 years and 2⅓ years), and the fifth group being those who even after 2⅓ years' schooling were still unsuccessful.

The first standard of achievement which has been taken (in Table 2) to constitute the difference between presently achieved success and at least interim failure, is the standard which is generally accepted in Britain as effective reading, shown in Table 1 by a dotted line. It has been generally accepted that children who are reading in Book IV have crossed a great divide and have achieved a level of success where their future learning will take the form of lots of practice in, and extension of, a reading ability which they have already learned: thenceforward they will virtually learn on their own. It is equally accepted that those reading in Book III and below are still in the process of rudimentary learning, and have not yet acquired that foundation in reading ability which is sufficient for success to have been already achieved, or to be in the future achievable save by continuation of a considerable teaching effort.

It may be assumed that the longer the time taken in schooling to reach that standard of effective reading (that is to say, to pass from above the dotted line which I have drawn between Book III and Book IV), the less was the 'reading readiness' of the four groups who in course of time succeeded, and the greater the lack of it in the fifth group, those who did not succeed even after $2\frac{1}{3}$ years. The figures of Table 1 have been set out as in Table 2, thus distributing the two

TABLE 2

Reading readiness	Successful in i.t.a. %	Successful in T.O. %
Most ready for reading	20·6[1]	3·3[1]
Next most ready	$(56·2 - 20·6) =$ 35·6[2]	$(27·9 - 3·3) =$ 24·6[2]
Next in readiness	$(74·5 - 56·2) =$ 18·3[3]	$(47·1 - 27·9) =$ 19·2[3]
Next in readiness	$(84·9 - 74·5) -$ 10·4[4]	$(55·1 - 47·1) -$ 8·0[4]
Least ready	15·1[5]	45·0[5]
	100·0	100·1

[1] Total of all in Book IV or above after 1 year.
[2] Total of all in Book IV or above after $1\frac{1}{3}$ years less those in group 1.
[3] Total of all in Book IV or above after 2 years less those in groups 1 and 2.
[4] Total of all in Book IV after $2\frac{1}{3}$ years less those in groups 1, 2, and 3.
[5] Total of all not yet in Book IV after even $2\frac{1}{3}$ years.

carefully matched populations in accordance with their readiness for reading when judged by their five degrees of success or failure.

If it be accepted that both populations, i.t.a. and T.O., were indeed carefully matched, then the differences found in the successes of the two populations lay not in any difference in 'reading readiness' between the two populations but in the difference in ease or difficulty of the two learning media in which the two populations were taught, and we arrive (as in Table 3) at a comparison of facility for learning as between the two media for each of the five groups.

Some may suppose that this standard of competence in reading is too low for a reliable and convincing comparison, and moreover, since it is one involving competence in i.t.a. before the transition to

TABLE 3. Comparison of facility in learning when taught in one or other of two media (i.t.a. or T.O.), reflecting the differences in duration of schooling needed to achieve the standard of reading ability defined above by learners of an equal 'readiness'

| | i.t.a. | | | | T.O. | | | |
	Successes %	Delayed successes %	Frustrations %	Failures %	Successes %	Delayed successes %	Frustrations %	Failures %
*Reading readiness**								
Most ready	20·6	nil	nil		3·3	nil	17·3	
Next most ready	35·6	nil	nil		24·6	nil	11·0	
Next in readiness	18·3	nil	nil		19·2	0·9	nil	
Next in readiness	10·4	nil	nil		8·0	nil	2·4	
	84·9				55·1			
Least ready (Failures)				15·1				45·0
				100·0				100·1

* Taken from Table 2.

T.O. has been attempted, that I have chosen a standard which thus shows i.t.a. to unfair advantage.

That has not been the case. Indeed if the standard of success be raised to 'Beyond Book v' (i.e. to reading in T.O., the i.t.a. learner having made the transition to T.O.), the comparison is even better still. The percentage distribution of readiness for reading, measured by the new level of achievement at the end of the four periods, now appears as in Table 4.

A second table of comparisons in facility of learning, comparable to that in Table 3, as in Table 5, may be compiled to show the differences in success of reading at the higher standard of reading, namely beyond Book v – that is to say, when the transition to T.O. has been made.

These findings shown in Table 4 below may then be set out as in Table 5 below, to show for the higher standard that comparison which was shown in Table 3 for the lower standard.

The comparisons of success at the two standards at Tables 3 and 5 may be conveniently studied in Table 6.

The i.t.a. children were by the first and lower standard (in Book IV or beyond) after one year more than six times more numerous than

TABLE 4

Reading readiness*	Successful in i.t.a. %	Successful in T.O. %
Most ready for reading	5·7[1]	nil[1]
Next most ready	$(33{\cdot}6 - 5{\cdot}7) =$ 27·9[2]	7·4[2]
Next in readiness	$(66{\cdot}4 - 33{\cdot}6) =$ 32·8[3]	$(30{\cdot}6 - 7{\cdot}4) =$ 23·2[3]
Next in readiness	$(78{\cdot}1 - 66{\cdot}4) =$ 11·7[4]	$(37{\cdot}8 - 30{\cdot}6) =$ 7·2[4]
Least ready	21·9[5]	$(100 - 37{\cdot}8) =$ 62·2[5]
* Taken from Table 1.		
	100·0	100·0

[1] Total of all beyond Book v after 1 year.
[2] Total of all beyond Book v after $1\frac{1}{3}$ years less those in group 1.
[3] Total of all beyond Book v after 2 years less those in groups 1 and 2.
[4] Total of all beyond Book v after $2\frac{1}{3}$ years less those in groups 1, 2 and 3.
[5] Total of all not yet beyond Book v even after $2\frac{1}{3}$ years.

the T.O. children; by the second and much higher standard (beyond Book v) after one year there was no comparison – they were infinitely more numerous since there were in fact no T.O. children successful

TABLE 5. Comparison of facility of learning when taught in one or other of two media (i.t.a. or T.O.), reflecting the differences in duration of schooling needed by learners of an equal readiness for reading to achieve reading success *in T.O.* to a common standard of reading ability – having finished the last book in the series

Reading readiness*	i.t.a.				T.O.			
	Successes %	Delayed Successes	Frustrations	Failures %	Successes	Delayed successes %	Frustrations %	Failures %
Most ready	5·7	nil	nil		nil		5·7	
Next most ready	27·9	nil	nil		nil	1·7		
Next in readiness	32·8	nil	nil		nil		23·2	
Next in readiness	11·7	nil	nil		nil		7·2	
	78·1						36·1	
Least ready (Failures)				21·9				62·2
*Taken from Table 4.				100·0				100·0

as against 5·7 per cent successes in i.t.a. It will be noted from Table 6 that after $1\frac{1}{3}$ years (the first time at which there were any T.O.

TABLE 6. Distribution by percentage of the successful proportions of the i.t.a. and T.O. comparable populations, after varying periods at school – success being measured by two standards

Lower standard (*attainment of Book* IV *and beyond*)

Cumulative successes

	i.t.a.	T.O.
1 year	20·6	3·3
1⅓ years	56·2	27·9
2 years	74·5	47·1
2⅓ years	84·9	55·1
Balance (unsuccessful)	15·1	45·0

Higher Standard (*beyond Book* v)

	i.t.a.	T.O.
1 year	5·7	—
1⅓ years	33·6	7·4
2 years	66·4	30·6
2⅓ years	78·1	37·8
Balance (unsuccessful)	21·9	62·2

successes) there were more than four times (33·6:7·4 per cent) as many i.t.a. as T.O. learners who had been successful at the higher standard. Moreover those who were least ready are shown (in both Tables 2 and Table 4) to have had a much better chance of avoiding failure. There were three times fewer failures after 2⅓ years at the lower standard (15·1:45·0 per cent – Table 2), and again virtually three times fewer failures (21·9:62·2 per cent – Table 4) at the higher.

These are percentages of the two research populations. When these percentages come to be considered in relation to the total number of children in Britain and in America (900,000 and 4,000,000 per annum) who each year start their task of learning to read and write, an indication is given of the degree of delay, frustration and failure which may be expected from continuing the use of T.O. as the learning medium. It ought also to be recognised that an improvement in the learning of reading and writing (and through them of language) is likely to yield also improvement in the learning of all other subjects in the curriculum, seeing that they are taught through language in one or other of its manifestations.

In the words of John Downing, when reporting the main conclusions of his comparisons, the following is unequivocal:

'From the proposition that T.O. is an important cause of difficulty in the early stages of learning to read and that a system in which grapheme-phoneme relations are more simple and regular would make this learning task easier, four hypotheses were derived which may be summarised as follows:

Children in classes where a simplified system (i.e. i.t.a.) is used should show superior achievements in reading and writing to those in classes where T.O. is used. More particularly:

1. the pupils using i.t.a. should make more rapid progress through their basal reader series;
2. they should achieve higher scores on reading tests in which lower-order decoding skills have an especially important role in solution;
3. their written compositions should be longer; and
4. their writing vocabulary should be more extensive.

All four of these hypotheses were strongly supported by the data from this first i.t.a. experiment.'*

The tables above show the great degree of the improvement which underlay the research report on the first of these hypotheses.

The next most important question is that of the transition. Will there be a need to unlearn and relearn, or will the transition be easy? The findings of the research and those of teachers working with i.t.a. are agreed that there is apparently no unlearning, and that whatever relearning there may be, the end result of teaching with i.t.a. is a better standard of reading in T.O.

Here as Table 7 is Graph 28 from *The i.t.a. Symposium*. It is to be noted that a test score of 25 in this (Schonell) test is the par score for children 'at the beginning of the third year' (aged 7⅓ in Britain).

There are, furthermore, two points on the testing of the transition:

1. that the superiority of the i.t.a.-taught children when so tested in T.O. is greater the higher the standard of reading achieved;
2. that (see column 2 of Table 1) only 33·6 per cent of the i.t.a. children had yet been supposed by their teachers to be ready for the transition and been put onto books in T.O. when all 100 per cent of the sample were (thus prematurely) tested in T.O. Thus an undeserved appearance of meagreness in performance is given to the results by the two thirds to the left-hand side of the graph, in that children were tested in T.O. who were patently not ready to be tested in that medium.

---

* *Evaluating the Initial Teaching Alphabet*, by John Downing (London: Cassell, 1967) p. 223: italics in text.

TABLE 7. Scores on Schonell Graded Word Reading Test (in T.O. to both groups) over ten ranges of achievement

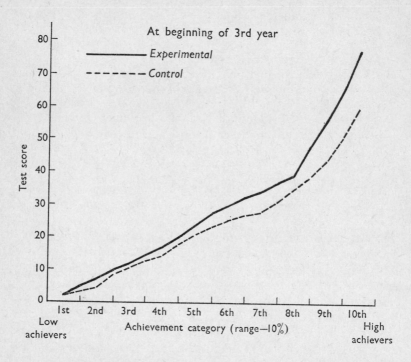

The poor results of those who had not yet met T.O. before they were tested in T.O. were made even poorer by the unsuitability for them of the test in question. Such children, if tested in T.O., ought to be tested with words in context carrying a message of meaning, not with single words. The Schonell Graded Word Reading Test, being a test in single words, was thus clearly most unsuitable for those who had not made the transition to T.O., and unsuitable too for those who had made the transition but had not made the transition sufficiently early, and who had thus not enjoyed for a long enough time the considerable reading experience in T.O. necessary to be able to read by look-and-say recall words misleadingly spelled (e.g. *light* and *nephew*).

It will then be asked – if the transition in reading has been found indeed to involve no unlearning and no significant relearning – has

apparatus who collectively have financed the hundreds o
s of pounds' worth of i.t.a. items (there are now over two
titles or items). American, Canadian and one Australian
g houses are numbered among these eighty independent
eurs, who must each have made a cautious and very careful
nt before investing their money. The success of i.t.a. has
enomenal in growth and in its degree of enthusiastic
ce in all the English-speaking countries. After Britain
got off to a good start), the United States, Canada and
a are the widest acceptors of the proposal and of its proven
It is impracticable to ascertain and report here the quantities
tance outside Britain, but America is top of the league
estimated excess of ten thousand schools, and New Zealand –
ightly controlled and authoritarian official regime – bottom.
een, i.t.a. has reached such far and exciting cities as Singa-
d Hong Kong, and many of the places where 'dependent'
are conducted by British and American defence forces.
s been used very successfully in remedial reading, and at
om 7 to 65!

ritain three cities have gone 100 per cent i.t.a. I understand
e public opinion of parents is in the end overwhelming, and
ven the most reluctant (and complacent) of headteachers
nbs in the end to parent pressure and decides to try i.t.a. –
which the future of that school is a foregone conclusion.
long-awaited report of the Schools Council by the late Pro-
F. W. Warburton (Professor of Experimental Education,
tment of Education, University of Manchester) and Vera
gate (Lecturer in Curriculum Department, School of Edu-
, University of Manchester) was published in September
* It completely vindicated the *a priori* contentions of great
sh and American men, beginning with Sir Thomas Smith in
that English literacy needs its own alphabet and was inade-
ly provided for by the roman alphabet. The evaluation of i.t.a.
eferred to the Schools Council by the Minister of Education,
Association of Education Committees, the National Union of

.t.a.: *An Independent Evaluation* – 'the report of a study carried out for
chools Council in the use of the initial teaching alphabet as a medium for
nning reading with infants' (London: W. & R. Chambers and John Murray,
).

transition in writing been found to be equally easy? Will the children taught with i.t.a. be doomed to be even worse spellers than the children taught with T.O.?

The process of transition in writing is a slower one than the instantaneous process in reading.* Those children who are fluent readers in i.t.a. and are sufficient masters of the language to be able to understand fully all the words they read, and to be writing in i.t.a. copiously, make the reading transition overnight and with no apparent effort if tested in context (not in single words); however, even those children who are fluent writers in i.t.a. take a considerable period to learn to spell correctly in T.O. But so do the T.O.-taught children also. The misspellings *sed* and *cum* appear frequently in the writings of T.O. children. Thus a comparison at a later date is likely to be the more reliable. Table 8 reproduces the graphical comparison between the T.O. and the i.t.a. children after $3\frac{1}{2}$ years when tested in spelling in T.O. by the Schonell Graded Word Spelling Test, as given in Graph 34 from *The i.t.a. Symposium*. The superiority in spelling of the i.t.a.-taught children is evident; also the inference will be drawn that it takes time – and effort – to learn to spell in T.O.: a point which will be brought up later in this chapter.

Before turning to consideration of what i.t.a. is not (even the thin end of a wedge for spelling reform), a word ought to be said about a further finding of the research – the great benefit which i.t.a. gives to the child when expressing himself in writing. This benefit, which was stated to have been found in the research (see (3) and (4) in the quotation from John Downing on pp. 14–15), is possibly the greatest of all the joys of teachers who use i.t.a. Their children become released from all inhibitions – and indeed any tension in writing. They behave with pencil and paper just as they behave with their vocal organs and the air which carries their speech. If they want to write anything, if they want to say anything, they write it or they say it because they have the confidence and the power adequate to match their will to communicate. Speaking is indeed satisfying to the child: writing is slower, but it is something which lasts and can be admired and shown to others. Thus this new power to communicate is a source of great delight to the children.

* This instantaneous transition is made by those who were or have become 'ready for the transition' if they are (1) reading i.t.a. fluently, and (2) fully understanding what they read.

TABLE 8

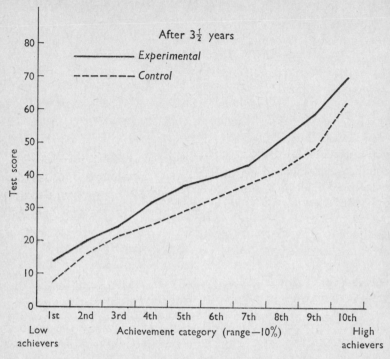

Much has been written about the Hawthorne Effect. The first, and easiest, reaction to findings which appear uncomfortably favourable to i.t.a. has been to raise this particular 'explanation' of the good findings of the research and to seek thereby to brush off the phenomenal spread of i.t.a.. We humans resist change. Thus to learn that we ought to change is an idea which we seek to keep at bay. Still more are we averse to change if we have brought to such an innovation a preconception that the proposal to teach reading with a new alphabet and new spellings must be indefensible (and to how many is this not axiomatic?), because we have then to recant our preconceptions and admit that we have been wrong. To do so goes greatly against the grain.

There is no indication, much less authority, to justify the suggestion that children aged 4 or 5 are susceptible to the Hawthorne Effect, or, if they are, to indicate that the effect is persistent for so long a duration as the periods covered by the research. It is in

respect only of the teachers (as adul
for asserting that the Hawthorne E
even if there be an effect upon ch
generating enthusiasm, there arises t
that enthusiasm, or some of it, is the
success experienced by the child and
innovation itself, and the situation of
publicised (even as an anonymous e
stimulating to enthusiasm – so too su
proved results, particularly on a scale
Tables 1 to 8. Teachers identify thems
are devoted to them. Surely it is a cause
enthusiasm of their children? This was w
ing on pp. 36 and 37 of *The i.t.a. Reading*
Bros, for the University of London Ins

'5. *Greater enthusiasm for reading and
i.t.a. classes*

The majority of headteachers are
Eighteen of the 19 headteachers found t
for reading, but one of the 18 believ
applies only to his brighter beginners
member of the group felt that it was di
school as there is generally a high lev
beginning reading classes and he felt th
enthusiastic as ever about reading in scho

Most heads feel that enthusiasm for 1
and that the children show a greater love
in the library corner. . . .

It is important to note that this increase
for "reading" as an official activity of the s
applies especially to the books in the library
can go to in free-choice periods of the sch

Can any innovation be imagined more im
into the conservative practices of British edu
Yet with only twenty schools, as short a time ag
the first experiment, the tally has grown to o
Britain alone. Can any investment by a publishei
hazarded than to publish books (or to manufa
i.t.a.? Yet there are over eighty publishers an

B

ment and
thousand
thousand
publishin
entrepre
assessme
been ph
acceptar
(which
Australi
success.
of accep
with an
a very t
In betw
pore an
schools
It h
ages fr
In E
that th
that e
succu
after
The
fessor
Depa
South
catior
1969
Engl
1568
quat
was
the

*
the
begi
1969

Teachers and the i.t.a. Foundation.* The report was to take into account not only the results of many researches but also the experiences of Directors of Education, Advisers, head teachers and class teachers, Her Majesty's Inspectors of Education and parents.

It was followed on 2 December 1969 by a press release jointly issued on behalf of London University Institute of Education and the National Foundation for Educational Research – the two bodies who had backed the launching of, and had been responsible for, the first and possibly most important of the researches. That statement was as follows:

'In October 1960, the University of London Institute of Education and the National Foundation for Educational Research jointly sponsored a major series of researches into the efficacy of i.t.a. as a teaching medium.

From the work done by the Reading Research Unit set up in the University of London Institute of Education, and from the evaluations of that and other work reported in the *i.t.a. Symposium* and *i.t.a. – An Independent Evaluation*, two findings clearly emerge. The first is that the medium has substantial advantages over traditional orthography in the early stages of teaching children to read. The second is that attention has been drawn to the great need for exploring further through research and experiment the critical two or three years in which children are taught reading.

Beyond this, however, lies another problem which concerns the role of research in determining policy. Some at least of the resistance to change lies in a rooted unwillingness to consider evidence. Few other areas of educational method have been as well and thoroughly explored as this. We would therefore urge teachers and others responsible for the important decision as to how and by what means reading should be taught, to examine the evidence and to recognise that on what they decide depends the welfare of countless children – especially those who now have difficulties.'

It was widely expected that, because the Report and the Joint Statement had so unequivocally convicted T.O. as the initial learning medium, there would immediately be a great expansion of the use and acceptance of i.t.a. (and of the other media such as Colour, Unifon, Professor Edward Fry's Diacritical Marking System, etc.),

* The non-profit organisation established to continue and formalise the functions of persuasion which my grandfather and I have pursued successively since 1843 and to absolve London University Institute of Education and the researchers from the embarrassment of being implicated in persuasion.

seeing that so many head teachers, Directors of Education and the pundits of the educational 'Establishment' were known to be sitting on the fence 'waiting for the Schools Council Report'.

The response, however, was not immediate, and the expansion was soon seen to be slow and steady rather than rapid and great.

Perhaps those who expected open-minded attention and swift action to follow as the fruits of research were too naïve, and indeed oblivious of the record and of the hostile attitude to research which is usual in the social sciences – in a most unfortunate contrast to the attitude to research results among those engaged in the physical and mechanical sciences.

The example of Joseph Lister's research into the causes of gangrene poisoning in surgery (by reason of which 90 per cent of those operated upon died) should have been in mind and the lesson learned from the murderous time-lag of forty years which intervened between the publication in 1858 of Lister's report and the final acceptance of his thesis that septic operating procedures caused gangrene and death, and ought to be discontinued.

How does it come about that well-intentioned and intelligent men and women in the social sciences are prone to reject the results of research and continue what have been shown to be no more than professional prejudices, basing themselves solely on the ignorance of the past? Why do they, and apparently only they, take so long to accept new knowledge? There is no such time-lag in the material sciences. Almost within a week metallurgists in America, Japan, Germany, Russia, etc., will eagerly accept and enthusiastically adopt new knowledge discovered by, say, English research. Research leads immediately to action.

But if research does not lead to immediate action, it is to be hoped that it will not take fifty years before those who stick to long-standing and 'generally accepted professional opinions' will seek to base themselves less on prejudice and more on evidence – in which case those who conduct and those who pay for research will need less to ask 'what availeth research?'

Meanwhile it is interesting, though sometimes exasperating, to note the almost generally professed mugwumpery of those who sit on the fence when debating innovations, even long after the publication of authoritative investigations and of thorough research by people of unchallenged repute. Such a posture of so-called 'open-minded neutrality' is – while not open hostility rather one of veiled hostility or hypocrisy – since such an equivocal attitude to evidence seeks to avoid the implicit consequences of thought and action, even when the evidence – as in the case of i.t.a. – is accepted and commended by such responsible and independent bodies as the N.F.E.R. and the University of London Institute of Education. Gallio had some reason when he 'cared for none of those things', but those professionally engaged in teaching some six million new entrants to school every year can hardly justify such irresponsible carelessness when results with T.O. are known to be as deplorable as they now are.

Virtually all research workers seem fearful of a positive attitude: qualifications, reservations, saving clauses, abound. Even in the report of the Schools Council there are many such examples. For instance, what starts as two forthright conclusions:

'There is no evidence whatsoever for the belief that the best way to learn to read in traditional orthography is to learn to read in traditional orthography. It would appear rather that the best way to learn to read in traditional orthography is to learn to read in the initial teaching alphabet.'

is immediately followed by:

'On the other hand, the evidence is not convincing that i.t.a. is the superior medium *after the transition to T.O.*' (italics in the report)

an evasion by what is after all an irrelevancy. At the outset in 1960 and throughout, the intention has been made clear that 'it is intended that when the beginner is fluent in this medium he should be confined to reading in the traditional alphabet.' Nevertheless the saving clause saves face as it was intended to do.

Cassandra was not believed when she prophesied woe. How comes it that research results which prophesy joy should be regarded askance? It is a poor soul that never rejoices, and a poorer one still which refuses to take joy when joy is even unexpectedly presented. We must press on in hope that the conditions in the 1970s are sufficiently different from those of the years of Queen Victoria, and that the spread of i.t.a. will be steady and inexorable, and faster than that of aseptic surgery, notwithstanding the anxious fears of those whom prejudice is driving to pray against the coming tide.

If, as I believe, the general acceptance of i.t.a. is inevitable, then 'If it were done . . . 'twere well it were done quickly'. Such success and acceptance will enormously benefit millions of children every year.

I turn now to the negative purpose of i.t.a., 'whiç is not, as miet bee suppœsd, too reform our spelliŋ, but œnly too improov the lerniŋ ov reediŋ'.

This success will remove the only *practical* ground for hope of Spelling Reform – at any rate as most spelling reformers have hitherto interpreted Spelling Reform – because the transition to reading in T.O. has been found to be so immediate and apparently effortless. It will hereafter be even less practicable to persuade publishers and printers to discontinue publishing and printing their wares in what I have called our traditional orthography and instead to publish and print them in a new, to-be-agreed spelling. This will be so because in time their customers will have had so little difficulty in learning to read and in making the transition, and so many years of practice in reading and writing in T.O. that there will be little benefit and possibly harm to the great majority of the English-reading world to accompany a vast disturbance.

It was the late Bernard Shaw who cured me, once and for all, of any such expectation and of any intention to attempt what he showed me was anyhow an impossible task. As he pointed out, the great barrier to any reform of the medium in which we read is the fact that our T.O. works so well – for those who have learned to read and write. Thus reform is anathema to those who know how to read, and virtually impossible to bring about, since those who know and prefer T.O. are the vast majority of the voters. Moreover it is clear that many of the very peculiarities, the host of redundancies in T.O., have a positive merit for those who have learned to read. When we read 'It was Brown' instead of 'It was brown', we are greatly helped to quicker and more accurate understanding by the redundant capitals I and B. The redundancies play their part in alerting the reader to the need to accept the beginning of a new train of thought, just as the full point and space indicate the end of the preceding one. The employment of the capital B signals advance notice of a noun, a proper noun, just as, by way of contrast, the lower-case b indicates an adjective (one of colour). Thus two quite different trains of thought are given a directional precision by the conventional use of redundant characters. In the same way the spellings *there*, *their* and *they're* give a precision which is most desirable – an advantage which speech does not enjoy, and which a reformed orthography would destroy. To have abolished all of the redundancies would ill serve not only those who have learned to read T.O. (and who insist on continuing to read in T.O.) but also those in future generations who, notwithstanding that they have learned to read with i.t.a., will at transition time switch with great ease to the redundant medium. They all wish to do so because it is at that time just as easy for them to read in T.O. as in i.t.a., and because they know well that they will have greater advantage in life if they do make this switch to T.O. and so join those who insist on continuing with the medium (T.O.) which is the more efficient for reading. At that later stage in the child's upbringing it will have become irrelevant that T.O. would have been much less easy as a medium for *learning*. What will have become compulsive in the changeover will be two considerations – the very vast volume of communication available in T.O., and only in T.O., and the need to become sufficiently habituated to reading in that medium.

No doubt it has been because of such signals as these that reading man is able to accept messages at a speed three or four times, sometimes ten times, faster than listening man. Bernard Shaw was probably right when he said that not improvement but only damage could follow from the exertions of 'tidy-minded' do-gooders who have not sufficiently understood the issues.

I would not ordinarily have given so much space to a negative purpose were it not that I have been leading up to one of the important concomitants in the *future* of i.t.a.

I am confident that one of the by-products of i.t.a. will be an eventual acceptance of permissiveness in the *spelling* with the existing cursive alphabet. We can change the characters of our cursive alphabet no more at this late hour than we can change the characters of our upper-case and lower-case reading alphabets, but we can at any rate adopt a permissive attitude to spelling of all but the common words when we receive memoranda and letters from those who write to us.

We already allow our friends a very great tolerance of form in the pronunciations of what they speak to us; we do so too in the particular forms of handwriting of that alphabet in which they write to us. If then we accept individualised speech and individualised handwriting, why should we reject individualised spelling? Why should spelling differ from speech and from handwriting? Is there any more practical advantage in a Draconian spelling of the less common words, seeing that there seems to be no Draconian pronunciation for any word nor any Draconian copperplate handwriting for them? Why is it right to demand in spelling alone a precise conformity to a particular set of arbitrary conventions when they serve no purpose? Why do we demand such conformity in the uncommon but nevertheless very usual words as, for instance, *accommodation*, *supercede*, *harassed*, *inocculate*, *battalions*, *rivetted*, etc., in which very few of my readers will in fact lay their hands on their hearts and say whether the skilled printers at R. & R. Clark Ltd., Edinburgh, have printed them all with their usual admirable accuracy or whether (and in which words) they have been influenced by me in allowing me to set some of the spelling traps which I spring upon friends to test their quite pointless expertise.

I believe that thanks to the one breakthrough of i.t.a. in the field of teaching of reading, there will come in due course another breakthrough in the field of teaching of spelling. At some future time educationists will be asked whether children who have learned to read T.O. should any longer be *required* to master a useless and vast expertise in writing it. Their individualised spelling will undoubtedly conform largely to what they have read. They will be, say, 97 per cent accurate, and that which they write for the remaining say, 3 per cent will be immediately intelligible, because they will have conformed to one or other of several 'generalised spelling rules' which are self-evident among the 'regular' and 'regularly irregular' words of the 97 per cent which they will write with T.O. spellings.

Words such as at, and, end, bed, left, it, in, if, our, not, up, under, etc., etc., are the same in T.O. as in i.t.a., and will be automatically spelled rightly by *all* learners of *T.O.* spelling. Words such as then, thus, ship, shall, when, whip, king, sing, etc., etc. will equally be automatically spelled rightly. Even those highly *irregular* spellings which recur so frequently that they are read and written over and over and over again (such as woz, wuns, hœʃ and aut) will also be automatically spelled accurately as *was*, *once*, *whose* and *ought*.

Those of us who are brought up to pronounce *Marshbanks*, *Chumly* and *Beecham* are amazed to learn that we are expected to spell them Marjoribanks, Cholmondeley and Beauchamp. In our ignorance, however, we fail to recognise that words pronounced as *wuns* and *woz* are just as amazing – and just as confusing to the speller – until he has overcome the difficulty and become so conditioned to it in early life that his amazement has become a willing acceptance.

I am already too old to expect to see the day when educationists decide no longer to waste the time of teachers and pupils in the useless exercise of arbitrary spellings of what could be easily read in a number of other forms. I am confident however that those younger than I will live to see the innovation when neither the recipient of a letter, nor a teacher, nor an examiner, will concern themselves with the precise form of a spelling – only whether it is immediately comprehensible. What we write will be judged solely on its content, its message in a then-to-become-acceptable form of communication.

During my lifetime I hope to see the intention 'tω imprωv ʃhe lerniŋ ov reediŋ' realised, and to see the new medium superseding the old as the medium in which children first learn to read. This positive purpose is to *defer*, and only to defer, the difficulties of learning to read the medium with which English-speaking peoples have persistently struggled during their earliest stages of learning, and for over 600 years.*

In no other branch of our educational curriculum has antiquity been tolerated as the final arbiter: in no other educational subject have difficulties in the path of the learner been accepted with no effort to mitigate them. So obvious are these difficulties, and so obvious too the means of mitigating them, that there can surely be no doubt either that T.O. will be for ever eliminated from the curriculum in the earliest days of school, or that i.t.a. will be the medium which will take its place.

How then do we eliminate from our 600-year-old T.O. the difficulties, and how do we evolve the simpler alternative?

The starting-point must be the word *as printed in T.O.*, because reading is related to sight. Note here my deliberate omission of sound and of hearing with the ear. Reading, skilled reading, needs to be a

---

* See *As DIFFICULT as ABC*: the case against the traditional orthography as a *learning* medium, by Sir James Pitman (London, 1966); in which the spellings of the hundred most common words of the English language are set out for the six earliest English Bibles from Wyclif in 1380 to the Authorised Version of King James in 1611, demonstrating the early date by which our present-day spellings had already become fixed.

silent process, one in which the meaning is obtained silently. Indeed a totally deaf child, one who has never heard the spoken language, can be taught to read. We must also remember that for those who can hear it matters not at all to a listener whether the precise sounds of the message which he *hears* are or are not that precise collection of sounds which he, the listener, would *speak*, were he to be speaking instead of listening. Indeed it never can be precisely the same sounds because even the same speaker would not repeat precisely the same sounds were he to reiterate the message. A man's voice is different from a woman's, and a Lancastrian man's pronunciation as well as voice is different from an American woman's, yet each will understand the other. No more than an approximation to what he himself speaks is what the listener expects – and indeed receives. He never expects or receives the exact sounds which he himself would speak. Speaking is highly individualised; listening highly generalised.

In an alphabetic reading system (in contrast to an arbitrary non-alphabetic reading system such as Chinese ideograms) the form of the symbol has a generalised value, never a particular value in the *representation* of sound: not a particular sound but a wide variation of sounds, or, in the terms of the linguist, the character represents not a 'phoneme' but a 'diaphone'.*

But there clearly must be a limit to the band of tolerance of such variety. Thus 'diaphone' is the name given to that group of phonemes which, notwithstanding their variety, enjoy the power to be understood because they have a place in the band of tolerance which listeners accept. For instance the phoneme used by the Cockney Londoner for pronouncing the word 'I' is peculiar and local, but is nevertheless understood by a generality of listeners. In most of the rest of the English-speaking world the Londoner's phoneme would do duty in the word *oil* / oi /. Again the American southerner and the Ulsterman will pronounce the word 'I' as / ɑ /, and a Bloomsbury Londoner will be found to pronounce it / æ /. Between these wide extremes there are a host of variants, each one a

---

* By Bloomfield's definition, the phoneme is 'the minimal unit of distinctive sound-feature'. The diaphone has been defined as (1) 'all variants of a phoneme occurring in all the utterances of all the speakers of a language (French tongue-trilled as against uvular *r*)' (Webster III); (2) 'a phoneme of one dialect corresponding to but phonetically different from that of another dialect (the British and American sounds of *o* in *not*, *pot*, or of *r* in *very*)' (Mario Pei, *Glossary of Linguistic Terminology*, Columbia University Press, 1966).

different, because 'individualised', phoneme, but each one an effective communication in the ears of the listener.

T.O. has always enjoyed this flexibility, which springs from the fact that print is silent. The letters never 'say' any sound. If there is a sound to be heard it is the particular one uttered by a reader. Thus T.O. has enjoyed the power to represent satisfactorily a wide range of diaphones. The new medium also enjoys this flexibility because it too is a reading system. It is irrelevant, in T.O. or in i.t.a., that a symbol such as ie may be variously pronounced as /ie/oi/u/ or /æ/, but it is essential that the use of each symbol should be restricted to its own particular diaphonic range. A given character must never represent more than its diaphonic value or else it makes the reading system *pro tanto* unalphabetic.

Thus the starting-point for an initial teaching medium must be an acceptance of the diaphonic nature of pronunciation and a recognition of the desirability of so designing the new characters and of so choosing the new spellings as to retain as far as possible both the alphabetic principle and maximum resemblance to the T.O. forms – to which the teaching medium must lead. The new forms must be as far as possible alphabetic (to make the learning easy) but they must retain as much similarity to the T.O. forms as possible (to make the transition easy).

The reader would certainly not be able to understand some words if he were to read them phonetically. For instance he would be lost were he to hear a person say / onky upon a timmy /, which is what *once upon a time* alphabetically represents. All readers will, however, easily be able to read 'wuns upon a tiem', even though each may clothe the word 'wuns' with a different vowel sound / w◌ns /, w◌ns /, wans /, and even / wauns / as well as / wuns / – and clothe the other words too with a corresponding accent, i.e. diaphonic variety. Thus the starting-point is not the *actual sound*, but the *diaphonic value* of the characters in the new reading system related to the sight-forms of the old, our Traditional Orthography.

The i.t.a. is a *reading* alphabet; it starts with the traditional *shapes* and adapts them only so far as may be necessary to eliminate the grosser difficulties in reading. Thus there is no need to change at all letter, dustbin, handcuff, or even the second half of 'sœldiery.' There are no gross difficulties in recognising these words, notwithstanding that the first three are spelled with a (generally) superfluous *t* and *d* and the fourth with an *e* and a *y* which would not be included in the visual form, were a writing alphabet to be employed rather than a reading one.

After all, while a *writing* system may well discriminate between *midday* and *middle*, between *innavigable* and *innocent* (many speakers make a real but barely detectable pause in *mid-day*, *in-navigable*, which is absent in *middle* and *innocent*), it is clearly unnecessary to suppose that the young reader has any need to have such sophisticated distinctions made for him in order to read effectively.

Because i.t.a. is not a writing system but a reading one, it matters not at all how he spells when writing in i.t.a. provided his spellings are intelligible. It matters little how he writes the i.t.a. version of the T.O. word *you*. Any of the twenty-seven possible alternatives is acceptable, varying from ɛɛœ (which I have seen in a child's writing in a composition which was nevertheless displayed, rightly I thought, on the classroom wall) to the form which is used for i.t.a. reading purposes, namely yœ. Nevertheless the learner very soon comes to write, as by rote, that form yœ which he reads so frequently in all of his i.t.a. books. On the other hand, if he reads 'uenieted stæts' only infrequently, he may well write yœnieted – and if he does he will still have been gloriously right in a medium in which the form he writes will in any case be no more than a transitional one.

It seems to me that the history of the first ten roman numerals, mostly digraphs, and their virtual supersession by arabic numerals, all ten (0–9) of them monographs, was due to the very fact that a decimal numeration needed ten ciphers, and that the only three roman ciphers (I, V, X) used to express those ten concepts were inadequate. It was soon found that the new arabic form 4 was better than IV, the new 6 than VI, 9 than IX, and 8 than VIII, just as ʃh in biʃhop, fiʃh, etc. gives an important distinction from the *sh* in *mishap*, *mishearing*, etc. Thus the other monographs þh, ŋ, ω, œ, etc., are better, because less confusing to the learner, than *th*, *ng* and *oo*. They are no doubt also more easily read as well as more easily learned. At any rate research has shown that even 'for numbers between 1 and 9 Arabic numerals were read fifty per cent faster than Roman' (D. K. Sperry, 'Speed and Accuracy of Reading Roman Numerals, *Journal of Applied Psychology* (Oct 1952) 346-7, as reported by Herbert Spencer, Royal College of Art, London, 1968).

Just as I rejected the use of digraphs, so I rejected diacritical marks. I concede that s̲h̲ (with the two characters diacritically marked by a line underneath) is one possibly satisfactory, but barely satisfactory, way of conveying the positive information that sh and s̲h̲ are to be regarded as radically different symbolisations. I consider however that sh and ʃh are better because more distinctive, more memorable and easier to learn, while imposing no significant extra burden either at the transition or in the handwriting of the learner. I cannot accept that ö̇ is a satisfactory way of symbolising a number of *different* sounds when spelled as now, with an o. If simplicity in learning be desired in a reading alphabet, there can surely be no exception to the principle that any character must in *no circumstances* be used to represent more than one (listening) diaphone.

What other futures do I foresee for the use of i.t.a.? Remedial reading, language instruction (in speech as well as in literacy, and the two virtually simultaneously, that is to say without the present timer gap between learning the auditory and learning the visual), fo-English as a *second* language, for teaching the mother tongue to those who are deficient in their mother tongue, for the deaf, the blind (with an Initial Teaching Braille now being tried by Dr Randall Harley, of the George Peabody College, Nashville, Tennessee, and Mrs Rachel Rawls, of the Governor Morehead School, Raleigh, North Carolina). I foresee also applications *mutatis mutandis* to other languages – because a principle which is a valid principle is applicable 'across the board'.

New windows have been opened. The all-importance of the child's linguistic competence in learning to read will lead – already has led – to new teaching procedures. The two main causes of so much reading failure have been isolated: our traditional orthography and the limited language skills of so many children.

We in education are now accepting a challenge which will assuredly lead us far afield. The years ahead are thus likely to be busy ones which will see many consequent innovations also.

2 Reading Retardation

Ernest W. Rayner

DEFINITION AND FREQUENCY

Difficulties in learning to read have existed as long as the written word, but it has required social change to highlight it as one of the largest problems in the sphere of education.

In former days there existed many alternatives if a person found that he could not read, and his standing socially and at his work did not necessarily depend so much on literacy as it does today. Gradually this has given way to a state of affairs where not only is literacy imperative, but a higher grade of education is demanded for adequate functioning in society.

With this greater demand for literacy more and more cases of disturbed ability have been uncovered and over the last ten years we have seen, with great satisfaction, the gathering together of many disciplines to tackle the problem. If I had to record the most important development in the field of reading disorder, I would suggest that it is this close co-operation of many workers in different fields in this important area; and through this co-operation, the uncovering of multiple aetiologies and the development of more adequate therapies.

Reading retardation therefore does not belong to any one discipline but requires the working together of many in both diagnosis and treatment.

Definitions of reading retardation have changed with the years and the present one, though serving a good purpose, is still far from satisfactory and we hope that the future will bring further modification to fit increasing insights.

A reading retardation exists when the reading age (R.A.) of a child (as measured by reading tests) is at least two years behind that of the child's intellectual capacity or mental age (as measured by intelligence tests).

Some intelligence tests, especially the group intelligence tests, rely heavily on reading; which will, if the child has a problem in reading, cause a faulty assessment of the intelligence. It is wise then to use those tests that have a minimum of reading items.

It has been suggested by some authors that the reading age be measured against the child's chronological age or his grade at school. If this is done, difficulty would arise in those children who have a higher than normal, or a lower than normal, intelligence. An eight-year-old child, for instance, with a mental age of ten years, who reads at an eight-year-old level on reading tests, would be considered to be normal, whereas in reality he is two years behind his capacity, and so should be classed as a reading retardation.

The two-year gap between the reading age and the mental age is an arbitrary figure, and although it is satisfactory in most cases it becomes a problem when testing a child's ability to read in the first few years of his school life, when a two-year gap cannot be obtained. A child of six or seven years of age cannot have the required two-year gap between the R.A. and M.A. if his M.A. is average or below average, as reading tests do not extend to this lower age group. Yet it is in the first few years that it becomes imperative to discover existing reading difficulties so as to institute immediate treatment. As reading retardation is only a symptom of a much wider disorder, we may well be advised to be aware of the various other associated disturbances when we evolve a more adequate definition in the future. As we continue we will see that reading retardation very rarely stands alone as a disorder and invariably is associated with many other signs and symptoms, and it is the recognition and understanding of these that play an important role in diagnosis of the condition, especially at an early age.

The frequency of reading disorders has been variously expressed as from 4 to 30 per cent of all school children, the average being 10 per cent (50, 51, 52).* These figures will include all reading retardates reflecting all causes.

Reading is one aspect of learning, having both general features and specific features of its own. We must now deal with both the general and specific features for a comprehensive understanding of the poor reader.

* Numbers in parentheses refer to works listed in the Bibliography, pp. 260-3.

FACTORS UNDERLYING THE NORMAL AND ABNORMAL READING PROCESS

Reading is not an activity suspended in a vacuum. It is a process which the child with certain endowments performs in a specific social setting. The actual process of learning to read is still a mystery, but we are aware of several factors necessary for its function:

1. Adequate brain function.
2. Social, cultural and educational factors.
3. Psychological factors.

Brain Function

We are aware of the outside world only because of our sense organs, stimulation of which produces electrical impulses conveyed to the brain via the sensory nerves. These impulses are received in portions of the brain called the primary sensory areas, which make us aware that we have been stimulated. This process is that of sensation, and it involves no more than an elementary awareness.

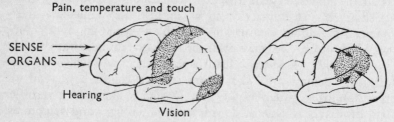

PRIMARY SENSORY AREAS   SECONDARY SENSORY AREAS

FIG. 1

Disturbance of the sense organs or sensory nerves cuts off the supply of information to the brain and so reduces the awareness of the outside world. Reduction of sight or hearing in the very young child, due to disease or defect in the ear, eye or their nerves, can interfere with learning. This interference leads to a general defect in the ability to learn, a part of which will be reading.

Once the sensory impulses have reached the primary sensory areas, they are conveyed to other areas for elaboration, co-ordination, storage and coding (secondary sensory areas). It is in these areas of the brain that meaning is made of all the incoming electrical impulses. One appreciates that there is a gradual building-up of memory and a gradual formation of concepts over the years before one can use these areas adequately for complex perceptual purposes. The process of making sense of stimuli is perception, and the full story of what it constitutes has not been written; but it is in this sphere of brain activity that a child develops his *reality*. He learns: where his limbs are in relation to his body; where his body is in space; what is left, right, up, down, in, out, etc.; what time, length, shape, texture are; and how to code and decode symbols of his culture. (The most important of which is language, reading being one part of language.) We must emphasise that reading is only one aspect of language, which is a function of the wider perceptual ability. The interlinking of all these functions produces a dependence one upon the other, so that if one is disturbed the chances are that we will find others that are disturbed too.

What is fed into these secondary sensory areas is extremely important. Feeding too little, too much, or feeding the 'wrong' information would shape a *reality* of the child which may well deviate from the norm. Secondly, the capacity and capability of these areas determine how the incoming material is processed. If the function is adequate and the incoming material is satisfactory we would have a normal reality – one which would coincide generally with that of his peers. If there is a defect in the elaborating mechanism we can have distortions of reality in any portion of it.

Defects in these areas can occur in three ways:

*Constitutional Defects.** Through inheritance the child may have fewer brain cells, or they may be incorrectly connected, or the activity of the cells may be lowered or absent. Whatever the defect, function is lost and the brain is less efficient than the average brain.

It may involve many functions of the brain or may single out only one. One of these functions, as we have seen, is the identification and understanding of symbols, which is the basis of reading.

Damage due to Disease. This is disease or injury to existing brain tissue, and the results are very similar to those due to constitutional defect.

Stimulus Deprivation. It has been observed that certain steps in the maturation of the child's brain require external stimuli at certain

* See p. 188.

critical periods* for their final emergence. If these stimuli are lacking at these critical periods, maturation is delayed or completely lost. This means that certain functions may not emerge even though the child may mature in all the other functions. If aspects of perception are so hampered we may find that language (and reading) are defective.

When one relates the above information to the learning of reading we can see that:

1. There are areas of the brain which are involved in the process of reading. We do not know their full extent, but those areas outlined in Fig. 1 show the most important.

2. Sensory input can be at fault and we will have a general learning deficiency, one aspect of which is reading difficulty (26).

3. Secondary sensory areas may be disturbed, either as part of a general brain disorder, or as a local disturbance involving perception only (29, 46). In the general disorder we will expect many signs and symptoms; and only one will be that of a reading disturbance. This is seen in diffuse brain damage, in mental defect,† and cerebral palsy,‡ where the learning problem is only one aspect of a large disorder. In a local disturbance affecting the perceptual areas only we will see a more restricted symptomology, where reading will be disturbed along with other perceptual defects. It is very rare to have a reading disturbance existing alone. When reading is disturbed as a result of organic disorder it is called dyslexia (or alexia when there is a complete inability to learn to read). We see too that dyslexia can result from (*a*) constitutional defect (often called constitutional dyslexia or genetic dyslexia (16)) and frequently runs in families; (*b*) brain damage (traumatic dyslexia); and (*c*) lack of external stimuli, which could be called maturational dyslexia.

4. One can imagine a range of brain defect, from the extensive to the more focal, and from the severe to the mild (minimal): see Fig. 2. If there is minimal brain disease over a wide area it will cause widespread minimal disorder. This is one kind of minimal brain dysfunction.

Further Notes on Brain Function

1. Because the secondary sensory areas are closely associated with

* See p. 82.   † p. 183.   ‡ p. 37.

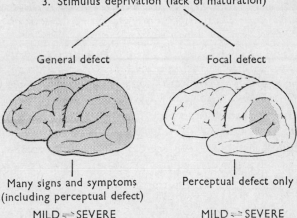

CAUSE:
1. Constitutional (defect)
2. Disease (destroyed tissue)
3. Stimulus deprivation (lack of maturation)

General defect   Focal defect

Many signs and symptoms   Perceptual defect only
(including perceptual defect)

MILD ⇌ SEVERE   MILD ⇌ SEVERE

FIG. 2

the motor areas of the brain there may or may not be, in cases of disease or disorder, associated motor dysfunction such as inco-ordination, which will show up as poor handwriting and clumsiness. These children are frequently accused of laziness and punished, but it must be remembered that they are incapable of smooth lettering as their nerves and muscles will not allow it.

2. Much has been written on the ophthalmological aspects of reading disorder (26), especially on the movements of the eye during the act of reading. The question is still unsettled whether the disturbed ocular movements that often accompany reading retardation are the cause or the effect of the condition.

3. The degree of consciousness will also determine the capacity of the child to learn. The disturbances of consciousness most commonly seen in schools are those due to brain disease, drug therapy, and those due to petit mal epilepsy. In the latter there is a momentary loss of consciousness (lasting only for a few seconds) in which the child loses touch with his surroundings, and as there may well be many hundreds or even thousands of attacks in one day, he will have lost much of his ability to attend to his learning.

Social, Cultural and Educational Factors

One need not linger too long on the many social and cultural factors which cause learning difficulties, as they add up to those which prevent the child attending school, and those which undermine his health and prevent his attending to his lessons. There are those families which keep their children at home during family crises or to assist with the household chores; the problem families which allow non-attendance and condone truancy; the poor families with lack of clothing and food, which may lead to malnutrition. All these factors will contribute to a lower level in learning, a part of which will be reading.

Educational factors are embraced by the concept of good teaching, lack of which once again will hinder the learning process. Poor and misdirected teaching more often results in an overall poor learning in the child, but occasionally may cause a specific reading difficulty.

Psychological Factors

We shall examine the personality structure of the child for two reasons. The first is to determine what factors in the personality contribute toward the child's inability to read; and secondly to find which factors help or hinder the child who is already dyslexic. Much has been written on this aspect (22, 23, 24, 25, 27, 28, 35, 39, 42, 43).

When a child arrives at school he brings with him various attitudes, feelings and responses which he has developed over the years in his family group. As these are the only ways of behaving he knows, he will apply them to his new environment. The development of these attitudes and responses is a gradual one, being the product of a moulding tendency of the family on the child in so far as the child's inborn constitution will allow itself to be moulded. This dynamic interaction between the child and his environment produces behaviour which will constitute his personality make-up.

Despite the infinite number of families, it is recognised that many have very similar patterns of dealing with children, and there are family types that stand out as fairly well constituted, and they will serve here as examples.

The Kindly Authoritarian Home. In this home the parents create an environment for the child which is kindly and loving. They are concerned with and for the child and wish him to do well. He is encouraged to act at a high level, but at times this is quite beyond his capabilities for his age. When he fails he is made to feel guilty and their response is frequently felt by the child as withdrawal of approval and love. 'If you do what I wish you to do then I will love you, and if you don't, then I won't' is the feeling the child eventually acquires, though this essentially may be an incorrect interpretation. He loves his parents and will try harder so as to avoid disapproval. He becomes obedient, neat and tidy, and in general fits well into the routine and rituals that the parents demand. He is an achiever and tries hard at any task. He doesn't want to fail, as this means withdrawal of affection by those who are important to him.

He becomes the perfectionist (or obsessive-compulsive) personality. These children are a joy in any classroom, and his willingness to learn is legend; and unless there is a dyslexic (organic) factor in the child he will usually learn to read well and easily.

There are, however, three ways in which the perfectionistic child can fail at school.

(a) When his personality traits themselves interfere with learning. He may become so concerned with perfection and ritual that he may not be able to move beyond a certain point, and his learning comes to an abrupt halt. These are the children who tear out pages from their books when they have made a mistake or will rewrite a whole notebook of notes into a brand new book because a word or drawing is incorrect.

(b) When he fails to achieve he often becomes depressed and with this depression there is a hopelessness. External evidence of this is a withdrawal from social contact, daydreaming, crying for no apparent reason, and a falling-off in his work at school.

(c) He may become neurotically involved with the meaning or with the shapes of words, and they may have some disturbing symbolic relevance to his inner conflicts. This may cause him to refuse to read, or to read only certain words. In (a) and (b) the learning difficulty is a general one, and must occur in the child's first or second year at school to interfere with reading to any extent. In (c) reading is involved alone and is one type of specific reading difficulty.

The Overprotective Home. As the name implies, in this home the child receives 'protection' by his parents, but to a degree quite beyond that which a child requires. Small dangers and simple tasks are overemphasised and the child eventually finds life a tremendous burden and is unable to perform the simplest thing without help from others around. He is afraid to try anything on his own for fear of failing, and he would rather just sit waiting for someone to help him, or, better still, for them to take over the whole task. In other words he never becomes autonomous and we call him the passive-dependent personality.

At school they are the children who cling to their parents for the first few days, but they do eventually settle down and become quiet, timid souls, never peeping out of their shells, never making a move until told to do so. They are so quiet that they may be 'lost' in a big classroom of children. They learn because they must, but the more the teacher pays attention to them the more they will try. If no attention is directed to them they just sit awaiting the next prod. In a small class it is possible to move these children to their full potential, but in larger classes they founder and show all grades of learning difficulties.

If only one subject is retarded in these children it is usually the result of a traumatic association with the subject. This is usually seen in the grades when the child is beginning to learn to read or write or do arithmetic. Homework done with a parent can provide this trauma, where the child experiences fear or terror due to harsh treatment, and as a result of a conditioning situation the subject will thereafter be associated with hurt and strong emotion, and the child will be paralysed whenever a book is produced. This conditioning process can occur in any personality, but it is most frequent in the more dependent child. If reading is the subject involved the child will develop a specific reading retardation.

The Overindulgent Home. The parents of this type of home find it difficult to discipline their children or may have a disturbed view as to what constitutes discipline, and so allow the children free rein with their whims and wants. The child comes to view the parents as 'all-giving' and he can always rely on them to get him out of trouble, and he may well expect others to react to him in the same way. As he is not well disciplined he has little or no control over his emotions and responds to situations with immediate emotional outbursts, whether it is hate, anger, jealousy or love. He is demanding and attention-seeking and histrionic. He is friendly and capable of going anywhere without anxiety – he is sure that someone will come to his assistance if he is in trouble. He is the hysterical personality.

He goes to school willingly and is soon at ease with the teachers and the other children. However, he soon finds that the work is routine and does not hold his full attention for long, and he wishes (and expects) to do something else – like going home. A skilful teacher may be able to get him to conform and do a certain amount of work, but he is often complaining, defying, asking for help, and if too much pressure is put on him he may explode into rages and temper tantrums, and run back to Mummy, who he is sure will fix everything as she has always done. Forced back to school, he can develop a wide range of physical complaints such as headache, abdominal pains, etc. Learning is frequently a problem with these children, but once again, unless there is an organic defect preventing him learning to read, he usually picks it up quickly and gains a lot of enjoyment from it – and pleasure is what he craves.

Reading problems can occur in two situations. Firstly, where an inept teacher clashes with the child over the subject and he digs his heels in, refusing to co-operate. He is able to learn, but certainly will not. Secondly, with constant pressure he may become very depressed and this depression may forestall any learning, including reading.

The Inconsistent Home. It is a truism that an inconsistent home produces anger in the child; whether the inconsistency results from two parents with differing disciplines, or both parents showing different attitudes at different times.

One kind of inconsistent home is said to produce a child who hates authority, routine, or any restriction in his pleasure-seeking. He lives for himself and makes little emotional contact with others. He is the sociopathic personality,* and at home and at school he is a very great problem. Fortunately this disorder is not that common, but one usually finds half a dozen in any school.

It is said by some that the sociopathy results from a constitutional defect, and a strange fact is that many of these children have a specific organic reading defect (dyslexia) which may be the result of the same organic deficit which prevents them responding to any discipline. Many others, however, are good readers and find pleasure

* See p. 44.

in reading. If a reading disorder results from psychological disturbance it is due to a general educational lag resulting from defiance, truancy or both.

The Neurotic Child. Neurosis uses the same mechanisms of adjustment as in normal personality development, but they are used uneconomically and to a greater extent. We find then that learning problems arise in the same manner as above, but with greater frequency.

The Psychotic Child. These children are gravely ill and the main feature of their disorder is a lack of contact with reality coupled with bizarre behaviour. They show from the start gross educational difficulties of all types, but very rarely with reading disorder as the main problem.

To recapitulate, reading can be disturbed for psychological reasons in many ways:

As Part of a General Learning Difficulty
(*a*) Any severe emotion, such as anxiety, fear, jealousy or depression, can cause an inability to learn.
(*b*) As an act of defiance in an unaccepting situation.
(*c*) As a conditioned response to an unpleasant learning situation.
(*d*) In the psychotic child.

Involving Reading Alone
(*a*) Where the act of reading is involved symbolically in the child's conflicts.
(*b*) Where the reading has become involved in a traumatic situation with an authority (parent or teacher). This is a conditioned response.
(*c*) Where reading is involved in a neurotic ritual so that the child cannot move from one task to another.

Notes on the Psychological Causes
1. Psychological and organic factors can coexist in one child.
2. The types of homes and personalities just mentioned are those that we meet in everyday life, and range from the mild to the more disturbed and disturbing. It is essential that the teacher

become conversant with every aspect of personality in order to distinguish normality from abnormality, and to trace some of the causes of learning difficulties in the child.

RECOGNITION OF THE DISORDER

The Child at School

Bearing in mind the causes of reading difficulties, we can see that the reading disorder can present itself in several ways:

As a Reading Problem. It is unusual for a child to be presented only as having a problem in reading; but if he is it is more often a severe case of dyslexia and this can show up in the first year of schooling. The child shows, from the beginning, no idea of how to read or what it is all about. At this early stage he may not have developed the secondary emotional disturbances. Less severe cases are detected a little later, perhaps in their second or third year at school. It is not uncommon, however, for them not to be detected at all, and they may go under the guise of 'naughtiness' or 'stubbornness'.

As a Behaviour Problem. As the reading problem is often part of a wider disorder, it may present with the associated signs or symptoms of that disorder. In 'minimum brain dysfunction', the restlessness, lack of concentration, the frustration and temper tantrums are usually the features which impinge more sharply upon the teacher and her endeavours to teach, and very soon there are complaints about difficulties in class and the mother is advised to seek medical help.

This hyperactive child may be so disturbing as to cause the school to seek help in the child's first year. He may be less disturbing, and two or three grades may be achieved before help is called for. Once he is recognised as a 'brain-damaged child', and once an explanation is given that he has associated perceptual defects which preclude him from the normal class routine, this is sufficient to have him sent for special education. The mental defective and the psychotic child can also show grave behaviour difficulties which single them out very early on in their schooling.

As an Emotional Problem. There are two clinical pictures which are fairly clear-cut:

(*a*) The child who comes to school with an emotional disorder and as a result of this has problems with learning. His emotional disorder is seen from the beginning and his relationships with his teacher, his peers and his parents can clearly be seen to contribute to his inability.

(*b*) The child who starts off at school with an apparently normal emotional state, but as he progresses shows increasing emotional disturbance. He may well be an undetected dyslexic who is endeavouring to perform a task which he obviously cannot; and his failure leads to increasing frustration and depression. His later reactions are determined by his previous personality make-up and these can include truancy, school phobia, antisocial behaviour, hysterical symptoms, anxieties and depression. These children if given intelligence tests may obtain very low scores and give the impression of mental defect (the pseudo-defective child). Group tests are notorious for this and it is always wise to retest any child who has obtained a low score, using a test that does not rely too heavily on reading. Retesting should also include tests for organicity and perceptual-motor function.*

Practical Factors in Assessing the Poor Reader

(i) The Act of Reading

In the first two grades the act of reading for the severely disturbed child is one of complete bewilderment and confusion, and he fails to grasp the very essence of what is expected of him. He learns to 'read' by heart to overcome his problem.

The less severely disturbed child reads with the same difficulties that the normal first-grader has in learning to read. There is a jerkiness and hesitation; he mouths his letters as if he wishes to hear the letters before he can say the word. It seems easier for them to join the letters through hearing than through sight. They make wild guesses, using some outstanding letter or letters, the form of which acts as a clue. They may learn their reading by heart, giving the impression of knowing, but are lost when the words are shown to them

* See p. 46.

out of context from their reader. They concentrate too hard on the mechanics of reading and lose sight of the meaning of what they have just read.

They find no pleasure in reading, and they rarely pick up a book except to look at the pictures. Increasing resistance is met with by teachers and parents in the reading situation and, as time goes on, both at school and at home there are problems with doing homework. Nearly all the problem readers show all or most of these features irrespective of the aetiology.

(ii) Reading Process Disturbances

These disturbances are the result of visual and auditory associational defects, and from directional confusion and temporal disorientation; all of which appear to be the basis of the child's reading difficulties. A normal child, before he learns to read, seems to possess the same problems, but they are with diligence, adequate training and maturation soon overcome.

Children with emotional, social and educational causes for their reading difficulties do not overcome these problems till much later, there being a lag of two or three years. Only the very severe psychological disorders can cause a long delay in the acquisition of reading.

Children with organic dysfunction (dyslexia) are unable to solve these difficulties at all, and they remain with the child to a greater or lesser extent all his life. Modern therapies are directed towards this end, but to date they have only managed to improve the situation and there is still a long way to go. The reading process disturbances show themselves in many ways. There is poor visual discrimination and letters are confused with each other: letters such as *p*, *b*, *d* and *q*; *m* and *w*; *n* and *u*; and *c* and *o*. There is difficulty in blending the letters or syllables together, and an inability to analyse letter shapes. They reverse letters in the words that they are reading such as *was* for *saw*, *no* for *on*. Some have associated hearing difficulties in being unable to discriminate sounds, and they confuse words such as *red* and *rid*, *pet* and *put*.

(iii) Associated Problems

These are not seen in the reading difficulties resulting from emotional, social and educational causes; and are evidence of a more severe and lasting organic dysfunction.

(*a*) *Speech Delay*. Slowness in learning to speak can occur in many conditions, but those that concern us are firstly mental defect, in which there occurs a general delay in all the developmental steps of the child as well as general delay in the learning process; and secondly the organic disorders of language areas (either inherited or acquired), where there is often a delay in speech only. In the dyslexic child it is not infrequent to obtain a history of delayed speech, and in the young child prior to going to school it may point to a future language problem.

(*b*) *Syntax Difficulties in Speech*. The problems that a child will have later in reading are sometimes reflected in his speech (32). Errors in grammar, displacing words in sentences, a twisting of letters in the words: all are heard while the child is speaking. This difficulty usually remains long after any normal child has corrected his errors.

(*c*) *Verbal and Non-Verbal Ability*. These children often show a general paucity of words in their vocabulary and may use gestures to a much greater extent than the average child. He may speak as volubly as any other child but this 'word-count' is smaller for his age. He often prefers non-verbal activities, such as model-making, carpentry, mechanical toys and outdoor activities. This emphasis on the non-verbal aspects of his activities is confirmed by psychological testing, which reveals a group of dyslexics who have a high non-verbal score and a low verbal score on intelligence tests. We must not forget, however, that all we have just stated may have resulted from a secondary compensatory mechanism on the part of the child.

(*d*) *Perceptual-motor Difficulties*. Tests for errors in perception, both visual and auditory, are often positive in these children. The Bender-Gestalt (53), the Benton Test (54) and the Frostig Test (20) are all useful in this respect. These errors in most cases cannot be detected in the classroom situation and require these special investigations, although hints of their presence can often be obtained. A feature of some of these children is an associated motor inco-ordination, which is seen in the difficulty they have in learning to catch a ball, in learning to ride a bicycle, in buttoning a coat and tying a tie. They can't hold a pencil properly and their handwriting is very poor. This scratchy, blotty and shaky handwriting is a disorder of co-ordination and not a problem in motivation, to be punished or shamed. They just can't write neatly; but they can with encouragement improve to a large extent. The probability that their handwriting will always remain to some extent untidy is great. It is said that many dyslexics are not right-handed, being either left-handed or mixed in their handedness. The problem of cerebral dominance in these children is well discussed elsewhere (14, 44, 45, 49).

(e) *Neurological Signs.* It is obvious that the more severe the brain disorder or disease the greater the neurological deficit, and the greater the chance of other signs showing themselves.

The electroencephalogram* is also reported to be abnormal in over 50 per cent of dyslexic children (21).

(f) *Family Incidence.* Genetic dyslexia (16), as its name implies, runs in families, and it shows a predominance of male over female in the order of 6 to 1. It is said to be a sex-linked recessive inheritance that produces the disorder.

Twin studies have shown a 100 per cent concordance in monozygotic twins, and a 30 per cent concordance in dizygotic* twins. Hallgren (51) has shown that 88 per cent of dyslexics have other members in their family with the same condition.

The Preschool Child (Predicting Reading Failure)

The majority of schools make no attempt to assess the child's readiness to attend school, relying only on the age of the child as a guide to whether he should or should not begin his studies. That he is capable of performing adequately will then show up as the years progress.

Some schools, however, do try to predict the child's capacities before he starts his first grade. The tests (17, 18, 19, 30) that are used include an intelligence assessment, a reading readiness test, and some evaluation of the emotional state. Underlying these tests is the knowledge, as we have seen, that learning in general (and here reading in particular) relies on many factors. In the older child it is clearly seen that both neuro-physiological defects (i.e. disturbance of central nervous system) and psychological factors play a major role in the child's inability to learn. It is argued that if one could follow these defects back to an earlier age and tackle them before the child started school, one might give him a better chance of success. There

* See p. 182.

is increasing evidence to suggest that appropriate testing at the age of 4 or 5 years can reveal future reading problems, and if suitable remedies are applied at this age they contribute substantially to the future learning of reading.

It is unusual for the uninitiated person to be able to detect the future reading problem at this young age, but there are a few pointers which are available which can direct attention to a future problem, and persons dealing with the preschool child can discover the child who is 'at risk'. These are:

The Slow Developer. This is the child whose development is slow and whose milestones are behind the average. This is seen in the mentally defective child, in whom all educational milestones are tardy. In the aphasic child and the child with the 'maturational lag', speech alone is delayed and the other milestones are normal.

The Hyperactive Child. The child with minimal brain dysfunction exhibits restlessness, lack of attention, a quick temper, and is difficult to discipline. These patterns occur very early on in the child's life and make one aware that there will be a problem later on in his life when he begins to learn to read.

The Emotionally Disturbed Child. This child is always 'at risk' where learning is concerned and may well be backward in all subjects and very occasionally only in one.

The Inept Child. The one who finds it difficult to catch a ball, to learn to skip, to ride a bicycle. He can't hold a pair of scissors easily, or colour in pictures within the lines. He can't stand on one foot, or hop. He is generally clumsy and awkward. There are grades of this awkwardness and the minor deviations require close observations over time. Many tests have been devised to discover these minor changes in activity (20, 29, 30), which can be used with great effect.

Family History. This may give a hint, as in some types of dyslexia several members of one family are found to have similar reading disabilities, or are not right-handed or are amusical (unable to carry a tune).

A Differential Diagnosis of Reading Retardation

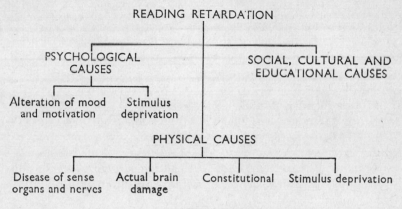

FIG. 3

In a classroom of thirty children, at least three will have a mild or severe reading difficulty. In order to determine the nature of the problem we need, in many cases, a team of diagnosticians. Once the initial label has been placed on the child – that he has a reading retardation – he will require a thorough investigation and it would be negligent to suggest that he is 'just a slow learner' or 'he has some emotional problem' or 'he hasn't matured yet, let us wait till next year and see how he does'. The rule should be in every case – quick and thorough assessment and immediate treatment.

As many of these disorders are 'silent', that is, they do not show up in a spectacular way, it is necessary for careful and detailed examination in every case to unearth the cause or causes.

It is worth repeating that the child with a reading retardation is not the special property of any one discipline, but needs the full multidisciplinary approach in diagnosis and treatment. He will require:

1. The initial diagnosis of a reading retardation (37, 13, 38), that is, that his reading age is at least two years behind that of his intellectual level. This is usually made by the teacher, but can be done by the pediatrician, the psychologist or the psychiatrist.
2. Intelligence assessment, using tests that rely less on reading.
3. Personality assessment.

4. Full physical examination. This will include tests of hearing and sight, and a speech assessment.
5. Special tests. These include perceptual–motor tests and an electroencephalogram.

The above scheme is an ideal, and as much as one feels that a full investigation is necessary in every case, many of the cases certainly do not have anything so comprehensive. Several factors contribute to this lack:

1. The presence of the 'limpet syndrome', in which a specialist in one discipline grabs hold of the problem, feeling that he can do all that is necessary for the child.
2. Many physicians themselves are not aware of the full implications of reading disorder and cannot participate to the full. Much needs to be done in disseminating information about the problem.
3. One usually has to work within a framework of existing staff, many of whom do not have the qualifications to handle the disturbed child.
4. The majority of cases are not recognised from the start and never reach the initial stage of diagnosis. Solutions of these difficulties are slow, but progress is being made in every direction.

THE RIPPLE EFFECT

If we throw a child with a reading retardation into the social pool we can see the ripples of his disorder grow wider and wider, seeming to touch everyone with whom he has contact.

The Child Himself

The vast majority of these children have secondary emotional disturbances, and these disturbances depend upon his own personality structure and the support that is offered by his family, teachers and friends. There is firstly confusion and bewilderment when he comes into contact with reading – in some much more than others. He soon realises that he cannot do something that the next child can, and his response to this may be either withdrawal from the task, greater application to the task, or some other way of adjusting.

Withdrawal is common and occurs in the more passive-dependent child. Stress of this nature (being unable to learn to read) brings on crying spells and depression and an unwillingness to remain at school. He may also show somatic symptoms such as abdominal pains and headache.

The achieving child tries for longer, but he too will eventually fail, with subsequent depression and withdrawal; although he often will attempt to achieve in some other area, such as in sport, music, or in another school subject.

Other techniques used by children in their adjustment under stress include a variety of attention-seeking and acting-out behaviours. These tend to take the teacher's (and the parent's) attention away from the basic reading problem and focus it upon something else. Early on in their schooling there are few children who admit to failing in reading; instead they will say 'it is a stupid subject' or 'I hate books' or 'I prefer sums', or they may project their difficulties upon their teacher, their parents, the class bully, or some recent illness.

These methods of adjustment are influenced greatly by the support (or lack of it) that the child finds at home. Some homes are able to contain the difficulties for years before noticeable emotional problems arise; while others add to the child's stress with extra pressure and recriminations, and the child breaks down much sooner.

The image that the child develops of himself as a person is very important, and the child with a reading disorder eventually develops an image of himself as being different from his peers. It is imperative that he be made aware of the true nature of his condition, as he may conjure up some distorted image of himself as being 'abnormal' or 'mad'.

With a limitation on his reading prowess he will organise his life accordingly, and this restriction hampers his full personality development. Unless others take over the role that books normally play in a child's life in vocabulary formation, the child will fall far short of his colleagues in his ability to use words. His inner fantasy world will become threadbare owing to lack of stimulation and his ability to conceptualise may become restricted. In therapy this lack must be made up by active measures ensuring that the child becomes aware of words and concepts through other means.

C

Parents and Siblings

Psychological stress involves three aspects. What is the meaning of the stress to the person concerned? How can it be avoided? Will it occur again and how can it be prevented? The meaning which a failing child has for his parent can range from identification with the child in his misery and failure, with subsequent help and emotional support, through to feelings of guilt at having produced such a creature and endeavours to place blame on the child, the teacher, or the other parent.

Solving the problem produces either extra lessons, extra homework hours, coaxing, punishment (physical and emotional), outbursts of temper, etc.

As the condition occurs again and again the family soon uses up the adjustive techniques that the home has at its disposal and this situation leads eventually to a request for outside help.

Relationships within the home of the child with a reading problem are placed under great strain and unless the bonds are good there is soon internal strife involving all the members. Mother fails in her homework sessions, and blames the child or the father for not helping. Father accuses mother of not doing the work properly with the child and may even take on the task himself. He too will fail with severe deterioration in relationships between the parents, and between the parents and the child. Outside help is sought or the school becomes the scapegoat.

Siblings are brought into the disorder and teasing, competition and comparisons result.

The Teacher

One frequently forgets that teachers are also human and subject to all the human emotions and motives. We expect them to be above all these baser things! They often work within a framework which requires a certain standard of work from the children within a certain period of time. Class population is sometimes too large for adequate individual supervision, and the child who fails to keep up with the rest of the class may get 'lost'.

A teacher's responses to a failing child extend from the helpful to the not so helpful. There may be an active attempt to find the root cause of the failure, and special attention is applied to the child's work. Parent Teacher Associations are very useful adjuncts in this respect if they are functioning as they should, and can contribute immensely in solving some of the problems associated with the failure. The teacher may not recognise the condition at all but will still give extra time and perhaps extra lessons after hours. In the milder cases this may achieve the desired effect, but usually this only adds to the burden of the child. The child may be considered lazy or stubborn and the teacher will institute punishment to remedy this. Underlying this punishment often lies a degree of guilt or fear in the teacher. She may wish to maintain a certain standard in her class and the failing child thwarts her in this. There may be a more malignant neurotic conflict which drives her in her actions.

Some failing children are completely ignored by the teacher, with inevitable deterioration. She may project the failure onto others, and accuse the parents of laxity in homework supervision, or of producing an emotionally disturbed child.

The teacher's handling of the problem will depend on her own awareness of the vast range of causation of the condition, and this in turn will depend on adequate tuition and training in college while a student. It is probable that in most cases book-learning on the subject is reasonably adequate, but one wonders if student teachers ever have practical experience with these children under competent guidance, and are made aware of the signs and symptoms in the classroom setting.

Friends and Social Activities

Some reading retardates show no great difference in their social activities, but most do show a characteristic pattern of adjustment to their social world.

They indulge more in outdoor activities and prefer the active use of their limbs in running, climbing and in all kinds of sports. Children suffering from the severe disorders of organic origin that show the associated motor inco-ordination may find these activities a problem, but they still prefer outdoor to indoor pastimes.

Their hobbies and interests cluster around the non-reading activities such as model-making, carpentry, knitting and sewing, collections of stones, etc. Even these may be hampered by their inability to read, as they often require written instructions and patterns, the reading of which will fall on helpful friends and relatives.

Friends are chosen to fit into their non-reading activities, and one may find the child choosing friends who have similar educational difficulties, or he may find younger children to play with. It is said that some reading retardates tend towards delinquent behaviour much more readily than the average child; and surveys of delinquent children have shown a high proportion of retarded readers. It is probable that the disorder that underlies the reading difficulty may also underly that which causes the delinquent behaviour. Parents frequently complain that these children are unable to stick to any task for any length of time, even to the extent of not completing a model that they are making, or a scarf they are knitting. Their abundance of energy is rarely directed to goals of which the parents approve, and is used up in random movement. This lack of perseverance is by no means usual and is probably associated with the brain-damaged child.

THE TREATMENT OF READING RETARDATION

Treatment must be directed to all areas that are deficient. Frequently there are many causes for the disorder, and in fact it is rare to find a child with a reading disorder who has only one facet to remedy, be it cause or effect. This being so, several disciplines will be used in the handling of the problem, with a great deal of overlapping of the treatments they apply.

Educational Treatment

This is the sphere of educationalists, and educational treatment is of primary importance in every case of reading retardation, no matter what the cause. Before starting therapy it is important to consider several aspects:

The State of the Child. The cause of the reading disturbance must be amply understood and liaison with other disciplines maintained.

The severity, the length of time the child has been at school before the condition was discovered, and any associated emotional factors must be carefully weighed in the planning of a treatment programme.

The Physical Setting. A decision has to be taken as to whether the child is to be treated at his own school by his own teacher, or at his own school by a remedial teacher; whether he needs to receive tuition at a special school catering for all subjects of the curriculum, or at a special school which handles only remedial reading. This depends wholly on the facilities available, and in many countries one is not able to choose the most desired treatment. This does not, however, prevent future planning for optimal treatment facilities.

In practice it has been noticed that the child responds better in a setting away from the one in which he has so often failed, and remedial education away from his school is not infrequently indicated.

The Milieu of the Treatment Programme. This embraces not only the physical environment of desks and books, but rather the inter-personal contact that is made by the teacher. The result of the treatment depends so much on the personality of the teacher, which in turn reflects her confidence, sincerity and interest; her ability to identify the difficulties that the child is having; the ability she has in adapting the programme to the child; her training and experience as a teacher; and the enthusiasm accompanying the treatment programme.

The Frequency of Treatment. It is difficult to state categorically how frequently the child should obtain therapy, but certain points do stand out as important in considering this. The cause of the condition often sets the time pattern. Where poor teaching is the cause, treatment involves remedial work in the classroom and will be patterned on the average classroom routine. Behavioural symptoms of a psychological nature often succumb to a short intensive educational training period, during which the psychological factors are being handled with psychotherapy. Organic causes involving perceptual defects will need long and maintained therapy if improvement is to be sustained. Such treatment will be given daily and will probably be found in special schools, which are able to incorporate the therapy in an otherwise normal school routine. Associated psychological factors may hinder progress in reading therapy to such an extent that continuous and frequent remedial reading is required.

Factors such as distance may alter the programme, as children living in remote areas would be required to attend an intensive course of remedial reading no matter what the cause, and they will return to their usual school on completion of the course. Change of domicile has been advocated in severe cases, if the parents are able to do this, thus enabling the child to have the appropriate treatment.

The Method of Treatment. There are many methods available for helping the child who cannot read (33, 34, 11, 36, 48, 8, 2), and each advocate is convinced that his or hers is the one that will succeed. The ultimate object of any method is to enable the child to learn to read and to derive meaning from what he has read. On looking closely at the methods available it becomes obvious that there are many things common to all:

(a) The maintainance of the child's interest by the use of graphic and interesting material.
(b) The overcoming of negative emotional responses to reading (41).
(c) The use of other sense modalities for learning, such as touch and the kinaesthetic sense.*
(d) The repetition of the material in many forms and in many ways, even to the extent of the gimmick.
(e) The obtaining of co-operation between parents and teacher in the handling of the child.

Perhaps the most important factor in the handling of these children is that the teacher should have the ability to adapt herself to the child's defect and his immediate emotional state, being able to move from one method to the other to accommodate the child and not expecting the child to fit into any one method of tuition.

Medical Treatment

Treatment is directed at the disease causing the condition, or the associated symptoms. Diseases of the brain, the eye or ear, any chronic debilitating condition, petit mal epilepsy, etc., must be treated appropriately. Symptoms associated with reading retardation

* See p. 84.

include restlessness, short attention span, outbursts of temper, acting-out behaviour; all of which prevent the child concentrating on learning.

Excessive medication also has its dangers, in that the drug given to prevent these symptoms may cause drowsiness and the cure may be worse than the original condition. Teachers and parents must co-operate with the doctor in assessing the optimal dose of the drug and in observing and reporting on the degree of sedation or tranquillisation.

Of late reports are to hand (31) concerning the efficacy of conditioned reflex therapy.

Psychological Treatment

There are various grades of psychological treatment, each depending on the degree of psychological insight of the therapist and the training that he has had in psychodynamics. These extend from that available to medical practitioners, psychologists, teachers, social workers and ministers of religion, to the more advanced training of the clinical psychologist and the psychiatrist. It is a wise person, however, who has sufficient insight into his own capabilities and deficiencies in the treatment programme to know when to refer the child and his family to a more competent therapist. Psychological therapy is aimed at the child, the parents and the teacher.

The Child. Therapy depends on the extent of the emotional disorder in the child and can be either supportive or a more extensive uncovering of disturbing conflicts. Important, too, are the gradual insights he obtains concerning his learning disorder.

Supportive therapy is given by a teacher in her everyday contact with the child, or by the clinical psychologist or psychiatrist if he has been referred to them.

More extensive therapy can only be given by trained persons, and it is most unwise for the untrained to embark on this kind of action.

The Parents. Counselling of the parents of the child is essential in every case, so that they can understand the child's disorder. Release from anxiety and guilt is aimed at by this discussion; and the various psychological complications of the disorder are gradually worked through by the parent under the guidance of the therapist.

At times the family disorder which has resulted is treated by therapy of the whole family together (family therapy).

Guidance of the parents on the handling of the child is very essential. How to conduct his homework sessions, what methods of discipline should be applied; the way in which he could be encouraged; the types of books he could read; how to train the child in other ways in order to build up an adequate vocabulary and concept formation, etc.

The Teacher. Many teachers are fully aware of how to handle the reading-retarded child, both educationally and psychologically. But many are not, and discussion of the problem with a therapist may be useful to both. An understanding of what constitutes a reading retardation, and an appreciation that it has specific aetiologies, may often allay guilt that the teacher has about her attitudes to the child and provide a new foundation for a more adequate relationship.

It is also useful for the teacher to become aware of the problems that exist in the child's home and of how emotional difficulties have arisen between the parents and the child.

This understanding should develop into a stronger working relationship between the teacher, the parents and any other therapist that has been called in to help. The average Parent Teacher Association fails miserably in its duties in this sphere, its members' main concern on the whole being fund-raising, and they tend to forget that their prime objective is to obtain a closer working relationship between the teacher and the parent for the benefit of the child.

PROGNOSIS OF READING RETARDATION

If we examine a group of adults who have had the benefit of school education, we rarely find one that cannot read at all. So it would seem that, even though they may have had a reading retardation as children, they have acquired a certain facility in reading as time has gone on. It is often asked, if this is so, what is the necessity for the urgent remedial education and other therapies which are so frequently adovcated. The answer lies in a closer examination of these adults. If this is carried out, several facts emerge.

Although they may be able to read, their reading is not fluent, nor can they read aloud without hesitations and mistakes. The extent of their reading is often limited to the newspaper or that which their work requires. They are invariably poor spellers, and their verbal facility and thought content is limited. This limitation will have directed the choice of work and interests, so we may find a person with a reasonably high intelligence who is functioning at a much lower level than his intelligence would warrant. In some cases, it is said, the intelligence test shows a low score as a result of this lack of stimulation, which is lower than the one that he had when tested as a child. Long-term follow-ups are scarce, and the subject offers a fruitful area for research.

Prognosis of reading retardation depends on the cause of the reading disorder (40), educational and social causes allowing the best prognosis. Prognosis of retardation due to psychological causes once again depends on their severity. Psychotics and grossly disturbed children have a poorer prognosis while the milder emotional disorders have a better one. The organically caused reading disabilities (dyslexias) are much more difficult to cure and some are quite impervious to the most forcefully applied therapy.

On the whole, however, there is usually a general improvement and figures given suggest that 80-90 per cent of all cases improve under therapy.

3 The Teaching of Elementary Mathematics

Leonard Sealey

INTRODUCTION

One of the most interesting and persistent reform movements in schools relates to the teaching of mathematics. Reform has transcended national boundaries, has broken down at least some of the barriers between schools, industry and institutions of higher education and drawn upon various disciplines for a theoretical rationale. We are now in the second decade of the reform of mathematical education and it is possible to look back over an extended period of turbulent movement away from the well-established practices of the traditional curriculum.

It is not surprising that reform should take place. The exponential growth of technology, associated with advances within the field of the physical sciences, is the major genesis. But it is not only the physical sciences which have focussed attention on the sterility of mathematics at the school level. A fresh appraisal of techniques which are basic to the social sciences and to efficient management of institutions of many kinds also contributed to the view that the majority of young people were subject to outdated studies. However, it was not merely the present and pressing needs of society which led to concern. There was a growing feeling in schools that pupils were being denied access to stimulating ideas and to a way of thinking which was fundamental to a full life in a changing world. Precious time was being wasted on a curriculum cluttered up with much dead wood. Unless fundamental changes were put into effect, children would be totally unprepared for the unknown future. In consequence, both the quality and content of mathematical education have been given close attention in many parts of the world.

Changes have not been limited to subject matter. Research relating to cognition, to the learning process, and concerning the nature of growth and development of children, has made it clear that many teaching practices are also in need of major reform.

The consequent upsurge of interest of educators, mathematicians and psychologists led to a diversity of fresh approaches, the establishment of a great variety of 'projects' and the expenditure of very considerable amounts of money in serious attempts to create a 'revolution'. To suppose that such a revolution has taken place would be naïve, but very considerable changes have occurred and the movement continues unabated.

Concern to bury much that was old led to the common usage of the terms 'new' and 'modern'. The adjective 'modern' is prevalent in Europe and 'new' more frequently met in continental America. Unfortunately both terms have led to confusion and a degree of emotional reaction by some teachers and parents. Looking back, we see that the words have come to mean several things.

First, we have the inclusion of fresh content in the mathematical curriculum. In fact, much of this material is 'new' only in the sense that it is unfamiliar. Mathematicians are constantly inventing really new mathematics of a highly sophisticated nature, but much of it has no ready application to the solution of existing problems and is therefore unlikely to find a place in any contemporary curriculum. The new content derives from mathematics of the last hundred years or so, and an example is the inclusion of some of the newer algebras and geometries.

Second, there is the upgrading of certain topics and their reformulation in ways which reveal the underlying structure and the interrelationships of concepts. The view that children should develop an understanding of the nature of mathematics, of its internal logic, is comparatively recent. The placement of topics in learning sequences often worked against such growth. Much of the mathematics of the early school years was learned in discrete parts, closely associated with facts and techniques which were presented in isolation and rote-learned. Because mathematics has been invented by man and is one of his supreme accomplishments it may be seen as a manner of thought. One thing leads to another to form a whole comprised of interrelated patterns. No child can be said to be learning mathematics unless something of the nature of mathematics and of mathematical thinking is gradually unfolding to him. An example of upgrading and reformulation is the introduction of the early study of number systems and reference to their underlying structures, such as that of a group.

A third meaning of 'modern' or 'new' relates to curriculum modifications which give an earlier awareness of the importance of certain ideas and topics in the world of industry and commerce. The inclusion of elementary statistical techniques and the associated use of simple mechanical or electrical calculating machines in the curriculum is one example, as is the introduction to elementary linear programming.

Perhaps the most significant meaning of the terms relates to new approaches to teaching which stem from psychological considerations. For a long time the mathematical education of young children was unaffected, even though patterns of learning and teaching of other subjects became significantly different and the evidence of the need for change was almost overwhelming. In particular, the developmental psychology of Jean Piaget in Geneva and the work of Jerome Bruner and others at the Centre for Cognitive Studies at Harvard University suggested that existing teaching methods needed overhaul. When the changes eventually came about, they were quite dramatic, particularly in Britain, where the approach to mathematical learning in many primary schools, based upon the wide use of concrete models, became established in a decade. Elsewhere there has been less enthusiasm for such an approach, which requires the child's use of materials which are structured and manipulated so that fundamental mathematical ideas are conceptualised. The extensive use of the environment, with each child directed towards a build-up of generalisations as a result of his own activity and 'discovery', which is another characteristic of this approach, is still largely confined to Britain and small areas of experimentation across the world.

It is necessary to keep all such changes in perspective. There are many misconceptions. Some educators are of the opinion that the curriculum as it is now being modified, allied to the revised teaching methods, will lead to a great upsurge of interest in mathematics and the attainment of much higher standards. There is some evidence to support this view, but such gains are far from general. It is also felt that the major difficulties have been overcome and that the 'new' curriculum can now settle down to become the normal mode. This is not the opinion of many of our leading mathematics educators, or the mathematicians themselves. The Report of the Cambridge

Conference on School Mathematics, *Goals for School Mathematics* (1963), leaves us in no doubt that many more fundamental changes will be required if we are not to slip back to the former state. The teaching of mathematics at all levels must be continually reviewed.

Perhaps one of the major difficulties, which must now be addressed urgently, concerns the training and retraining of teachers to handle the revised material in the newer ways. One remarkable aspect of the process of mathematics curriculum reform has been its circumvention of the teacher training institutions. The foci have been at the operational level of work in schools, or the curriculum development groups which exist either outside any system or under the umbrella of university departments other than schools of education. In Britain, and in certain other countries, the degree of national concern is contributing towards an early solution of this problem, and colleges of education are fast catching up. In the United States of America this is far from true, despite the ever larger number of summer and in-service training institutes which are associated with the many projects and supported by national organisations such as the National Science Foundation and the various professional mathematical bodies. Everywhere the publication of new texts has precipitated change and the sad fact is that many teachers are quite unprepared. Many educators now consider that much of the new work will fall into disrepute unless strenuous attempts are made to provide adequate and continuous in-service training, together with a complete redesign of the preservice training courses for elementary school teachers. It is significant that the most recent report of the Cambridge Conference (1967) faces the question in *Goals for Mathematical Education of Elementary School Teachers* and that the publications of the English Nuffield Mathematics Project are all addressed to teachers rather than children.

A further problem which has not been resolved satisfactorily is that of evaluation. The majority of teachers who are involved with updated work are convinced that children are learning more, achieving better understanding of fundamental ideas, and developing more favourable attitudes towards mathematical activity in general. But such subjective assessment, by itself, will not satisfy many. Unfortunately, evaluation techniques and procedures have lagged behind for many years and this is perhaps one reason why mathematical innovation was slow to start. Certainly there have been few innovations in regard to evaluation itself.

Some of the more promising developments are related to the definition of behavioural objectives. Content is seen as secondary to process, and performance descriptions are used to classify pupil behaviours. With such a taxonomy it is possible, by relating it to the conceptual structures of mathematics and the skills which depend upon them, to elaborate a hierarchical series of pupil behaviours which provides checks on what is being learned. The Nuffield Mathematics Project, in association with the Institut des Sciences de l'Education at Geneva, has designed such a series of 'check-ups' for the youngest children, and publications such as *Some Behavioural Objectives for Elementary School Mathematics Programs*, prepared by the Colorado State Department of Education (1966), are indicative of the thinking in some parts of the United States of America.

As far as attainment and attitudes are concerned, it is really too early to generalise about the effectiveness of recent work. Not only are existing measurement instruments imprecise, but many children have been brought up on a 'mixed diet' and it is not easy to attribute strengths or weaknesses to one approach or another. The writer's own research in English primary schools at the nine-year-old level (1964) suggests that the use of structural materials for arithmetical learning leads to a better understanding of the conceptual structures, particularly in girls, and that anxiety associated with mathematical activity is reduced. These results were clearly significant when the approach had been maintained for several years. Other research, particularly in the United States, must be interpreted with an understanding that the use of actual materials is severely limited and that class teaching from texts is much more common. Changes have largely been confined to content. Even so, certain investigations show that programmes with a modern content lead to significantly better understanding of conceptual structures.

We must now consider some of the characteristics of the newer approaches in greater detail.

SOME CHARACTERISTICS OF NEW APPROACHES

The newer approaches to the teaching of mathematics at the elementary level share a number of characteristics. First, there is the change in name from 'arithmetic' to 'mathematics'. In practice, arithmetic embraced counting and computation, with applications of the ideas to measurement. Such activity did little to encourage individuals to think and work creatively, and no general attempts were made to teach the underlying conceptual structures. The major purpose of the primary school experience was to enable children to calculate with accuracy and speed in preparation for the study of mathematics at the secondary school stage. In fact, by using demonstration and practice methods allied to rote learning in a non-permissive atmosphere, many children reached a satisfactory level of achievement. They could 'do sums' and get the right answers. Unfortunately few assimilated any of the basic ideas of which computation was the expression, and the change to the secondary school left them bewildered and anxious. Mathematics may be described as the abstract science of number and space, and mathematical activity cannot remain at the level of superficial arithmetic. Elementary notions of space as the set of all points and a beginning study of the properties of figures in space must also be taught.

One consequence of the change from arithmetic to mathematics has been the characteristic, now shared by all approaches, of continuity of experience. This is not to say that children are necessarily following strictly programmed paths, and they are certainly given ample opportunities to generate their own learning activities. We shall discuss this further when specific approaches are considered in some detail. But the newer work does provide a logical ordering of topics and also attempts to stress the interrelationships of fundamental concepts. For example, the operations of addition and subtraction are no longer learned separately with perhaps many weeks between. Because the operations are inverses of each other they are learned together. Similarly, because the number line is often used as a 'model' for such operations, the notion of a line as a set of points extending infinitely outwards in both directions requires an introduction to points, line segments, rays and lines. If the operations of addition and subtraction on numbers find analogues in corresponding set operations, then children will also be considering elements, sets and subsets.

Such approaches point to another common characteristic, the emphasis on structure. At one time it was thought that young children were not prepared to inquire beyond the obvious, indeed, that it would be inappropriate for them to do so. One of the real problems relating to mathematical learning concerns the deductive nature of the subject. The axiomatic approach implied by this would be quite unsuitable for young children because their basic learning style is to work inductively. That is, generalisations are gradually 'discovered'. In order to have an appreciation of the structure of the subject it is necessary for pupils both to become aware of the axioms and to have some feel for the recurring patterns of ideas which bind the diverse topics into a meaningful whole. Many of the newer approaches have begun to resolve these difficulties and to demonstrate that children, even at the level of the primary school, can grasp underlying principles and ideas and use them with growing power and imagination.

It hardly seems necessary to state that a further common characteristic of recent work is the rejection of rote learning of techniques and procedures. Such terms as teaching for 'meaning' or 'understanding' are frequently used to describe approaches which put children into situations in which abstractive learning takes place. Abstractive learning should not be confused with 'abstract' as it is applied to mathematics. Mathematics is a study in abstractions. There is no corresponding reality. Nobody has ever seen a number or a point. A natural number is an idea in the mind, an abstract property of a set of objects. The objects are real enough, but the number is not. One of the important characteristics of mathematics is its abstract nature, and children must eventually come to understand this. Some of the new approaches to the teaching of elementary mathematics attempt to give children an earlier feel for this quality. But most are more concerned that pupils should, through the *process of abstraction* from appropriate experiences, come to have a firm grasp of fundamental ideas without necessarily appreciating their abstract nature. For example, the design of experiences which cause children to understand the need for the extension of the set of natural numbers to the set of integers to make subtraction always possible is given more attention than experiences which lead them to understand that positive integers and natural numbers are isomorphic and that both kinds of number are not in any way 'real'.

The design of learning experiences suggests another characteristic of new methods. It is the concern for the creation of positive attitudes towards mathematical activity. In general, this is achieved by paying attention to motivational aspects. At one time, arithmetic was sometimes disliked because wrong answers to problems or inaccurate computation led to penalties of one kind or another. The motivation was negative. Pupils who did badly often became worse and over-anxious. There was a specific anxiety associated with numerical work and many suffered as a result. Indeed, the crippling effects are still visible in many adults. Up-to-date methods often play down the emotional level of the teaching situation. Projects such as that known as the Madison Project, directed by Professor Robert Davis of the University of Syracuse, prefer the emotional neutrality of 'true' or 'false' as opposed to the emotionally charged 'right' or 'wrong'. Levels of praise or blame are also controlled and there is com-paratively little positive motivation in terms of rewards. This, and other, projects prefer to aim at inherent motivation, putting their trust in the fascination and challenge of the tasks and materials with which the pupils are presented. Levels of aspiration are also open-ended, each child being relatively free to set his own. In these ways anxiety has been considerably reduced and many children have achieved levels of thought and activity which have far exceeded our expectations. More important, children have maintained their initial interest in mathematical activity and look forward to the work that will come later.

Such an approach suggests that teaching has been individualised; that children are now encouraged to work in accordance with their personal learning styles and rhythms. This is not yet the case with all newer approaches. Some are far too inflexible for this to be so, relying as they do on the continuation of an orchestration of whole class or group activity by the teacher. In Britain the role of the teacher in relation to mathematical learning has altered considerably, and individual or small group work with a wide variety of materials of many different kinds is much more common than elsewhere. The *Report of the Central Advisory Council for Education* (*England*). (1966), often referred to as the Plowden Report because the Council worked under the chairmanship of Lady Plowden, suggests that between 10 and 20 per cent of English primary schools 'have com-pletely rethought and organised their mathematical syllabus and teaching methods'. In the United States, and in other parts of Europe, much more emphasis is given to discussion by the class as a whole. Recent innovative approaches in the United States, such as that known as Individually Prescribed Instruction, directed by Professor Robert Glaser of the University of Pittsburgh, are attempt-ing to redress this imbalance. The use of computer-assisted methods, such as those of Professor Patrick Suppes of Stanford University, also hold promise of partial solutions to problems of matching each mathematical learning experience to the diagnosed needs of the individual while maintaining a high quality input.

One further characteristic must be mentioned. It is the reform of the language of mathematics. There is now much more precision in the use of both words and mathematical symbols. This is long over-due. Some approaches have introduced new symbols to replace the old. For example, the conventional use of literal symbols, such as x and y to represent variables, has largely disappeared. We now find $\Box$ ('box') and $\triangle$ ('triangle') common to many approaches. Such shapes have more meaning for children. The new way of writing positive and negative numbers is an example of the attempt to avoid confusion. For example, formerly positive nine might be called 'plus nine' even though 'plus' normally referred to an operation. The use of the symbol form $+9$ or, more correctly, $(+9)$ also led to difficul-ties. The new form $^+9$, with the positive sign level with the top of the numeral, identifies the number uniquely. Many teachers have been surprised how readily young children have taken to the more precise language of the newer work, and pupils can now proceed without having to unlearn inappropriate terms at a later stage.

Mention has already been made of the use of concrete materials in the mathematical education of children. Although such use is widespread, it is by no means universal. We shall understand its introduction more easily by turning to some of the new views of learning.

NEW VIEWS OF LEARNING

It has been suggested that the modification of classroom practices as a result of recent psychological findings is one of the most important aspects of the 'new' mathematics, but it is clearly impossible in this brief overview to give a comprehensive survey of the field.

Perhaps the most important work is that of Professor Piaget and his associates. Their developmental psychology considerably affected the teaching of elementary mathematics in England, once it became widely known, and is now reaching out to influence practice in America. The central importance of Piaget's work concerns his identification and description of stages of learning and their association with the growing child.

Of the main periods of development, that of 'concrete operations' is the most important as far as learning in the primary school is concerned. Piaget suggests that children build up their 'schemata', which might be considered as personalised interpretations of their experiences, which are then used to deal with their world, as a result of their own activity and the mental processes of 'assimilation' and 'accommodation'. He further suggests that the child, during the period of concrete operations, must interact with things 'concrete', that is with actual objects. If this is not possible, ideas will be confused and conceptual growth will not take place. The period of concrete operations is followed by that of 'formal operations'. At the formal operational stage, children are no longer tied to the here and now and to material objects, but can formulate ideas and see their interrelationships in the manner of the adult. Further research supports the view that children in primary schools are at the stage of concrete operations for much of their time.

The implications of such research are obvious. Ways must be found for children to interact with materials that are physical embodiments of the fundamental ideas of mathematics. This is not an easy problem. The abstract nature of mathematics works against acceptable solutions.

There have been a number of important contributors to the design of materials which have close associations with mathematical structures. Catherine Stern was an early worker in the field, closely followed by Caleb Gattegno, who recognised the power and significance of the Cuisenaire Rods. Zoltan Dienes, in England, was able to bring his own mathematical and psychological interests to bear on the problem and was able to work closely with other innovators in Leicestershire. Dienes not only developed a comprehensive set of materials over an extended period, but also added new thinking about the nature of the learning process. His work suggested that constructive thinking was typical of the primary school child and that analytical thought came later. More than this, he proposed that the child's activity should follow a cycle of preliminary activity analogous to play, followed next by structured experience and, finally, by a stage of practice to make the idea secure. He also established a perceptual variability principle at the structured stage, pointing out that concepts can only be assimilated as a result of a variety of perceptual experiences. In other words, there must be multiple embodiments of any one idea. Such work had a considerable influence in Britain and led to the wide use of structural materials of many kinds. The work was later further developed in Australia, Canada and elsewhere.

In the United States the work of Jerome Bruner and his associates is considered to be of great importance, but much of it is of a theoretical nature. Bruner, however, represents the viewpoint that children are capable of learning conceptual structures and that their potential in this regard is largely unrealised. His theory of mental growth is also of great interest. Bruner describes three stages, the 'enactive', the 'iconic' and the 'symbolic'. The enactive stage is that during which the child acts out his thoughts and so learns. At the iconic stage, the child uses not his body but objects which, for him, represent ideas. The final stage, the 'symbolic', is the time when symbol systems are used as the normal mode. It is interesting to compare the e developmental stages with those of Piaget. It will be readily observed that there are close correspondences between Bruner's iconic stage and Piaget's stage of concrete operations.

The combination of the work briefly described focuses attention on the inappropriateness of the conventional approach to the teaching of elementary mathematics. Teaching by telling, that is, the use of a sophisticated symbol system with its verbal stereotypes to describe mathematical ideas, is unlikely to lead to intellectual growth at a time when children need to deal with reality. The use of one concrete embodiment of an idea is better than nothing, but the generality of any concept will only be appreciated if children have a variety of experiences from which they can abstract.

We are still in doubt about the nature of learning, despite the promising work which continues. Meanwhile, it is necessary to take a closer look at some of the developments relating to the teaching of elementary mathematics in a variety of schools and curriculum projects.

WORK IN SCHOOLS

Although there were no national mathematics teaching projects in England until recently, work of a very interesting and highly innovative nature has been proceeding for some years. At first this was centred on progressive Local Education Authorities, or even individuals, but was later disseminated and extended by the Department of Education and Science, which seconded Miss Edith Biggs, H.M.I., to be responsible for organising courses and other activities for teachers across the country. The work and publications of the Association of Teachers of Mathematics also contributed a great deal to the spread of ideas and to the great upsurge of interest in reform.

The spirit of much of the work during the period from 1959 until 1964 is expressed most clearly in the Schools Council Curriculum Bulletin No. 1, *Mathematics in Primary Schools* (1965), which was prepared for the Council by Miss Biggs herself. The publication should be read by all who teach in primary schools. It is full of examples of children's work and clearly shows how the results of research findings have been built into classroom procedures.

The work described is a skilful blend of the use of special materials, such as structural apparatus, and everyday objects and experiences in an attempt to provide a mathematical education for primary school children which is both challenging and relevant. Stress is placed on children finding and solving their own problems, many of which associate mathematics with other subjects of the curriculum in imaginative ways. The approach is based upon real experiences. Experiments and investigations are carried out and recorded, with the teacher ever present to ask the significant question and suggest the next work. The complexity and variety of the tasks may confuse the casual observer. Yet anyone who first sees the film 'I Do and I Understand', which shows a large class of English children at work, will be impressed by the keen interest of the pupils and the confident way in which they work, even though the interrelationships of the various activities and their association with conceptual structures may not be obvious.

The activity in such classes has sequence and pattern, although it is closely related to each child's stage of development. Control is exercised by the teacher, who gives each child, or small group of children, an assignment which provides the starting-point for an activity. According to their abilities and interests, the children, after completing the tasks, are free to go beyond them. In this way, practice is assured and, equally important, each child develops some degree of confidence in his own thinking and action. Much of the work involves graphical representation and there is much descriptive writing about the activity.

Side by side with experimental work of this kind, many of the schools use structural materials, such as the Dienes Multibase Arithmetical Blocks or Cuisenaire Rods, to give an understanding of systems of numbers and of numeration and the arithmetical operations of addition, subtraction, multiplication and division. By making arrangements of sets of the pieces which comprise such materials, the child is able to enact the operations. Thus the written record of the calculation arises from experience. It is no longer mystical.

The work described in Curriculum Bulletin No. 1 and elsewhere represents a new approach to content which is still mainly traditional, although many topics have been upgraded and reformulated. For example, there is only a brief reference to sets and the geometry of transformations, but children meet simple statistics and calculate in number systems which have bases other than ten.

There is now one national project in England concerned with the teaching of mathematics to children between the ages of 5 and 13. It is the Nuffield Mathematics Teaching Project, sponsored by the Schools Council and financed by the Nuffield Foundation. The project is directed by Dr Geoffrey Matthews, and is mainly concerned with the production of teachers' guides. This is of significance. It presumes that the critical variables in relation to change are centred on the teacher and the headteacher, an assumption that has validity when schools have the degree of autonomy common in England. Elsewhere other points of intervention may have greater impact.

The Nuffield Project leans heavily on the earlier work but attempts to provide a greater degree of organisat on of the material and pays more attention to conceptual structures. A more rigorous notation is used and new content is included, but there is no regression to class teaching. The main themes of the various publications speak for themselves. They are 'Computation and Structure', 'Shape and Size' and 'Graphs, Algebra and Statistics'. There is a further series of 'Weaving Guides', which shows how the topics may be inter-related.

There is no doubt that the course is entirely contemporary and really does relate to the nature of children's thinking. Writing in *The Changing Curriculum: Mathematics* (1967), Professor Robert Davis refers to the approach as 'One of the finest and most carefully devised of all the 'modern mathematics' projects. . . .' Certainly it is having a considerable effect on practice throughout primary schools in Britain, and should do much to bridge the gap between work at the primary and secondary levels.

In his published review of the global scene, *Mathematics in Primary Education* (1966), Professor Dienes attempts to classify many of the new approaches. He distinguishes six major categories, 'the basic-set approach', the 'arithmetically oriented approach', the 'geometrically oriented approach', the 'symbol game oriented approach', the 'science oriented approach' and the 'object-game oriented approach'. The reader is referred to the UNESCO publication for a detailed explanation of the approaches. Two merit further consideration here.

The 'symbol-game oriented approach', in Dienes's view, is that most widespread in the United States. It relies upon game-like activities with symbols, rather than with concrete materials. We have referred already to two of the symbol forms that are commonly used, the number line and place-holders.

Arithmetical operations are symbolised by jumps on the number line. For example, the operation of adding seven to one and then subtracting two might be represented as follows:

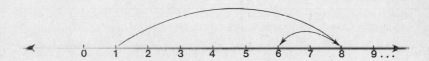

Notice that the number line suggests to the child that there might be numbers 'less than zero' and that the natural numbers go 'on and on' because that is what the line does. Using the number line, children find it easy to understand that the operation of addition on any two numbers is always possible, as is the operation of multiplication, but that subtraction is not always possible without extending the set of numbers beyond zero, and that division without a remainder is not always possible using the natural numbers. In these and other ways the need for the extension of the set of natural numbers to the set of integers, and then to the set of rational numbers, becomes clear to the child.

Place-holders, or 'pro-numerals' as they are sometimes called, are widely used in 'open' sentences, such as:

$$\square + \triangle = 10$$

The frames strongly suggest that numbers should replace or 'go into' them to make the open sentence into one that is true. The truth set of the open sentence shown above would be discovered by the child as a result of making a table:

$\square$	$\triangle$
1	9
2	8
3	7
4	6
5	5
6	4
7	3
8	2
9	1

In this case, using the set of natural numbers only, the set is finite. That is, only certain numbers may replace the pro-numerals. However, in an open sentence such as:

$$\square + \triangle = \triangle + \square$$

the truth set is universal. That is, it contains all the numbers. The truth set is universal because the open sentence is an identity which is usually referred to as the Commutative Law for Addition. It is an important element in the algebra of the number system.

Using this approach, children become familiar with the symbol forms and seldom depart from them. There is no perceptual variability. In contrast, an approach such as that of the 'object-game oriented approach' would involve the use of many perceptually different real objects to arrive at the same knowledge.

Very recent work, such as that of the Nuffield Mathematics Teaching Project, makes no attempt to have exclusive qualities. Instead, the best of many different approaches are interwoven.

A LOOK AHEAD

We are still some way from the goal of an effective mathematical education for all from the earliest days in school, although certain things are becoming clearer.

Ways must be found to match each child and the learning task. We have broken away from whole class instruction in some approaches, notably in England, and children are facing interesting tasks in situations which have a laboratory style. But it is by no means certain that the tasks really are the right ones. With the situation as it is in many schools, that is, large classes with ill-prepared teachers, the feedback system is inadequate to deal with the complexity of the situation. With the present state of computer technology, it is already possible to address this problem. Experiments in the United States show that each child can weave his individual path through a complex maze of experiences using computer-assisted techniques. But this is only one side of the issue. The computer will only respond to the information which it receives, which is based upon pupil behaviours exhibited by some form of test. Until such tests can be relied upon to reveal levels of mathematical thinking, we are still a long way from being able to make a really good match.

With regard to the tasks, there are still many differences of opinion in regard to both the approach and the content. There is much called 'new' which remains trivial and dull. Many children are not excited by the work. Too often the intellectual challenge is played down and children do not really come to grips with conceptual structures in any way which gives them a growing sense of their own power. Sometimes children are pawns in a game which seems to be designed for teachers rather than for pupils. Despite the new projects, texts continue to appear, and to be bought, which do not speak to children's needs.

Looking ahead, it seems clear that the training of teachers and their function in the classroom must change. We can expect to see much more help for teachers from central sources. National projects, local centres and on-site resource centres must place good materials and appropriate tools into teachers' hands. If some teachers cannot learn the mathematics and develop the attitudes essential to effective management in the classroom, they should not be allowed to remain as central figures in the mathematical teaching environment.

If children in primary schools do not get off to a good start, the matter is not easily put right later. It is better for them to learn nothing mathematical during the earliest days in school. Indeed, we may decide that mathematics and science should be combined, and that a form of 'pre-mathematics' which provides experiences of a very general nature, such as classifying in relation to attributes, would contribute much more to the intellectual growth of many young children.

One thing is certain: the present combined concern of mathematicians, psychologists, teachers and others will continue unabated until a sound mathematical education for all seems assured.

4 The Culturally Deprived Child

Brian Rose

The shortage of technological and scientific skills essential to an industrial culture in which increasing specialisation and diversification are taking place simultaneously, prompts a re-examination of human resources which may at present be inadequately developed.

Riessman states that approximately one child out of every ten in the fourteen largest cities in the United States in 1950 was 'culturally deprived'. By 1960 one in three were culturally deprived, and by 1970 the figure was expected to rise to one in two (1).*

The most satisfying reason for identifying and helping the culturally deprived lies in the probability that there is more latent high intelligence among the culturally deprived than among the culturally advantaged middle classes (2).

But since the symptomatology of cultural deprivation closely resembles that of dyslexia and mental subnormality, all three are sometimes grouped together under the term 'educational retardation' – with bizarre results. What are urgently needed at present are (a) generally acceptable differential definitions, (b) an adequate diagnostic strategy to identify each genre, and (c) a corrective approach that can be evaluated through successful change.

Much of the problem lies in the fact that the culturally deprived, the dyslexic and the mentally subnormal show similar behaviour patterns. Each may exhibit severe reading retardation, school aversion, problems in interpersonal relationship, and avoidance of verbal communication. Such a syndrome may precede deteriorating school progress, deviate social behaviour and early drop-out.

The dyslexic child is one whose learning difficulties result from some form of organic deficit or lesion or from perceptual dysfunction present at birth. The mentally subnormal child is one who, if his potential intelligence were actualised, would nevertheless perform at a lower level than normal children. The culturally deprived child is

* Bibliographical references to this chapter will be found on pp. 264-6.

one whose environmental thresholds are inadequate to actualise his genetically determined intelligence.

In terms of these definitions, both dyslexia and mental subnormality may be considered to be endogenous; though it must be agreed that properly devised educational therapies have raised the intellectual performance of dyslexic children. Social deprivation, on the other hand, whilst expressing itself in educational inadequacies and deviations, is environmentally induced.

The next problem – and this is a major one – is that of determining intellectual capacity or potential.

Until recent times when the whole matter has come under review (3, 4) it was usual to accept the I.Q. – which in any case is a relationship of increasing intelligence with increasing chronological age – as constant (5) until the potential ceiling of intellectual development was reached somewhere between the ages of 14 and 18 (6). Group tests have for some time been regarded as inaccurate reflections of the real intelligence of culturally deprived children (7). But whilst individual tests may well be more accurate, it remains true that, being constructed for middle-class children, they become just as culturally tainted for culturally deprived Americans as they would be (for example) for English-speaking Africans (8). Thus, as the author has pointed out (9), it is possible that many children who are not mentally subnormal may produce quotients which indicate subnormality. These results, as Haggard (10) has suggested, may be culturally conditioned by lack of motivation, skill, practice and reading ability. Whilst the Bossio study in Britain fails to clarify this point (11), it did show not only that the proportion of dull children in the sample was higher than among school children generally but also that emotional maladjustment was higher. Modern research frequently fails to differentiate between innate and learned factors. Were the children in this study dull because of social or genetic influences? Or were their intelligence scores masked by low threshold (12) variables?

It has generally been acknowledged that whilst the intelligence of normal middle-class children increases with age until the ceiling is reached (at which time the expression of intellectual potential as a quotient becomes meaningless), that of the socially disadvantaged child has a less positive relationship. Riessman conjectures (13) that this may be because such children are not exposed to the 'experiences and vocabulary presumed normal to the culture'. Chauncey

(14) supports this view and treats the preschool years as a critical period in the child's development which influences his intellectual growth considerably. The loss of development in one period, he maintains, cannot be fully recovered in another period. Koegler, a neuro-psychiatrist, supports this thesis of the 'critical period', and doubts whether the child who is deprived culturally until the age of six can ever catch up, even when given a sound primary education, a point that Silberman (15) supports.

The tendency of the culturally deprived to show up badly on standard intelligence tests draws attention to the predominantly verbal nature of most of them. Even the so-called performace tests are not free from verbal implications. The Brossio study showed that backwardness in language development was considerably larger than in intelligence or reading development, a conclusion that supported Goldfarb's finding (16) that 'the effects of deprivation tend to be more detrimental to a child's language development than to any other aspect of his developing personality'. It would seem (as Bossio also conjectures) that intelligence tests of a highly verbal nature militate against the culturally deprived and artificially depress their real intelligence. Because of verbal deficits, the I.Q. of the dyslexic child might also be depressed (17). In view of the modern trend towards streaming by apparent ability, both the culturally deprived and the dyslexic might very easily be reduced in status in the modern school system. (18).

The use of standard individual intelligence tests, and more especially of group tests, is questionable as an adequate diagnostic tool for *differentiating educational retardation which is socially conditioned from that which is genetically determined*. This conclusion is complicated by the fact that in some culturally deprived families both factors are present simultaneously. It would seem that a positive approach might be to follow up the work of Allison Davis (19), who reworded a number of tests in such a way that although the underlying facets of intellect were tapped, the language in which they were examined was culturally familiar. In view of Bernstein's analysis (20) of the language of working-class English people (to which we shall refer in greater detail later), it might well be possible that intelligence tests that are language-appropriate for the culturally deprived should be used for all children whose socio-economic standards fall below a certain level. Although educationists would still be left with the problem of the proper approach to such children, one would at least have established a reasonably reliable estimate of the innate intelligence.

There are two major problems underlying cultural deprivation in normally intelligent children. Firstly there is *language inadequacy*, and secondly there appears to be a *developmental deficiency*. It is proposed to consider the problem of language, though it should be appreciated that its separation from such experiential facets as sensation and perception (whilst convenient theoretically) is almost impossible in practice, as Piaget has repeatedly stressed (21).

EVIDENCE OF LOWER STANDARDS OF LANGUAGE ABILITY IN CULTURALLY DISADVANTAGED CHILDREN

Deprived children, says Riessman (22), are notoriously poor readers, a contention supported by the Plowden Report (23). Riessman refers to Haggard's experiment (24) of reading the test aloud to the children, a procedure that resulted in considerable improvement in results. The greatest block to the realisation of the deprived individual's potential, says Riessman, appears to be his verbal inadequacies. He points out that culturally deprived children seldom develop an *auditory set*: they are not accustomed to *listening* to adults at home. There is little informed conversation or discussion. Hence, when they arrive at school and are expected to listen to the teacher, they are confused and unpractised in comparison with middle-class children (25). The (often unrealised) task of the teacher is to train such children to *listen*.

The presence of language retardation in culturally deprived children may date back to the first two years of life (26, 27). As Jensen remarks, the sort of language that is in fact acquired shapes the child's intellectual development, especially 'the development of the ability for abstraction and conceptual learning. Poor development of this ability places a low ceiling on educational attainment' (28).

The work done by Bernstein and his associates in Britain has contributed to our understanding of the relationship between culture, language and the development of intellectual performance. In 1961 (29) he postulated two types of language usage, *the formal* and *the public*. Formal language is person-orientated, public language is status-orientated. Public language exhibits characteristics such as short, grammatically simple (often unfinished) sentences, less use of clause subordination, rigid and limited use of amplifiers (adjectives and adverbs). Formal speech is more precise and accurate, uses more clause subordinations, makes frequent use of 'I', shows greater verbal discrimination, especially of amplifiers. Lawton, working with a group of young adolescents in London, supported these postulates (30). Middle-class boys wrote 30 per cent more when given a story reproduction task and 100 per cent more when given an abstract essay. Using the term *restricted code* (instead of public language), Lawton points out that in each case working-class boys select words and structures from a narrower range. They are, at the same time, more inclined to concrete language than to abstract expression, a tendency that supports Bernstein's formulations. This study was followed by the publication in 1964 of Bernstein's further statement, in which he examined the differences of speech systems between middle-class and working-class groups. He characterised the restricted code (of the working-class group) as one which did not permit verbal elaboration of meaning, one which did not 'help the user to put into words his intent, his unique purposes, beliefs and motivations. It sensitises the user to a social relationship that is unambiguous, and in which authority is clear cut. It is a code that facilitates the ready transformation of feeling into action and in which changes of meaning are more likely to be signalled verbally' (31).

Bernstein states that the restricted code is not a speech system produced by innate intelligence. Nor, incidentally, is it necessarily (or only) class-linked, but will arise in closed communities such as the armed forces, prisons, or in peer groups. In fact, as he remarks, it will appear wherever the form of social relationship is based on some extensive set of shared identifications, self-consciously held by the group. Those using a restricted code would not stress the unique importance of the person, nor would they verbally elaborate this importance (hence the diminished usage of the personal pronoun 'I'). Bernstein suggests that the mother of a family that uses a restricted language code 'conveys her uniqueness non-verbally'; hence 'much of the awareness of the developing child of his mother is less available for verbalisation, because it has rarely been verbalised. A powerful bond of a non-verbal form is forged.' In terms of what is said verbally, he states, a restricted code is a *status-orientated* code, whilst an elaborated code (or, as he had previously called it, a *formal code*) is a person-orientated code. Status appeals rely on role appeal: 'Little boys don't do things like that'; 'Children should be seen and not heard'. Whereas the person-orientated appeal states 'Daddy wouldn't like that'; 'If you do that, you will hurt the dog'. In the status-orientated appeal, as Bernstein explains it, the *significance* of the act is the point at issue, whereas for the person-orientated it is the *feelings* of regulator that are crucial. The restricted code signals *social* rather than *personal* identity, and is concerned with the concrete 'here and now' rather than reflective, abstract relationship. The self is rarely the subject of verbal investigation. Hence a strong sense of social identity is achieved at the expense of personal identity. Work done by Hess in Chicago has supported Bernstein's main thesis and shown that it has applicability in America (32).

CRITICAL PERIODS

The concept of *critical periods* of development, accepted for some time in physiology and a probable growing point in Piagetan theory (33), has been stated by Mussen (34) as best understood in regard to the foetal development of such organs as heart, eyes or kidneys. He gives the instance of Erik Erikson's contention that the first year of life (some would extend this) is critical for the development of the child's capacity to relate to others. We have already seen that some educationists regard the period from 3 to 6 years as a critical period for cognitive development and hence for educability (35). The Plowden Report takes critical periods into account in discussing cultural deprivation (36). Writing in 1963, Martin Deutsch commented (37) that *stimulus deprivation* might well account for the underachievement of the socially deprived, a view already expressed by the W.H.O. Report in 1962 (38). This view is in keeping with Piaget's theory of cognitive development, as Flavell interprets it: 'The child should first work with the principle (of internalisation) in the most concrete and action-orientated context possible; he should be allowed to manipulate objects himself and "see" the principle operate in his own actions. Then it should become progressively more internalised and schematic by reducing perceptual and motor supports, e.g. moving from objects to symbols of objects, from

motor action to speech, Piaget's theoretical emphasis on the action
(and active) character of intelligence thus provides the rationale for
certain specific recommendations in the teaching process' (39). One
might comment in parenthesis that these conceptions are under-
strutting much of the modern teaching methodology of new maths
and modern science. The point that Piaget is making links into
Deutsch's observation that in deprived homes 'the urban slum with
its overcrowded apartments offers the child a minimal range of
stimuli. There are usually few if any pictures on the wall, and the
objects in the household be they toys, furniture or utensils, tend to
be sparse, repetitious and lacking in form and colour variations. The
sparsity of objects and lack of diversity of home artefacts which are
available and meaningful to the child, in addition to the unavail-
ability of individualised training [because the mother is usually too
busy supporting her large family] gives the child few opportunities
to manipulate and organise the visual properties of his environment
and thus perceptually to organise and discriminate the nuances of
that environment' (40). Discrimination of FORM is absolutely
essential as the basis for later reading readiness. Before a child can be
expected to read, that is to recognise and differentiate between a
standardised set of forms that we call the alphabet, he must have had
considerable practice in differentiating simpler forms. The recognition of alphabetical signals involves a process of symbolisation that
has been established in the sensory world early in the stage of
development that Piaget calls concrete operations (41). If the child's
environment is lacking in stimulation for (in this instance) recognition and discrimination, the culturally deprived child may already be
retarded in cognitive skills (as compared with the middle-class child)
by the time he arrives at school. Deutsch points out that a similar
impoverishment of VERBAL SKILL development would probably
take place, because verbal stimulation in his environment would for
the most part be meaningless noise which would promote inattention.
He comments that data so far collected (1963) at the Institute of
Developmental Studies, New York, shows that 'poor readers . . .
have significantly more difficulty in auditory discrimination than do
good readers. Further, this difference between good and poor
readers is greater in the lower class group' (42). As he comments
later, 'The acquisition of language facility . . . is particularly important in view of the estimate that only 60 to 80 per cent of any
sustained communication is usually heard.' The cultural impoverish-

D

ment of the child's environment in slum areas in particular therefore denies Piaget's dictum: *Penser, c'est opérer*. As Flavell comments
'Stable and enduring cognitions about the world around us can
come only through a very active commerce with this world on the
part of the knower. The student must be led to perform real actions
on the materials which form the learning base, actions as concrete
and direct as the materials can be made to allow. As actions are
repeated and varied, they begin to interco-ordinate with each other
and also to become schematic and internalised, that is, they are
transformed into Piagetian operations . . .' (43).

If the developmental schemata of Jean Piaget are accepted with
their underlying tenets of fixed sequence, it will be appreciated that
if the environment leads to stimulus deprivation, even the stage of
concrete operations is likely to show inadequacies. The probability
that the child will then develop its potential in the stage of formal
operations when an increasing degree of abstract thought and
logical organisation should be present, is remote. The inability of
Negro pupils to function with abstract concepts has been noted on
many occasions (44, 45). As McBroom of the University of California has remarked: 'The whole preschool period is now regarded as
critical: i.e. as another growth stage at which inadequate sensory and
intellectual stimulation can produce irreversible damage to capacity
which will be diagnosed as retarded development, be reflected in
low scores on intelligence tests, and form the base for cumulative
school failures, dislike of a school, lowered self esteem and defensive
attitudes' (46).

The dynamics of cultural deprivation are particularly important in
the United States, where the whole concept of desegregation is
threatened unless techniques can be evolved which can offset the
effects of environmental stimulus deprivation. At least one contention of the desegregationists was based on the assumption that
Negro admission to White schools would provide adequate educational stimulus for Negro children to overcome previous educational
deficits. There is evidence to show that southern Negroes had a
lower educational performance than northern Negroes, just as there
is evidence that southern Whites performed lower than northern
Whites (47). But early gains by Negro children made in school
districts such as Louiseville were maximal when whole classes of
Negroes were in fact segregated in the school under the instruction
of Negro teachers (48). To expect Negro children to handle the

highly complex web of emotional rejection at the same time as increasing their cognitive efficiency is, as Lazarus (49) and others have demonstrated, somewhat naïve. Evidence of the strain imposed on such children was given by Coles, who commented on Negro experience in White schools in Atlanta that such children showed 'all the medical and psychiatric responses to fear and anxiety. One child may lose his appetite, another may become sarcastic and have nightmares. Lethargy may develop or excessive studying may mask the apprehension common to both' (50). As far back as 1952 Lazarus *et al.* reported that 'the general trend on verbal performance has been that stress impairs efficiency on relatively complex and difficult tasks; while on simple tasks, stress has sometimes been shown to improve performance' (51). Lowered performance due to the disturbance of cognition caused by emotional factors in the environment seems to be the price that must be paid by the culturally deprived at present in America for education of a higher standard, such as may be expected in middle-class White schools. In 1963 Roberts pointed out that less than 3 per cent of Negro 'graduates' from segregated high schools would meet the standards of non-segregated colleges (52). Charles E. Silberman has noted that the I.Q. scores of Negro children typically drop by 20 points as they go through school, and that when such children participate in projects designed to improve their education, the reverse occurs (53). A similar problem exists at an acute level in England, where it is estimated some 15,000 gypsies present a small-scale problem to the educational authorities. The Adams and Smith Report, which is included (as appendix 12) in the Plowden Report (54), notes that (as frequently but not always occurs with Negroes) until World War II, gypsies 'were virtually unanimous in considering education a waste of time, harmful to health and to be avoided'. As in the case of the Negro, Gordon (55) in 1923 showed 'a considerable decline in mental ability with advancing chronological age in the group of gypsy children that occasionally attended school. A headmaster commented that, without "the normal home background of play and vocabulary, schooling was very difficult for the children".' Teachers reported that on arrival gypsy children were very withdrawn and some did not speak for three months. They appeared to understand brief verbal communications but not long sentences. Much the same problem has been reported for other children suffering from stimulus deprivation such as the Kentucky mountain children (56).

But, as D. P. Ausubel put the matter succinctly (57), the real problem – and one crucial in educational strategy – lies in the Piagetian concept of critical periods. If one defines a critical period as a moment in development that is not subject to reversibility, the implications for the culturally deprived are poor if we accept the preschool years as critical for educability. As Ausubel expressed the matter: 'If the organism is deprived of the necessary stimulation during the critical period, when he is maximally susceptible to it in terms of actualising potential capacities or developing in new directions, it is held that *some degree of permanent deficit is inevitable* [own italics]. The time of readiness can be advanced and the quality of development can be enriched by working with the children before they show overt signs of readiness.' But, he adds, in support of another aspect of the concept of critical periods, 'our work also indicates that if the time of readiness for developing certain abilities passes without being influenced by environmental agents [the home or school], these abilities may never be developed'. This contention raises once more the problem of 'irreversibility', mentioned above. Quite clearly, at the present stage of our knowledge, no conclusion can be reached, except that this is an area in which more research would be profitable.

TACKLING THE EDUCATIONAL PROBLEM OF THE CULTURALLY DEPRIVED CHILD

As has been contended in this chapter, although the culturally deprived child functions at a low level of intelligence (and hence would score poorly on any of the acceptable I.Q. tests), there is no reason to assume that his real or potential intelligence is in fact commensurate with his operative or functional intelligence. Ausubel points out that the concept of critical periods, although verifiable experimentally in other fields, has never been demonstrated empirically for cognitive development. What in fact Ausubel succeeds in achieving is a clarification: for while he demonstrates the lack of empirical support for a neurological concept of critical periods in the development of cognition, he is able to adduce considerable evidence for culturo-neurological critical periods. He makes what we may consider to be the very important statement that 'New growth . . . always proceeds from . . . the already actualised capacity, rather than from the potentialities inherent in the genotype', a statement that he at once interprets as meaning that if the child has experienced a consistently deprived environment during its formative years so that superior endowment is not actualised, the functional deficit limits the extent to which later stimulation can increase the rate of cognitive growth.

This finding has been supported by that of Moshe Smilansky, Chairman of the Department of Educational Sciences at Tel Aviv University. Summing up the tendency of modern findings (mid-1968), Dr Smilansky commented (58) that two broad generalisations were evident: (1) that to a large extent human ability is a social product, and (2) that the formal policy of equality (of educational opportunity) for all is not enough; the disadvantaged must have preferential treatment if they are to catch up.

Dr Smilansky is primarily concerned with the twin problems of prevention and therapy. Like many other exponents in this field, he contends that special attention is needed in the preschool years. But unlike some investigators, he is not prepared to accept readiness as a maturation concept based upon genetic determinism. Dr Smilansky warns against confusing the educational behaviour of the culturally deprived child with mental retardation, contending that such children should not be placed in special schools for the handicapped, where a slow tempo and a reduced range of content was supposed to answer to diminished abilities. As Smilansky comments, the culturally deprived child benefits neither from the ordinary school, nor from the special school. What he has been shown (in the Szold Institute) to need is a special curriculum, revised methods of teaching and special apparatus to fill his gaps of experience. Agreeing with other authorities in the field, Smilansky stresses the importance of the preschool years, and he states categorically 'After five years of experimentation in this field we can say that it is feasible to develop programmes for three to six year-olds that will lay a foundation for developing desirable behaviour, abilities and organisation of knowledge.'

The advantages of focusing 'rescue work' on the preschool stage are that there is at this age little gap between the advantaged and the disadvantaged; the child has experienced little failure; parents are generally reasonably co-operative; and intergroup prejudice is low. While he accepts the concept of critical periods in the broad sense, together with the concomitant concept of 'readiness' (reading readiness being the most commonly used term among educationists), Smilansky asserts that 'the time of readiness can be advanced and the quality of development can be enriched by working with children before they show overt signs of readiness'.

Ausubel divides his educational strategy of approach to cultural deprivation into three areas: (*a*) the selection of initial learning material geared to the learner's existing state of readiness; (*b*) mastery and consolidation of all on-going learning tasks before new tasks are introduced so as to provide the necessary foundation for successful sequential learning; and (*c*) the use of structured learning materials optimally organised to facilitate efficient sequential learning.

The problem of producing a curriculum specially tailored to the needs of the culturally deprived child is a considerable one, which meets with considerable resistance, particularly from those it is designed to help. Ausubel remarks, chiefly with the American Negro in mind, that the creation of a special curriculum should not be regarded as undemocratic, reactionary or as indicative of class bias or of a belief in the inherent ineducability of lower-class children (59). But the American Negro is not the only one who views special curricula with suspicion; it is the common reaction of many African communities, who see in the literary-orientated curriculum originally introduced into Africa by missionaries of the late Victorian era the ultimate in educational planning, despite the fact (as the author has himself seen) that a child who can say 'The King's coach drew up at the royal palace' would be completely nonplussed if you asked the price of a kilo of flour at the local store. Ausubel sums it all up succinctly when he says that 'to set the same initial standards and expectations for the academically retarded, culturally deprived child as for the non-retarded middle or lower class child is automatically to insure the former's failure and to widen the discrepancies between social class groups'. His insistence on consolidation is based on considerable research evidence that prior learnings are not transferable to new learning tasks unless they are first overlearned. Because of the stress on the structure and the sequencing of materials, Ausubel supports the use of programmed instruction as a learning method, but he prefers programmed book material to machine material. A number of attempts have been made to move educational planning on to the 'drawing-board' stage. Olson and Larson of Wisconsin published in 1965 a paper entitled 'An Experimental

Curriculum for Culturally Deprived Kindergarten Children' (60), which described with greater precision than is often found in educational intentions an approach to curriculum structure for a study group of deprived children. The tables, which act as a crude analysis of the skills, intentions and materials involved, may prove seminal for more detailed experimentation. Although persuasive evidence of the value of nursery school education in combating social deprivation has been assembled by Sears and Dowley (61), inadequate empirical work has been done to integrate classroom methodology into an acceptable developmental theory such as that of Jean Piaget – and it is this consideration that makes the work of Smilansky, who is concerned with materials and methods, so valuable. As Fowler commented in an important article, so much stress has been placed on the socio-emotional aspects of the child's development that research in cognition has lagged badly (62). Perhaps a breakthrough is beginning to take place in one important sector of cognitive development – that of language. British authorities are well aware of the implications of this, as the Plowden Report comments: 'Part-time attendance at a nursery school is desirable for most children. It is even more so for children in socially deprived areas. They need all verbal stimulus, the opportunities for constructive play and a more richly differentiated environment' (63).

Much can and has been done at a remedial level. But it is debatable whether corrective measures taken in adolescence should be regarded as educationally normative, or as a treatment of social pathology. The terms primary prevention to describe preschool mediation and secondary prevention to describe enrichment programmes during early adolescence have led (Smilansky mentions) to considerable gains, not only in I.Q. but in commitment to education. 84 per cent of the youngsters who participated in these programmes had completed their high school course to matriculation as compared with 62 per cent in the uncontrolled sample. Of those participating in 'enriched programmes', 83 per cent passed without any failure, as against 60 per cent in the control groups. Enrichment programmes were organised in centres outside the deprived neighbourhood, were voluntary, and consisted of two afternoons a week and a whole day during summer for three years (64).

Perhaps one of the weaknesses of current approaches to educational planning in many Western European countries is to be found in the traditional conservatism of educational thinking, which leads to an uncritical acceptance of underlying assumptions. Examination might show that many of these assumptions rest more on opinion than on empirical evidence. For example, when we consider the problem of planning effectively for the culturally deprived child, we are faced with two broad aspects: (1) the child to be educated, and (2) the corpus of existing techniques, syllabuses and curriculum content. We tend to consider this corpus as fixed and the child as a variable. In order to assess the degree of deviation of the child's cognitive response from this fixed corpus we employ a number of diagnostic devices such as intelligence tests, performance tests and personality inventories. In terms of the data obtained from these and similar testing instruments, we may label the child 'culturally deprived' or 'mentally retarded' or 'emotionally disturbed'. Whether the very considerable amount of time spent in these measurements (which are fashionable at least in part because they quantify the data and render one's work subject to statistical control) is well spent, is another matter. There may be, in fact, an untenable assumption that leads to the confusion of performance with potentiality. In addition, without realising it, many educationists have been influenced by the psycho-analytic format, which, stressing the infantile origin of neurotic behaviour, emphasises aetiology. There is no guarantee that a knowledge of 'who struck the match' will make us useful firefighters – and, as figures soon to be presented in this chapter will demonstrate, the idea of firefighting is not an extravagant one.

In practice the test results obtained after an examination of an educational deviant enable us to label him. Some modification of the classwork is then made; still too often a modification of *amount* of content, so that the difficult work is omitted and a generally slower tempo permitted in a syllabus that is shortened for that purpose. We seem to feel that such children should be able to cover 60 per cent of the syllabus instead of 90 or 100 per cent. But it seldom seems to occur to educational planners to *start with the child* and to design an entirely new course around the child's abilities and in terms of his existing level of skill and cognitive development. Putting it another way, suppose we regard the *child* as *the fixed point* (whilst recognising his immense capacity for change, which is learning) and suppose we regard subject matter, syllabus, etc., as mere tools to be adapted to suit the process of 'humanisation', which lies at the core of all

sound education — what then? Well, clearly, we have in effect
revolutionised our thinking, for we at present tend to regard the
child as *the variable* which must be manipulated into our systems –
we are, in fact, prisoners in mental constructs of our own design, our
educational systems. The primary importance of a study of cultural
deprivation lies not by any means only in the insights it offers into an
important 'minority problem' in education today, but in the leads
that such a study provides to our understanding of *all* education. If
new thinking is necessary in planning to help the culturally deprived,
it can only be made fully effective in a revitalised approach to education generally.

Since improved educational handling of the culturally deprived is
more economic of time, human resources and funds, why have we
made so little progress? The answer to this question lies partly in
the hierarchical organisation of the teaching profession – the chasm
that lies between the upper echelon of administrators, planners and
supervisors of all sorts, and the day-by-day practical work done by
teachers in the classroom. Many administrators are divorced from
daily personal contact with *children*, and hence much of the theor-
ising introduced is uncontrolled by the theorists responsible. Again,
educational planners seldom operate at a multidisciplinary level,
collaborating with specialists in other fields, such as sociologists,
psychiatrists and behavioural scientists generally. The need for the
cross-fertilisation of ideas and techniques and for an exhange of
insights cannot be stressed too greatly. Lack of informed constructive criticism in education can be costly. Whilst one can but admire
the massive projects mounted in America to reduce the effects of
cultural deprivation, it is worth noting that Fantini and Weinstein
(respectively of the Ford Foundation and Teachers College,
Columbia University) commented as recently as November 1967
that '. . . the most concentrated and widely heralded education
programs – New York's *Higher Horizons* and *More Effective Schools
Programs* and the Ford Foundation-assisted *Great Cities School
Improvement Project* – have not significantly improved academic
performance' (65).

Whilst it is almost facile to comment that the problem of cultural
deprivation resolves itself into two major areas, the cognitive and the
emotional, this division is organisationally helpful as long as we all
realise that in practice this type of Aristotelean duality has no practical basis. On the cognitive side we need to develop the seminal

thinking involved in Jean Piaget's developmental constructs, so that syllabus construction, classroom materials and books can be designed especially for the culturally deprived child. As long as we treat the middle-class child as the norm, we involve ourselves in an expensive and ineffective patchwork job with all other children (and that includes the exceptionally alert child as well). Research work has modified industrial techniques to a very considerable degree in the second half of the twentieth century, and because those who control the capital investment involved in such research sometimes evaluate this investment in terms of ultimate profits, it would seem that such research more than justifies itself. The contribution that education makes to the economy of a country is a matter of speculation, and although many countries have concerned themselves in trying to find an answer (particularly the Russians, who place a far greater value on education than do many countries in the West), it is difficult to demonstrate unequivocally that x amount of investment in education will invariably lead to y amount of profit to the nation. At present the Russians invest about 8 per cent of G.N.P. in education, whereas Britain invests 13 per cent of all public expenditure, South Africa 4·5 per cent of G.N.P., and America 6·62 per cent (66). Countries in the West need to increase educational spending and, more particularly, to create facilities on a major scale for top level research work in education, with liaison with all other countries that are willing to involve themselves. The domination of educational policy by philosophical concepts which no longer answer to modern needs costs the man in the street millions of pounds a year.

Much scattered but valuable research work has, of course, been going on. Smilansky of Israel, who is very much aware of the need to harness new techniques to developmental theory, regards educational contents and methods as his manipulable variables. Gray and Klaus (67), despairing of an effective sociological approach, have concerned themselves with applications of modern learning theory. In their excellent interim report of the (Peabody College) Intervention Project, they lament that 'short of a complete change of milieu in infancy we have yet to demonstrate that it is possible to offset *in any major way* [our italics] the progressive retardation that concerns us'. Also aware of developmental theory, their approach in this project was to develop attitudes and aptitudes conducive to school achievement. The authors used a system of positive reinforcement and supported their intensive summer vacation work by frequent visits to the homes of their pupils. Significant gains at the < ·01 level were reported. This project demonstrates one of several attempts to cope with the emotional aspects of the problem of the culturally deprived. But the point raised by the authors that educative work is to a considerable extent reduced by negative home influences – which have been demonstrated as causative – is a matter we cannot neglect. In Western countries a child is separated from its parents only with considerable reluctance and usually by judicial process. It has first to be established that being in the family would constitute a major hazard to the child's health and well-being, which – while easy enough in such extreme cases as the insanity or criminality of the parents – is much more difficult when parental behaviour emanates from ignorance, lack of intelligence or a variant culture pattern. It is generally accepted that a close relationship between child and parent is essential if a healthy personality is to develop, and the law usually tolerates a wide range of negative behaviour and relationship before ordering separation. In fact, then, we are not likely to find public support for a mass removal of slum children from slum parents, desirable as this may be theoretically from an educational point of view. Indeed, the solution would seem to be that 'Mohammed must go to the mountain', once again. Supportive educational work with adults must accompany any major educational attack on cultural deprivation. The alternative is schism: a child subjected to one set of standards, relationships and expectations at home, which are contradicted in the school. It should be possible to use married women teachers on a part-time basis as educational aides who would support the work being done in the schools in home visits. The value of seeking parental co-operation is instanced in the work of Orvis Irwin (68), who selected a group of children whose fathers were labourers. He asked the mothers to read for ten minutes a day to their children from the age of 12 months. Tested at 20 months, the experimental group showed significant language gains over the control group.

An often unrealised bottleneck in putting into action new educational plans is not so much the re-education of the *teachers* to carry out the work, but the training of *teacher college staff* who will be responsible for teacher training, a point stressed by Bloom *et al.* (69). Bloom's work presents the main deliberations, findings and recommendations of a research conference held in Chicago in 1964, and represents one of the best and most informed surveys of the problem of cultural deprivation to date.

Education is full of fads. Is the emphasis on the culturally deprived child a fad? Putting it another way, does it concern such a minority that serious attention to its solution would call for disproportionate effort? Riessman estimated that by 1970 one child in every two in the great cities of America would be culturally deprived (70). Frost and Hawkes estimated that in America each year a million children starting school are disadvantaged (71). Martin Deutsch, one of America's leading authorities on the culturally deprived child, says that 40 to 70 per cent of the total school population of America's largest cities consists of children from marginal economic and social circumstances (72). He adds that by the time these children reach junior high school, 60 per cent are retarded in reading by one to four years.

Cultural deprivation is not limited to slums. It is found in backward rural communities, in communities intentionally or accidentally isolated from the mainstream of society, and it is the hallmark of all those who, during infancy and early childhood, were (for whatever reason) cut off from communication with adults who had the time and inclination to care about them. It is an aspect of the depersonalisation that seems to result from population explosion with its inevitable reduction of creative leisure and its diminution of individual human values. Unless we are very careful, it is a condition we shall find expanding towards crisis in the immediate future.

Part Two

MODERN TRENDS IN
SECONDARY SCHOOL TEACHING

In this section we consider changes in science teaching, new approaches to foreign language teaching and the growing use of programmed instruction.

In introducing Part One, new mathematics *was treated as a bridge between new trends in the primary school and those developing in the secondary school. Piaget's insistence on the exploration of the sensual world and on the recognition of the child's 'thing-centred' thinking, which so largely understruts the strategies of new mathematics in the primray school, develops at the secondary school stage into what he calls* formal operations. *At this stage the young person is able to divorce* sign *from concrete* significant *and achieve a growing abstraction of thought. He soon escapes from the encumbrances of his home language into the abstract purity of mathematical expression.*

But mathematics is not the only discipline in which a determined bid has been to escape from rote learning and 'formula teaching'. Secondary school science, as Mr John Lewis comments, has had to struggle to escape from dreary techniques and unimaginative approaches which were effectively inhibiting the 'quest' that hallmarks the truly scientific mind: for science is much more an attitude *towards realities than a* fixed *corpus of fact to be memorised. Mr Lewis's close association with the Nuffield Physics Project and his association with UNESCO and O.E.C.D. as a consultant on science education give him a special credibility in this field. The need to help pupils to think critically, to maintain curiosity and to participate actively in the scientific process is easily stated, but in reality requires a major change in educational thinking – and something of a revolution in school laboratory method. Much of what Mr Lewis would have teachers practise is summed up in the Chinese proverb: 'Hear and forget, see and remember, do and understand.'*

Modern science is by no means opposed to the humanities since, in its ability to contribute to our understanding of the nature of man and of the values that predicate an enduring civilisation, it plays an important role in Man's quest for self-understanding. At the same time it is by means of scientific insights and skills that we are able to explore and to control the physical and psychological universes, and there is little doubt that the twenty-first century will be considerably managed and directed by those with skills developed during scientific studies. It is in an attempt to revivify secondary school practice that people like Mr Lewis have devoted so much thought and energy to science teaching.

One need hardly stress the need for the young modern to be multi-lingual. The geographical location of some communities favours the acquisition of languages in such instances as the Dutch and the Belgians, just as the insularity of Britain tends to promote a monolingualism. But, with the growth of the common market concept not only in Europe but in Asia, South America and Malaysia, the demands on effective multi-lingualism have considerably increased. The young modern who can command one or two languages other than his home language has a distinct advantage in commerce – and often in industry. The pressures towards the acquisition of foreign languages have been further increased by the expansion of world travel and more particularly of tourism, quite apart from a climate of internationalism that electronic communications and an awareness of common humanity and common peril have induced.

For the millions of pupils who are not in a position to acquire a second and third language through daily contact in a multilingual community, the traditional teaching methods prove increasingly in-adequate. Thousands of English people, for instance, had acquired skills in reading literary French without developing any corresponding facility in oral communication – especially in the racy idiom of colloquial usage. The growing need to be able to communicate with reasonable ease in foreign countries was not helped by such grammatical delights as being asked to express in French 'My grandfather's ear trumpet has been struck by lightning'. A new emphasis on oral language and a growing shift from academic niceties to daily pavement usage, de-manded a complete reorientation of intention and method at a time when the electronic industry was becoming more and more efficient in handling sound reproduction. While there is no doubt that the proper use of a language laboratory does relieve the teacher of much of the tedium he previously experienced, as an instrument of practice and drill there is nothing magical about machines. They are as efficient as the mind of their designer and as helpful as the programmer whose work the machine presents – and not a scrap more. There is in the use of any mechanical device an innate tedium such that, even in highly automated teaching techniques, one needs to return to two-way communication with other human beings if motivation is to be maintained. Even if few foreign language teachers would maintain that we have today achieved a generally accepted *theory, let alone practice, there is little doubt that the 1960's saw notable developments in this field, and J. Donald Bowen of U.C.L.A. has been at the growth centre of the new design of language teaching from America. His insistence on investigating difficult language problems in Africa and other parts of the world has, one feels, helped to integrate his theoretical approach into the highly practical situations in which he has been working. Those interested in foreign language teaching will soon recognise in Professor Bowen that rare theorist whose observations are pragmatically based.*

The third interesting trend that has caused much discussion among contemporary educators has been the development of programmed instruction, *a technique that found appreciative allies not only among language teachers but among mathematicians and teachers of the applied sciences and technologies. Developed initially by Pressey and matured in the work of Harvard's B. F. Skinner, programmed instruction owed much to the operative conditioning techniques of Razan and others of the modern school of behavioural learning theory. Like many new trends, programming has been at once oversold by its enthusiasts and undervalued by its detractors. It has been pushed forward by industrialists with vested interests in the sale of 'teaching machines', with the unhappy result not only of facile claims that bear little relationship to research fact, but of stifling further research that might necessitate* a change in machine design – *at least until the capital development has been amortised. But programming is a mental approach to the organisation of a learning situation, and in fact one could do without particular machines entirely. One of the most gratifying results of learning how to programme is not that one can use the hardware and gadgetry, but that one to some extent becomes 'a programmed teacher' – and the gain in efficiency is very considerable even if one were never again to write another 'formal' programme in one's life. There are many virtues in the underlying strategy of programming that every teacher in training ought to achieve.*

Of course, it is accepted that programmed instruction has its 'blind spots'. It is – usually – inept as a technique for teaching subjects of 'high value', *such as poetry appreciation or religious education, as against* high content *subjects, such as mathematics or science. But anyone who is looking for a universal teaching methodology is likely to search in vain. And the presentation of a programme by means of a machine has revealed unsuspected advantages too. Emotionally disturbed pupils whose relationships with teachers may inhibit learning, often work successfully with a machine – which after all, does* not *involve an* interpersonal relationship. *And machines, oddly enough, promote, rather than detract from, the pupil's individuality, since he can work at his own pace without having to use the class as a reference group for rate and progress.*

A scholar of careful approach and objective evaluation, G. O. M. Leith is an English authority on programmed learning, well-known at international conferences and in demand in other countries as a consultant and teacher. He has been intimately connected with the development of programming from the outset and represents today one of the most acceptable specialists in this field. Nor does his interest in his own topic lead him into unsupported claims or excesses, as the reader will soon discover when he examines this informed and judicious survey. There is no doubt that programmed instruction is making an important contribution to secondary school teaching in an increasingly technological era.

5 New Trends in Science Education

John L. Lewis

Since 1956 there have been considerable changes in science education throughout the world. These reflect both a dissatisfaction with
existing conditions and an increasing interest in education shown by
scientists, whether or not directly concerned with teaching. There
was apprehension about existing syllabuses: in physics there was
little awareness of any developments since 1900, the syllabuses were
heavily overloaded and there was an emphasis on factual knowledge,
perhaps mainly because it was easily examined. If the teachers were
dissatisfied, so too were scientists in industry and in the universities. They were concerned whether the young men and women
coming to them were in fact being adequately prepared. To quote
from the Bulletin of the Institute of Physics: 'If there is one common
complaint by science faculties about science students . . . it is that
they know but do not understand. The emphasis in all changes must
be on the improvement of the degree of understanding by the pupils'.

The surest way to assess the quality of teaching in a country is to
study its examination papers. In England it was too often true that
the safest way to pass a biology examination was to remember a lot of
names and to have the ability to draw a carefully labelled diagram.
In chemistry success often lay in memorising the properties of
different gases or what happens when x is added to y, rather than in
any ability to say why it should happen. In physics the standard
question in the G.C.E. 'O' level examination began by asking for a
definition of specific heat, a request which encouraged rote memory
rather than understanding. It then asked for a description of how to
measure the specific heat of copper or brass. In the standard experiment for this a block of metal was heated in hot water and transferred to cold water so that the specific heat was deduced from the
rise in temperature. This was an experiment which no practising
physicist would ever use. If the experiment were done it gave a
reasonable answer, as the heat lost by radiation in carrying over
the metal block was usually compensated by the water transferred

with it, but it was perfectly possible to answer the question by rehearsing the description beforehand whether or not the experiment had ever been done. Such a question always finished with a numerical part which amounted to substitution in a formula: if the formula were remembered correctly and the given figures were substituted, there was always a statistical chance that the arithmetic would be worked out correctly and the pupil would pass. Too often when he went out into the world to be a bank manager, a salesman or a lawyer, science for him was no more than a maze of formal definitions and ill-digested formulae. The idea that a scientist reasons things out, always seeking clues to a fresh understanding, might never have occurred to him.

The situation was no better in the G.C.E. 'A' level examinations. Again and again would appear: 'Define thermal conductivity. How would you measure it for a good conductor?' – a question which required an account of Searle's apparatus for measuring conductivity of copper. There would of course be changes: sometimes a *bad* conductor was asked about and a description of Lees' disc would be churned out by the pupils. Being 'A' level, the numerical part was more difficult, but it was basically substitution in a formula. The teaching necessarily followed the pattern set by these questions.

Equally unfortunate was the influence of the practical examination. In biology the dog-fish so often alternated with the rabbit, with predictable and tedious regularity (especially now that insecticides have made the cockroach a rarity). In chemistry volumetric titration and qualitative analysis dominated the work. As physics apparatus can be more costly, there was a dependence on a limited number of standard items. The variations that were devised for using the Wheatstone bridge or the potentiometer were only rivalled by the number of different ways that were found for finding the focal lengths of lenses. The practical exams were tributes to the ingenuity of examiners, but their influence on the teaching in schools was so great that practical work often became no more than a series of routine measurements. Many practical books were commercially available which consisted of no more than 'cook-book' instructions, which a pupil could carry out without any real understanding of the principles involved.

This criticism must not imply that there was no good teaching. Of course there was, and many devoted teachers aimed at teaching for understanding, despite the strait-jacket of the examinations.

Journals like the *School Science Review* testify to much that was excellent, but despite this there was much more teaching relying solely on rote memory.

As to 'modern' physics, the electron had no place in the School Certificate or 'O' level course, even though it was discovered in 1895. Radioactivity was completely omitted from school work and atomic physics was classified with relativity as suitable only for universities. The physics syllabuses reflected the state of physics at the beginning of the century, when the basic syllabus was drawn up. It was divided into self-contained compartments: heat, light, sound, magnetism, electricity and mechanics. The unity of physics was not at all apparent. Of course there were changes: a few new topics were added to the syllabus and rather fewer were taken out. This in itself led to the syllabuses being seriously overloaded. There was even less time for worrying about 'understanding', and so there was more inducement to rely on rote memory. It was certainly time for the reform which began in the late 1950s.

There was one other serious weakness in science education, though this weakness was not confined only to science. The system tended to be self-perpetuating. Young men or women on obtaining their degreee would go into teaching and teach as they themselves were taught. There was far too little opportunity for them to benefit from the ideas of others. They might spend a lifetime learning how to present each topic and by the time these skills were acquired, they would have to retire. Some of the present trends are beginning to change this repetitive tedium.

THE HISTORY OF RECENT CHANGES

In England the first moves towards revision were made by the science teachers themselves. In 1957 the Association for Science Education was encouraged to look critically at syllabuses in physics, chemistry and biology, and to make recommendations for the future. Their policy statement was followed shortly by detailed syllabuses in physics, chemistry and biology. It is perhaps a measure of the success of those syllabuses that most examining boards in the United Kingdom have now modified their 'O' level and 'A' level syllabuses on the lines advocated by the A.S.E. The planners of the new syllabuses certainly accepted the need to be relevant to the second half of the twentieth century.

In physics some 'modern' physics was included – even though this only meant physics since 1895. This raised even more acutely the problem of teaching. The new range of material could so easily be taught by dogmatic assertion; it was more difficult to make it a satisfactory educational exercise in which the pupils could see the evidence for themselves and exercise their own judgement. If the pupil was to be encouraged to think for himself, and to think critically, this 'modern' physics was not just a matter of a modernised syllabus. It was the method of teaching that mattered so much more, and this was where reform was most needed. (It is interesting to note that, as country after country in recent years has set about reform of its science teaching, it has usually started with syllabus reform and only subsequently come to realise that matter may be of less concern than method!)

The first effective call for a complete programme rather than a new syllabus came from the United States. A great debt is owed to Professor Zacharias and the late Professor Friedman, with their colleagues in the Physical Sciences Study Committee: the influence of the P.S.S.C. programme in stimulating reform throughout the world has been felt far beyond those countries which are using the actual programme. They saw the need to produce a textbook, a teacher's guide, a laboratory manual, a series of background books, new apparatus, films, test papers and examinations, all of which welded together to produce a teaching scheme complete in itself.*

There were other influences beginning to have their effect. The U.S.S.R. claimed that they had enough teachers, but they accepted that they would never have enough *good* teachers. For this reason they provided the wherewithal to enable an indifferent teacher to achieve a certain minimum standard. The teacher received not just a syllabus of topics to be taught, but complete details on the demonstrations to be shown and the experiments to be done by the pupils. He was provided with all the apparatus necessary and also various

---

* Although the P.S.S.C. scheme commands respect and influenced our thinking in the British Isles, it is never likely to be widely used here. A course of a relatively sophisticated nature for pupils aged 16 or 17, which is intended to last a year (though admittedly it could be extended to two), unfortunately does not fit our well-established tradition of secondary-school science teaching, extending over five or seven years for children from the age of 11 to 16 or 18.

visual aids, including the films to relate classroom physics to the
outside world. For this last important purpose provision was made
for relevant factory visits and tours of power stations. This organisation was intended to set a minimum standard; there was also
scope for the good teacher to develop additional ideas of his
own.

Another contribution to science education was being made in
Germany. The tradition for high quality demonstration apparatus
has always been strong in Germany, but their equipment has often
been too expensive for extensive use in many other countries. Their
contribution, however, comes from the pioneering work of firms like
Leybold and Phywe, which have turned sophisticated experiments
into classroom realities.

The work of the P.S.S.C. soon led to the development of complete programmes in chemistry and in biology. There were two
American schemes in chemistry and three in biology, each being a
complete programme, meeting the need for something more than a
new syllabus or a new textbook.

In the United Kingdom the winds of change blowing from the
United States and from the U.S.S.R. demonstrated that the work of
the Association for Science Education needed extension: complete
teaching programmes were required, suitable for British needs. It
was here that the Nuffield Foundation decided to assist, and accordingly made substantial funds available. Work began on the Nuffield
science teaching projects in 1962. There are now ten different
Nuffield science projects which have either been completed or are
in the process of completion:

1. Nuffield 'O' level physics course.
2. Nuffield 'O' level chemistry course.
3. Nuffield 'O' level biology course.
   These three are all five-year courses intended for children aged
   11-16.
4. Nuffield 'A' level physics course.
5. Nuffield 'A' level chemistry course.
6. Nuffield 'A' level biology course.
   These are two-year courses, for pupils aged 16-18. They follow
   the usual English 'A' level pattern, by which the pupils
   specialise on these courses to the extent of seven or eight
   periods a week for each subject for two years once they have
   passed the 'O' level stage.

7. Nuffield 'A' level physical science course.
   This answers the need for a single 'A' level subject, bringing together physics and chemistry.
8. Nuffield Junior Science Project.
   A project for primary school children aged 5-11.
9. Nuffield Secondary Science Project.
   A project for secondary school pupils who are not above average academically.
10. Nuffield Combined Science Project.
    This takes the first two years of the three 'O' level courses and welds them together into a single combined science course.

More and more countries are now appreciating the need for developing their own projects to meet their particular requirements. Some of these projects are modifications of existing programmes: in Sweden there is a Swedish version of the P.S.S.C., and in Tanzania there are modified Nuffield courses. Some, like the UNESCO projects in Latin America, in Africa and in South-east Asia, are new projects. The trend in all countries – in Israel, in Uganda, in Zambia, in Australia, in Ceylon, in Latin America, in South Africa, in Turkey, in Scandinavia, in the West Indies – is increasingly away from mere syllabus reform towards complete teaching programmes, designed to meet the particular needs of the country concerned.

Perhaps even more significant than this extensive development of science teaching programmes throughout the world is the similar philosophy that pervades so many of them. International conferences in the last ten years have confirmed this similarity of outlook.

Typical of this outlook are these words, written in 1961: 'a radical reform of physics education is urgently required. Although reduction of excess material is vital, little else will be achieved just by introducing new syllabuses since the same ideas will inevitably be taught. What is required is a critical attitude.' A year earlier we read: 'Great importance must obviously be attached to the subject matter of a course and the way in which it is developed as a logical whole. Of even greater importance is the way in which the teacher handles the subject matter.' The emphasis on understanding rather than rote memory is repeatedly stressed, accompanied by pleas for fostering inquiry: 'It is essential to lay a foundation of simple empirical studies in which pupils become familiar with the more striking phenomena of nature. Let this study be permeated, as far as we can arrange it, by a spirit of inquiry.' The science teacher has the advantage of the natural curiosity of the children. Any new programme should make a more conscious attempt to build on this.

Also typical were the pleas that a course should give children a broad picture of what modern science is about and the way in which scientists think. Professor Eric Rogers wrote: 'We want well-educated people to feel that they understand science and the people who practise it, and to know that science makes sense.' Also characteristic of Eric Rogers was this: 'I am thinking of our young people when they are grown up, not when they are learning science at school, but a dozen years later when they are out in the world: a young man in a bank presently to be manager, an important person in business or industry, a civil servant, a history teacher in school or university, or, above all, the parent of young children giving the next generation a first view of science.' How important it is for such people that science should not appear a collection of facts, formulae and definitions; how important for them to realise that science involves experimental knowledge, imaginative thinking and intelligent reasoning.

Although a programme is aimed at the general education of the future citizen, it may at the same time form a very good foundation for the future scientist or engineer. In the United Kingdom the evidence from the universities is that a sound knowledge of what science is about, with an understanding of certain basic principles and topics, is a better foundation for the future scientist and engineer than a vast number of ill-digested facts, improperly understood, and a quantity of formulae through which substitution can give a 'correct' answer without understanding of the principles involved.

What kind of programme should evolve in view of all this?

1. A programme should be complete in itself – not a partial course devised more with the future specialist in mind.
2. It should not contain too much material, but a few important ideas which the pupil can make his own.
3. It should build on the natural curiosity of the children.
4. It should foster a spirit of inquiry.
5. It should encourage the children to think, and to think critically.
6. It should strive for understanding.
7. It should give a broad picture of what modern science is about and the way in which scientists think.
8. It should be relevant to the world outside the classroom.

The programme materials would doubtless include books for pupil use, whether they be textbooks, question-books or background books. Experimental work by the pupil would be an essential part of any programme, and doubtless this would be amplified on occasion by demonstration experiments by the teacher. This would require apparatus and instruction, whether for pupil or teacher or both, on experimental techniques. Visual aids are now an accepted part of education and any programme would inevitably utilise them where practicable. There would be the need to provide guidance for the teacher, so that he can make the most effective use of the material available, and so that he can benefit from the experience of others. Finally, and most important, there would need to be new examinations to suit the particular programme.

It is along these lines that most programmes today are developing. They are certainly those that guided the development of the Nuffield Physics Programme, details of which are given in the next section to illustrate how programmes today tend to be constructed almost as a fabric in that the strands are all woven together.

CONTENT OF A PROGRAMME

It is now widely accepted that it is the method of teaching that is of first importance in developing a science programme. Nevertheless the course has to be built around certain topics, though these will certainly be fewer in number than has been customary in the past. Those that are included should attempt to form a connected programme, in which something learned in one place proves useful somewhere else, and something discovered later throws light on something worked with earlier: in this way it is hoped to show that physics is a unified fabric of knowledge, woven together and certainly making sense.*

In the Nuffield project, it was considered important that in the last year there should be some feeling for the relationship between experiment and theory. For this the development of the atomic

* For a teacher of Nuffield physics, what a wonderful moment it is when pupils doing experiments in physical optics suddenly start to say 'But this is just like the experiments we did with ripple tanks.' Suddenly they see the unity as different types of wave motion agree with each other. Of course the teacher might have pointed it out to the pupils, but how much greater the impact when the pupils themselves see it.

model might have been chosen; but this requires evidence from so many different directions that it was discarded as too complex. Planetary astronomy was chosen instead, a historical treatment showing how successive observations lead to the development of successful theory, culminating in Newton's grand design. As soon as this decision had been made, it required earlier work in Year V on circular motion, including an experimental derivation of V^2/R. This had to be preceded by quantitative work on Newton's laws, a study of momentum changes, of conservation law, and of kinetic energy in Year IV. This required an empirical approach to force and motion in Year III, including some work on projectiles. The concept of force, however, is first introduced in Years I and II, where various forces are encountered as pushes or pulls.

It was also considered desirable to include something on the uncertainties in science, in order to avoid the impression that 'science knows all the answers'. Year V therefore included a little work on electron diffraction, to show that electrons sometimes behave like waves, sometimes like particles: the treatment is not a detailed one, but sufficient to bring out the wave–particle duality. Another kind of uncertainty is brought out in work on radioactivity, also in Year V: the experimental work brings out the statistical nature of readings. The random nature of the process emphasises the uncertainties involved, and this helps to discourage expectation of a single 'correct answer'.

The work on radioactivity is used in the study of the atom, when atomic models are used to discuss the place of models in science. Some understanding of the part that 'models' play in scientific thought is developed throughout the whole course, showing how a model is only significant as long as it is useful, and is even then no more than a model.

The work on radioactivity and the atom requires earlier a study of electron streams and the effect on them of electric and magnetic fields. The work on motion in a circle, already referred to and required for planetary astronomy, again finds a use when estimating a value of e/m (the ratio of the charge to the mass of the electron). These cross-links, where one piece of work finds use in different contents, are characteristic of the Nuffield 'O' level physics course.

The work on fields necessitates earlier work on electromagnetism (in both Year IV and Year III), some electrostatics and some basic work on electric currents in Year II.

The study of the atom in Year v requires another important strand which runs right through the course: the approach to an atomic picture of matter. Year I includes a study of crystals, which suggests that matter might be made of particles. Work on pressure in the same year leads to a molecular model of air, for which evidence comes from the Brownian motion of smoke particles in air – an important observation which the Nuffield planners hope every pupil will make for himself. The pupils make their first atomic measurement when they themselves make their own estimate of molecular size by spreading an oil drop on a water surface. The atomic picture is taken further in Year II, when attempts are made to interpret the effects of heat. In Year III there is a more detailed look at the molecular model of a gas, Brownian motion is seen again, and further evidence comes both from diffusion and from Boyle's work on expansion. By Year IV the work on mechanics makes an important contribution, when Newton's laws, developed with trolleys on a large scale, are applied to the molecules of a gas. This enables quantitative work on the kinetic theory to be done. There is a calculation of molecular speed, and some simple quantitative work on bromine diffusion enables an estimate to be made of molecular diameter.

Wave motion is another key topic introduced experimentally in Year III, where there is extensive work by the pupils using ripple tanks. This is followed by ray optics, again experimentally developed and concentrating on image formation. There is further consideration of waves in Year v, with a study of interference, diffraction gratings and spectra.

The topic of energy pervades the whole course. It is met first in Year I, where the idea of energy transfer from one form to another is examined. In successive years the concept is treated with more and more sophistication, becoming quantitative in Year IV. Just as the topics chosen interlink and interweave, so energy appears again and again throughout each part of the course. Everything chosen is relevant to the whole, providing in the end the carefully woven fabric.

With this method for deciding on the content of the course, there are inevitably many topics omitted which appear in most traditional courses. There is no Wheatstone bridge; there is far less calorimetry, there is no statics – no point men, standing on weightless ladders, leaning against frictionless walls – and very little geometrical optics in the traditional sense. Some deplore the loss so strongly that the

Nuffield course is not for them. For others there are plenty of exciting new things, which have already been shown to capture the interest of pupils, who are able to gain from this work something of the fun of a scientific inquiry.

There is always a sadness felt by teachers when a particular favourite topic does not appear in a new syllabus: we each have our own item that we love teaching. But a syllabus put together as a series of topics – which was the traditional way of writing a syllabus – can never have a comparable unity. A sacrifice has to be made for the sake of the programme as a whole.

TEACHERS' GUIDES

With the trend towards laying the emphasis on the method of teaching, a teachers' guide must play a most important role in any programme.

A syllabus alone gives no indication of how deeply a topic should be explored: phrases like 'elements and compounds', 'crystal growth', 'radioactive disintegration', 'interference effects', all of which have appeared in some syllabuses, could be very differently interpreted by different teachers. They need guidance.

They also need to know *why* certain things have been included in any well-planned programme where something studied in one place is an essential basis for something coming later.

A guide can include experimental details which will enable the teacher to get the most effective use out of the apparatus. He can be advised on the best way to set up an experiment and be given hints and instructions where it might not be at all advisable to give so much detail to pupils. If their laboratory work is to be a true investigation in which the pupils feel the information acquired is their own, the real enemy to this is the 'cook-book' instructions that at one time it was customary to give pupils. Of course the new way takes longer and may not appear so efficient, but it is much more effective than for ever 'going by the book'. The instructions, however, need to be somewhere – and the right place is the teachers' guide.

This modern trend towards the giving of guidance does enable an indifferent teacher to achieve a certain minimum standard. There is no need for such guides to be a restraint on the good teacher: he will always want to devise and develop new methods of his own and should be encouraged to do so. But gone are the days when different countries can afford merely to give a man a degree in a scientific subject and then put him into a school to teach for the next forty years of his life without further guidance. A wise head of a department will always give help to a young man when starting, but he cannot do this to the extent that is possible in a detailed teachers' guide. It is not only the inexperienced teacher that can be helped: the good teacher always delights in learning of ingenious ways others have found to do experiments or awaken fresh understanding. There are always rewards to be gained by everyone from such guides, and, as they develop, their advantages will be increasingly employed and appreciated in future.

TEXTBOOKS?

Teachers following traditional courses almost invariably used a textbook. The P.S.S.C. scheme in the United States – the first of the new science teaching programmes – continued to rely on a textbook for use by the pupil. The Nuffield biology courses also relied on textbooks, but the physics and chemistry courses did not. This has caused much thought to be given to the place of a textbook in a science course, and there may possibly be a future trend away from textbooks in the traditional sense.

No one would question the place that the textbook has for the university student, and it is equally essential for the advanced level pupil towards the end of a secondary school course. What is questionable is how necessary a textbook is at the early stages of a secondary school course.

A textbook in a traditional course had to meet various needs and each of these should be considered.

1. *For Questions.* It is certainly necessary to have a collection of questions to put to the pupils, often for use as homework. This need will be felt whatever the course.
2. *For Background Information.* It is always agreed these days that classroom work should be related to the outside world so that the pupils themselves can see its relevance.

3. *For Revision.* Pupils find it helpful to have occasional summaries of the work: it gives them confidence.
4. *For the Teacher.* A textbook can be a guide to the teacher to show him what should be taught.
5. *For Factual Knowledge.* Perhaps the main purpose of having a textbook is for pupils to acquire information from it, though never as a substitute for what can be experimentally found out.

In the Nuffield Physics Project, it was accepted that questions were important and separate question-books were included in the programme for each year of the course. Occasional summaries of the work can also be included in such question-books in order to meet the pupil's need for 'something to revise'.

There is, however, a weakness when a volume tries to be too many things at once: a question-book is not the ideal place to include background information. So the tendency now is to produce separate background books, pleasantly illustrated and easily readable and it is likely that this pattern will be extended. However much a teacher may have used a textbook in the past as an indication of what should be taught at each stage of a course, this is clearly not the true purpose of a textbook, and the newer concept of separate teachers' guides should obviate this.

Lastly there is the provision of factual knowledge. If the tendency in science teaching is to encourage critical thought and to discourage an authoritarian approach to science, this aspect of the textbook's role must inevitably change, at least in the early stages of secondary education. How can we expect a boy or girl to find out something about electric circuits in order to make the knowledge his own if the answer is clearly stated three pages further on in his textbook!

So for all these reasons the textbook role is likely to change considerably in the next few years.

EXPERIMENTAL WORK

In all new projects there is great emphasis on personal participation in experimental work by the pupils: as the old Chinese proverb has it, 'Hear and forget, see and remember, do and understand.' If understanding is what a course is striving for, the pupil must be involved himself. There is therefore an increase in practical work. New apparatus has been designed for this, for the cost must be kept down if each pupil in the class is to participate in his own experiment. Some exciting new techniques have been developed in the last ten years and more are bound to follow.

There are other significant changes. In the first half of the century many schools would use an Attwood machine or a Fletcher's trolley, both extremely ingenious devices developed because of the difficulty of measuring small time intervals. But there is no longer a place in schools for such apparatus. Instead, with the advent of electronic techniques, a scaler can be used to make the necessary measurement of time, the experiment is much more direct and the pupil's understanding of the principles is so much the greater.

Other modern devices are now making a substantial contribution to science education: for example, centimetre waves developed for radar work now play an important part in schools when wave phenomena are being studied. The wavelength is much more convenient than that of light, and again greater understanding results.

Much traditional work was confined, as stated earlier, to routine measurements: finding the specific heat of copper or brass, measuring the focal length of a lens by innumerable different methods, or making various electrical measurements using either the Wheatstone bridge or the potentiometer. These were indeed the mainstays of much physics teaching. In the same way the tangent galvanometer may be an ingenious item of apparatus on which innumerable practical questions can be set, but where in the world is the physics laboratory that actually uses such a galvanometer? Such experimental equipment not only lacked relevance. The whole principle of ever more intricate elaborations on a limited theme, determined by restricted resources, has been necessarily superseded by a new emphasis on much greater variety in experimental work, facilitated by a wide range of apparatus made readily and widely available. Of course there is a place for an experiment which makes a precise measurement, but not all experiments should be of that kind. Greater variety should lead to a greater understanding of what science is about.

FILMS AND VISUAL AIDS

The powerful contribution that films and visual aids can make to science education is now generally appreciated. Elaborate experiments that could never be shown in a classroom can be put on film so that pupils can see them. Background films relating the classroom work to industrial applications are obvious assets. Films using time lapse photography have exciting possibilities, especially in biology.*

The 8 mm. cassette film has already proved itself a powerful aid, and there is no doubt this medium will develop in the next ten years. The expansion may in fact be alarming, for there is a tendency for every new project to want to produce its own cassette films and there is a danger of over proliferation. There are already too many bad films available, and a substandard surfeit may not be an educational advantage.

The value of the overhead projector is also appreciated. Transparencies for use with it are likely to be an integral part of future programmes.

One of the most interesting developments in educational films in recent years has been the series of films made in the United Kingdom by Esso Petroleum in association with the Nuffield project. These films are intended for teachers, and they are not suitable for showing to pupils. The problem of teacher training, or teacher retraining, is always a serious one and films showing new techniques can make a major contribution here. The Esso film on *Momentum and Collision Processes*, for example, indicates a possible approach to momentum, but its greatest value lies in the way it shows how apparatus can be used to advantage. Some films in the series show the experiments which might be done on a particular theme, for example *An Approach to the Electron* or *Introduction to Radioactivity*. Others devote themselves to showing how a kit of apparatus can be effectively used: *The Electromagnetic Kit* or *The Worcester Circuit Board* are typical of this.

Such films, however, can cover in fifteen minutes work which might take the pupils half a term. It would ruin the teaching if the films were seen by such pupils, and stress is laid on their being suitable only for teachers. They have been extensively used on courses in the United Kingdom and throughout the world. Deliberately they are kept simple, and they are made by practising teachers rather than Nobel Prize winners, in order to instil confidence: 'If

---

* Perhaps the most remarkable teaching film ever made is *Frog Development – Fertilization to Hatching*, made by Educational Services Inc. in the United States. By time-lapse photography, one watches cell division through a microscope: the creation of life for the child to see.

E

Bill or Jack can do it, so can I.' These films have proved to be power-ful aids, and we can look forward to more of their kind and quality. Their influence can extend far beyond the limited audience that sees them: they can affect many generations of schoolchildren.

EXAMINATIONS

It is the examinations that will decide the success or otherwise of any new science teaching programme. However much the teaching con-centrates on understanding and a critical approach, this will come to nothing if traditional examinations are set which rely on rote memory. The devising of test papers was considered essential to the American science programmes. In the United Kingdom the Nuffield projects were fortunate in getting the full co-operation of the various examining boards. They agreed to set alternative Nuffield papers, papers which reflect the aims of the course, both to the pupils and to the teachers. To assure pupils that there was no need to memorise formulae, a guarantee was given that all formulae would be provided at the beginning of the paper, and this is standard practice in Nuffield physics papers.

Perhaps nothing shows the present trend in science education better than to contrast examination questions. A School Certificate question in 1932:

> Define coefficient of linear expansion. How would you measure it for a metal rod?
> A steel tyre has a diameter of 99·7 cm. at 15° C. To what temper-ature must it be raised to enable it to be put on a wheel 100 cm. in diameter? (Coeff. of linear expansion of steel = 0·000012 per °C.)

From the same period an 'A' level question reads:

> Define latent heat of fusion.
> Describe the Bunsen ice-calorimeter and discuss its merits.
> The capillary tube of such a calorimeter has an internal diameter of 0·4 mm. When a piece of metal of mass 0·5 gram heated to 100° C is dropped into the calorimeter, the mercury meniscus moves 4 cm. What is the specific heat of the metal? (Specific gravity of water at 0° C = 1·000; that of ice at 0° C = 0·917; latent heat of fusion of ice = 80 calories per gram.)

Both questions rely heavily on rote memory. Both could be answered by a candidate who had memorised a standard experiment without having done the experiment or even without having seen the apparatus. The numerical part in each case relies on successful substitution in formulae.

By contrast, three recent Nuffield physics questions read as follows:

1. Members of a class assembled some model moving-coil ammeters from pairs of magnets, coils and some other items as shown in the diagram:

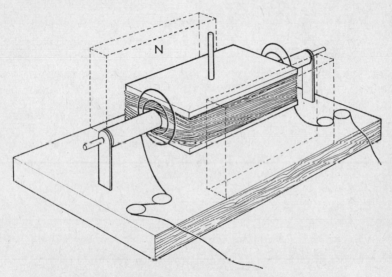

After using them members of the class were heard to say:
   (i) 'The magnetic field of the two magnets pushes the coil round.'
  (ii) 'How can there be only one magnetic field when there are *two* magnets *and* a coil?'
 (iii) 'What would happen if I had wound the coil round the other way?'
 (iv) 'What would happen if I wound one of the spirals round the wrong way?'
  (v) 'My meter will not work. But I am sure that the coil is all right.'
 (vi) 'I would like to make my meter more sensitive. What can I do?'

(vii) 'What will happen if I connect my meter to my cycle dynamo and turn the wheel slowly at first and then faster and faster?'
Write seven paragraphs commenting on each of these remarks. Offer explanations where they are necessary and illustrate with sketch diagrams.

2. Two skaters, gliding with different speed in opposite directions meet and clasp each other.

(a) In what circumstances will they both come to rest? Give your reasoning.

....
....
....

(b) In what circumstances will they move together in the direction of the one which had the slower speed? Give your reasoning.

....
....
....

(c) Give a brief outline of an experiment you would conduct to illustrate your answer to (b). Mention what measurements you need to make, and indicate how you would make them. (You may use trolleys, or frictionless pucks, or skaters themselves if you wish.)

....
....
....
....
....
....

3. (a) Many cloud-chamber photographs have been taken of the tracks of alpha particles from radioactive sources. It is rare for these photographs to show anything but straight line tracks, yet each alpha particle encounters more than 100,000 atoms along its path. On this evidence alone, what can you say about the nature of the atoms of the gas in the cloud chamber?

....
....
....

(b) Very occasionally a forked track is found, looking like Fig. 3(i) (in nitrogen) or Fig. 3(ii) (in hydrogen). In each diagram the alpha particle is coming from the left, and you may assume that no nuclear transformation takes place.

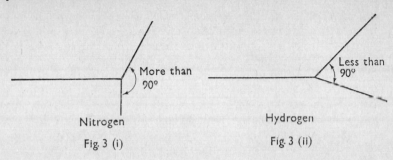

Nitrogen

Fig. 3 (i)

Hydrogen

Fig. 3 (ii)

What does this tell you about the mass of an alpha particle compared with the masses of a nitrogen and a hydrogen atom?

....

....

....

(c) If the gas in the cloud chamber is helium, and a forked track is obtained, then the angle between the forks is found to be 90°. What conclusion can be drawn from this?

....

....

(d) How would you demonstrate the same thing happening (i.e. 90° angle after collision) with 'carbon dioxide pucks' on a glass surface?

....

....

....

....

(e) State briefly any evidence, other than that obtained from collision experiments, which confirms your conclusion in (c).

....

....

....

The reasons for examinations are well known and do not need repeating here. There is one function which is often left unmentioned – to exhibit the aims of a course to both pupils and teachers, so that examinations become an aid to achieving those aims. Examinations control the success of any teaching plans.

Professor Eric Rogers wrote on this theme:

Consider a course in French literature: there, examinations raise an essential question; should we test grammar (with ease and accuracy) or test literary appreciation (with difficulty, doubt and unfairness)? Many teachers choose the grammar test, and most pupils prefer it. Yet the important thing for our pupils – whether the course is for their use as future ambassadors or for their general intellectual growth – is an insight into the thoughts and literature of another people; a feeling, perhaps, for 'how a Frenchman thinks'. The teacher of the course justifies his grammar examination by claiming that: 'while the test will serve for marks, the real value of the course is in the reading and class-room discussion; and the pupils know that'. Not for long. Even the most inspired pupil takes account of the examination and draws his own conclusion.*

There is a present trend towards multiple choice questions. They were extensively used in the P.S.S.C. project, as in other American programmes. In the United Kingdom there has been a reluctance to adopt this type of examination as it is still considered educationally desirable for a pupil to be able to express himself, to organise his material and to develop an argument as well as to recognise the right answer. But such is the pressure of examinations – the increase in the number of candidates and the shortage of examiners – that multiple choice questions may increasingly be set.

APPLIED SCIENCE

This account of present trends in science education would not be complete without some reference to applied science.

There are engineers who advocate that there should be separate courses in applied science, but it is often difficult enough for a young person to choose between science and the humanities – and if he had to choose between pure and applied science, he would be in even greater difficulties. It would be better if the basic course included more reference to applied science than to make it a separate course. This is a field in which very little work has yet been done: there should be some interesting developments in the next ten years.

PROJECTS

The place of project work in science education is also under review. Traditional experimental work was always confined within the limits

* Nuffield Physics Teachers Guide I.

of a single or double classroom period. Work extending over a longer period, however, can have educational advantages: it teaches the pupil pertinacity, he has to learn to overcome difficulties and setbacks as they arise, and he has to plan his work carefully.

Project work in biology teaching has been encouraged for some time owing to the longer time many biological experiments take. This approach may well now be adopted for both physics and chemistry.

TEACHER TRAINING

Reference has already been made to the importance of training teachers in the new programmes. The United States developed an elaborate system of 'summer institutes' for retraining teachers. Long and short courses have been run throughout the United Kingdom on the Nuffield programmes. Support for such courses will doubtless increase in the years ahead, especially when governments appreciate more and more the advantage in making it financially possible for teachers to attend.

CONCLUSION

This is an exciting time to be a teacher of science, so fast are the developments, and so far-reaching their effect. All the more must it be our hope that this world-wide activity will produce future generations of young people with a greater understanding of what science is truly about, as well as encouraging more and more to become good scientists and engineers, on whom the future prosperity of mankind will inevitably depend.

6 Recent Developments in Second Language Teaching

J. Donald Bowen

Second language teaching, particularly when the second language is English, has had about as much trouble getting named as getting recognised as a distinct academic area.* In English-speaking countries one studies (or teaches) French, German, Spanish or some other language without reflecting on the particular circumstances of the course and subject. These are, after all, languages which provide subject matter for courses in the typical school curriculum, alongside other courses, such as psychology, economics, music, etc. So too is English a course in the curriculum, at some levels divided into separate courses for literature and language, at other levels not. Thus in the traditional 'domestic' curriculum English has been taught as an academic subject to people who already speak it; other languages have been taught to people who do not speak them. This pattern has come to be accepted as the normal state of affairs, and the difference has not always been considered when English has been taught as a second or foreign language.

In America, Canada, Australia, New Zealand, etc., there have been quite a number of students of English who were not already speakers. These countries have accepted streams of immigrants, people seeking a new home and a new life, willing and even anxious to acquire a new language. If members of the first generation learned English imperfectly, they took pride in the accomplishments of their children, and by the third generation the ancestral language was often forgotten. The forgetting was frequently a source of pride to

* Some of the designations that have been used are: English for foreigners English for the non-English, English as a foreign language, English as a second language, English to non-English speakers, foreign-student English, English to speakers of other languages. All of these are to some extent inaccurate and descriptively inadequate, but the last, with the acronym ESOL, seems most likely to survive as a generic representation.

the second generation, accepted as a symbol of complete and satis-factory Americanisation, Australianisation, etc.

Assistance to immigrants in learning the new language was available. Special language instruction was offered in many places, usually in the larger cities, typically by the public school system. The effort was not really language training *per se*, but rather inci-dental, as part of the students' citizenship training. The usual pattern was attendance at part-time evening classes, with emphasis on the literacy requirements of the citizenship test. The instruction was not especially productive of results, and there was seldom any effective professional guidance.

Aboriginal peoples have formed another group in the large areas of the world which have been colonised as English-speaking coun-tries. In many instances, for example in American Indian areas, the needs of these people were for many years largely ignored. When the wars over land tenure and territorial rights finally came to an end, peace treaties usually included a specification of educational oppor-tunities to be made available. Special schools were established, with a standard curriculum minimally modified to meet the realities of life on an Indian reservation. It has been only in recent years that English has been taught with any recognition for its status as a second language in schools for American Indians.

England got its early experience with teaching English as a second language by establishing schools in the diverse and numerous lands where it exercised administrative control. A considerable body of literature has been built up providing texts and materials as well as outlining methodological approaches to teaching English in the colonies, based on the direct experience of teaching in colonial classrooms. Many nations today owe their competence in English as a language of wider communication to the efforts of British expatriate teachers who served throughout much of what was once the British Empire.

The basic idea of second language teaching – that a special kind of approach and methodology is necessary to teach a language not known by the students, and that this methodology should take into account the skills and habits the student has as a speaker of his own native language – was slow to be recognised and applied. In early times, when languages began to be 'studied', the classroom tradition seems to have been developed in classes for languages no longer spoken natively, i.e. classical languages: Latin and Greek. The learning goal for these classes was to be able to read texts, to make translations, and perhaps to write. For these purposes a knowledge of the vocabulary and a set of grammatical rules for stringing words together were needed, and a study of the lexicon and grammar made up the core of the course.

When modern languages (i.e. languages currently used as native tongues) came to be studied late in the last century, the same methods of teaching were applied. The grammars which had been formulated for these languages followed the tradition of grammatical description established for Latin and Greek. The latinate grammars worked reasonably well, since nearly all the languages of Europe are closely related to Latin and Greek. This close relation was not fully appreciated until scholars began to study languages that were vastly different. The idea of noun classification associated with natural gender can be applied convincingly to European languages, even though the domain varies enormously, as in two closely related languages such as English and German, but how do you interpret and label the ten or so noun classes of Swahili?

Scholars became a little uneasy with the classical model for the grammars of modern languages and began to look more closely at each language. The comprehensive grammars of English of the late nineteenth and early twentieth centuries (Jespersen, Poutsma, Kruisinga, etc.) included a catalogue of structures and expressions that were unique, or at least unusual, and were therefore 'interesting'. Teachers began to look for new applications for their classrooms. The fact that a student could spend several years studying a language and then not be able to communicate with speakers of that language was noted by some teachers with regret and even chagrin. Students who wanted to learn to speak a language were advised to go and live among the speakers. But some teachers tried to find other answers.

One interesting solution led to what was called the 'direct method', in which a classroom was established where only the foreign language was used. Translation was banned, and communication was limited to expression in the new language (supplemented by gestures, postures and mime). The direct approach emphasised the advantages of hearing and using the language, of associating language with actions and situations. It has a serious flaw, which many teachers soon recognised: in trying to separate completely the native from the new language by voluntarily avoiding the overt use of the students' language, the proponents of the direct method somehow failed to appreciate the fact that all the influence of the native tongue was still there, built into the habits and responses of the students. Merely avoiding the use of the first language does not overcome or suppress the covert influence. Indeed, pretending the first language is not there not only can be wasteful of classroom time, but adequate detailed guidance cannot be offered as it is needed, since sophisticated communication is impossible. Not many direct method teachers insisted on the rigorous exclusion of the native language at all times.

While the direct method attempted to recognise and teach the skill of oral communication, other teachers decided this was too big a task for the time allotted in the school curriculum – typically two years of secondary-level training. Since everything could *not* be taught, why not concentrate on a reduced number of skills that *could* be? The result was a course design with special emphasis on reading – in some cases of reading and translation. There was some justification for the idea of making the most of what was possible, or exploiting the feasible, but classes, at least at the beginning and intermediate levels, were seldom exciting for the students who laboriously plodded through pages of reading, often looking up fifty to seventy-five words per page in the glossary that was an integral part of every text. The apt and well-motivated students persisted and learned to read, but a high percentage of failures bothered the conscience of the serious teacher. The most unfortunate casualty was perhaps student morale. Language study came to be thought of first as uninteresting and unrewarding – later as unnecessary, even useless. One state legislature in the United States enacted a law which specified that no state-supported institution of higher learning could require the study of a foreign language as a condition of enrolment or graduation. There were more practical ways to spend classroom time.

There were other 'methods' and 'approaches'. William P. Mackey in his book *Language Teaching Analysis* lists and describes about twenty, some distinctive and others slight variations. Many of these are interesting and useful, but a perhaps more significant contribution to language teaching pedagogy came as a result of the need for intensive language training during World War II. The allies found that they must deal with peoples in many parts of the globe whose languages had never been taught and were almost totally unknown in English-speaking countries.

To solve this problem the planners turned to a small group of scholars whose interest in language was almost incidental: the anthropologists, who felt they had to learn the language of aboriginal peoples in order to properly understand and interpret their cultures. These scholars had done what only a few missionaries had previously attempted – to study intensively languages other than those of Western Europe. The cultural anthropologists, and particularly the anthropologically oriented linguists whom they encouraged, responded to the request for assistance by offering the techniques of a discipline that could logically be related to language teaching: descriptive linguistics.

Several assumptions from linguistics were promptly and willingly passed on. One was that language is first of all speech (all cultures have oral language, but only a very few of the advanced cultures have writing). The pedagogical corollary was that the spoken language should be learned first, with reading and writing to be postponed until the spoken language was mastered (just as in the case of one's first language learning experience). A second assumption was that speech has a definite, describable structure, a system with dependable consistency, which meant it was subject to scientific observation. The pedagogical corollary is that grammatical patterns as such, not just random sentences, should be learned by the students, principally by the techniques of repetition and substitution, with the control of an extensive vocabulary to come as a later goal. A third assumption was that language is used by people to communicate and interact. The pedagogical corollary was to extend the domain of the classroom situation beyond the traditional single sentence of the drills. To dramatise a real speaking situation, the dialogue was adapted to classroom needs. The result was a capsule situation enacted by two or more participants who uttered sentences with a discourse relation between each of the sentences in sequence. A good dialogue provides the illusion (even though rarely the real substance) of reality and offers the students an opportunity to participate vicariously in a situation that seems authentic, providing more realistic practice in learning the language than was previously available.

An emphasis on teaching English as a second language in the United States coincided with the development of descriptive or structural linguistics. At this time, roughly the forties and fifties, linguistics came to have considerable influence on language teaching.

One result was more concern for the spoken language, which meant more attention to details of pronunciation, particularly the details that distinguish word meanings: the phonemic contrasts. For many teachers linguistically oriented language teaching was closely associated with lists of minimal pair words, such as *fit/feet*, *den/then*, *dish/ditch*, *pilot/pirate*, etc., that were to be recognised, identified and produced in a great profusion of practice. The distinction of minimal pair words was not the only characteristic of teaching languages 'linguistically', but it was certainly conspicuous.

Along with greater interest in accurate and fluent pronunciation there was a concern for unambiguous notation of sounds, particularly in English, where a single sound is often represented in the spelling in a variety of ways. Several phonetic (or phonemic) transcriptions have been utilised for their convenience in representing English sounds in a satisfactorily consistent way, to avoid such look-alikes as *dose/rose*, which in spite of similar spellings are not rhyme words.

The technique of repetition is widely associated with linguistically oriented language teaching, even though the basis for its application is a principle from behavioural psychology: operant conditioning. The assumption as usually stated is that one will learn faster and more thoroughly an item or expression that one hears and/or uses many times. The application is to repeat in the classroom a sentence over and over again until it becomes easy and natural to produce it – so that it can then be recalled when necessary in a real communication situation.

It is assumed that learning items should whenever possible be presented one at a time, that a new sentence pattern should be introduced with familiar words, that new words should be given in known sentence patterns. Once presented these are practised in new combinations. Typically for this purpose substitution drills are used. If the sentence 'I bought a new house' has been learned, and the word 'car' is subsequently presented in a sentence like 'The car is red', then the student can be led to say 'I bought a new car'. This is done by means of guided analogy, with controls to ensure that the task will be within the capability of the student, and an immediate correction in the event of his making an error, like 'I bought a car house'.

Three techniques, then, have dominated language teaching as it has been influenced by structural linguistics: imitation, repetition and substitution. All three techniques have frequently been used in chorus drills in order to provide more active practice with the language for more people. Explanations of the grammar were brief, often postponed on the assumption that problems would be clarified by seeing the language in use. Using the language rather than talking about it was considered to be the priority need of the students.

The results of this philosophy of language teaching have been encouraging, particularly in the students' ability to pronounce and communicate in the spoken language. Occasionally classes may have tended to become a bit boring if imitation and repetition were carried too far, but good teachers were aware of this and tried to provide enough variety in their techniques to keep student interest alive.

Structural linguistics had another important influence on language teaching, through the encouragement of contrastive analysis – the point by point comparison of two languages (native and target) in as much detail as possible. Contrastive analysis focused on structural differences, points of interference that explained learning problems. The explanation of course didn't make the problem go away, but it did show why an error was persistent (system conflict rather than student non-interest or non-co-operation), underscoring the need for special emphasis and drills where they would most help. Contrastive analysis didn't necessarily reveal secrets previously unknown to language teachers, especially those who were observant, but its predictions allowed teachers to anticipate student needs and to understand the specific nature of particular learning problems. Even though the contributions to effective language teaching by contrastive analysis may have been overstated, it has been helpful, and continues to make useful contributions to teachers and text writers.

In the last decade the science of linguistics has developed at a rapid rate, much faster than the applications to language teaching could be worked out. There are a number of new theories on the linguistic horizon today, but the most promising is probably transformational analysis, sometimes referred to by the fuller designation 'transformational-generative analysis'. The transformationalists have been interested in language acquisition, but have so far concluded that their theories do not satisfactorily explain how humans learn languages. They reject the explanation of language behaviour as habitual responses to recognised stimuli, pointing out that language is a highly innovative activity, that sentences are usually created, not 'repeated' from the memory of an earlier performance. Speaking a language is best explained as the ability to produce and interpret sentences following sets of various kinds of rules, such that all grammatical and no ungrammatical sentences are allowed. The complete specification of these rules lies well into the future but the complexity of the rules presently offered might make a language teacher wonder how a child of five or six has managed to assimilate the rules to produce such complicated behaviour.

Nonetheless the transformationalists have greatly benefitted language teaching, even if all the answers are not in sight, by raising questions about procedures that seemed to be on the verge of becoming dogma, a set of assumptions that were to be considered beyond question or discussion. They have expressed healthy doubts about exclusive reliance on analogy as a means of learning new rule applications, since these can be complicated and sophisticated (i.e. the 'exceptions' of the grammatical generalisations), and the recognition of a distinction between deep and surface structures underscores the complexity of applying analogies.

English spelling has been partially rehabilitated as a reasonable system for representing the language, one which usefully shows relationships which would be obscured by a strictly phonemic or phonetic transcription. The related meanings of contrasts like *able/ability* and *divine/divinity* are shown more clearly in traditional spelling than they would be in a respelling transcription which followed pronunication: *éybǝl/ǝbílǝtiy* and *dǝváyn/dǝvínǝtiy*. Even those useless 'silent letters' can have a useful purpose – to show deep structure relationships – as in *resign/resignation* and *doubt/indubitable*, where the *g* of *resign* and the *b* of *doubt* are lost in the surface realisation (i.e. the pronunciation) of these two words, but retained in *resignation* and *indubitable*.

Another theoretical contribution of the transformationalists – not necessarily a new idea, but one they have given a solid footing by providing a reasonable, logical explanation – is the difference between *competence* and *performance*. *Competence* is the capacity a native speaker has for producing grammatical sentences following the rules of pronunciation and sentence formation if the language. *Performance* is the realisation of utterances on a single occasion, including such things as slips of the tongue, deliberate rule violations used for artistic effect, or modifications ascribable to incipient bilingualism. We no longer feel, for example, that we must include šw- in the inventory of permitted initial consonant clusters in English just because some English-speaking student of German has learned to pronounce the name Schwartz as šwárts instead of the anglicised form swárts. At the same time we can better understand some of the processes by which change is introduced into language. If a feature of performance is copied and generalised, if šwárts becomes the common pronunciation and if other words in the language allow šw-, then the patterns of competence must be modified to explain it.

Transformational analysis has encouraged an interest in related sentences, particularly those with similar meanings. Sentences like 'John won the election: this was a blessing' can be paraphrased as 'John's winning of the election was a blessing'. Drills based on such relationships have proliferated to a point where the application of transformational analysis to language learning may well be characterised as paraphrase drills. Some of these have been understood and used in language classes for a very long time (e.g. active versus passive sentences), but other comparable relationships are being defined and described in ways that are very helpful for language teachers. Excellent examples can be seen in a recent book by William E. Rutherford, entitled *Modern English*.

Other ideas of transformational grammar, though interesting as theoretical concepts, have not as yet found an application in the language classroom. One of these is the expansion of the concept of language universals. Some transformationalists assign all of the language deep structure to linguistic universals, with differences between languages limited to the rules that derive surface structures from deep structures. There seems to be little difference in the learning problems, however, for the student, whether he finds differences between languages in the deep structure or in the transformational rules; the differences are still there and must be mastered.

Language teaching has been changing in ways other than through the influence of linguistic theory. Some of the ideas for applications of linguistics to language teaching (especially structural linguisitcs) are being reconsidered in the light of current studies in psychology, and excesses are being modified. A very interesting book by Wilga Rivers, called *The Psychologist and the Foreign Language Teacher*, challenges the operant conditioning basis of repetitive drills, stressing the need for the student to understand what he is practising and why, as a means of providing adequate incentives to study an unknown language. Traditional teaching relied heavily on analysis; linguistic orientation has stressed practice and analogy. Rivers seems to be suggesting a combination of the two in whatever mix produces optimum results.

Language teachers have been looking in many directions for answers to their problems. One of the answers that seemed to hold great promise in the fifties was mechanisation: the language laboratory. The 'hardware' was introduced with great enthusiasm, with the virtues of the laboratory enumerated more or less as follows: (1) The lab is a tireless servant – it works as many hours a day as necessary, always repeating utterances in exactly the same way to avoid irrelevant inconsistency. (2) The lab can take over the 'mechanical' chores of instruction, modelling for repetition or drill, freeing the instructor for more creative teaching and more attention to individual students. (3) The lab can be used as a multiplier, adding to the weekly hours of contact with the language available to the student. (4) The lab can add versatility and realism to language instruction, providing a variety of voices, male and female, mature and young, etc., in dramatic and contextual situations. (5) The lab would help compensate for individual differences among students. Those who needed more time to keep up with the class would not have to drop further and further behind, but could put in extra hours in the lab to keep abreast.

The lab has not often fulfilled all these promises. Perhaps it was oversold by the hardware salesmen and the enthusiasts in the profession. It has in many parts of the world become an educational status symbol which any school presuming excellence in instruction must possess, in spite of the absence of convincing evidence to prove the contributions claimed. There are at least two probable reasons for the failure of the lab to produce. One is that language is an essentially human activity, and *any* attempt to mechanise practice is bound to affect the students' motivation. The fact that all responses to stimuli from a recording–playback device must be predictable may tend to discourage efforts at realistic communication, the essence of which is unpredictability: there is no purpose in asking a question if one already knows the answer. The second reason is the extreme difficulty of providing effective laboratory recordings. Neither commercially nor locally prepared tapes seem to be able to fill this yawning gap. And far from freeing the teacher, the lab demands more teacher-time investment, with a knowledge not only of lab management and effective drill procedures, but also of mechanical skills such as tape editing (and a knowledge of minor maintenance procedures for the machines is certainly helpful if not requisite). Furthermore lab administration turns out to be difficult and demanding, especially if large numbers of students are to be served.

Perhaps the most difficult problem the lab has to solve is evaluation. How is the student to know if his performance is satisfactory? The teacher can't tell him; even if the teacher is busy monitoring student performance, only one student can be heard at a time, a procedure even less efficient than in a classroom, where an individual error can often be picked up while listening to several students at once. In pronunciation drill, which the lab is especially designed to support, since it produces the oral language, there is really only one answer: the student must be taught to evaluate his own performance. But to teach him to do this may be more difficult and time-consuming than to teach him to pronounce. And if he is capable of effectively monitoring his own performance, he probably won't need laboratory practice. No easy answer is available to rescue lab instruction from this dilemma. Far from encouraging students to be alert and active in the correction of their errors, most lab programmes tend to be soporific.

Perhaps language laboratories will yet fulfil what theoretically ought to be their potential. So far I think they have not.

Another new answer to some of the problems of language learning is programmed instruction, or P.I. as its proponents like to call it. Again the enthusiasts are generous with their claims, and again the results have so far failed to live up to expectations. Programmed instruction has its theoretical appeals: (1) Learning problems are formulated in easy steps to facilitate learning by a large student audience with a wide spread of abilities. (2) Easy steps minimise errors; the student practises correct language performance. (3) Learning is individual and can proceed at the optimum rate for each student. (4) Instruction requires student involvement; he is asked questions to which he must provide answers. (5) The student is informed immediately of the adequacy of his answers, corrected if in error and encouraged if correct. This prompt information serves as a reward to maintain student interest.

The programme is said to be self-improving. If students have problems at some point, the programme is blamed and an effort can be made to remedy specific ills. After trial and refinement, the programme should be improved to a point of genuine teaching efficiency. Why hasn't this attractive design of problem specification and learning reinforcement been more successful? Perhaps one reason parallels the experience of the language lab: language is employed naturally in human-to-human communication, and students find working alone with a series of questions and instructions for an extended period of time to be unsatisfying. They need to employ, even display, what they are learning. Another reason may be in the design of programmes currently in use. Learning problems are specified in such detail, a careful step at a time in frame following frame, that all details serve to construct a background, with nothing focused in the foreground. Students have been known to progress satisfactorily through a programme and then at the end of the experience fail to produce a significant answer that they passed (and answered satisfactorily) along the way. Perhaps the structure of learning demands some giant steps to occasionally provide real excitement when these steps are mastered, and the same content is dissipated when broken into small bits with an action (a frame) for each bit.

It might seem that if one were wise enough one might be able to foresee the best sequence to preserve interest, learning and retention. But perhaps no single sequence will serve the needs of all students, and if this is so, then one of the principal advantages of programmed instruction – individualised learning – will be seriously prejudiced. Experience has shown that many programmes which meet the criteria of achievable steps, logical progression and adequate subject coverage are still dull to read through. Perhaps programme construction can be improved, but in the meantime it would seem wise not to abandon more traditional methods of presenting material to students, methods which can capitalise on an unplanned opportunity for making a point – impossible in the detailed pre-planning necessary for language laboratory lessons and programmed instruction.

Other recent developments have come to the field of second language teaching. Early in this chapter the different patterns of teaching English to persons who already speak it and teaching other languages to people who are starting from a position of no knowledge or skill were mentioned. In other words, English has been taught traditionally as a first language in English-speaking countries, other languages as second languages. In more recent years English has been taught, extensively, as a second language, to immigrants, indigenous non-English speaking peoples, visiting foreign students and other visitors. The extensions to the field of English as a second language include first language instruction to non-native speakers of English and second language instruction to native speakers of English.

Teaching other languages to their native speakers is a consequence of accepting a new educational philosophy: bilingual education. An excellent example is the instruction given to Mexican-American children in the American south-west. The pattern is designed to produce students literate and versatile in both of their languages, Spanish, which they learn in their homes, and English, which they must acquire – in the schools if necessary – in order to participate meaningfully in the wider society they are a part of. In the past Spanish has been neglected, with unfortunate results if the statistics relative to poor social adjustment can be relied on (school drop-outs, juvenile delinquency, prison populations, welfare rolls, etc.). It has been suggested that many of the Spanish Americans are frustrated by the conflict between the demands of their native culture and those of the English-speaking world they must live in and adjust to. The suggested solution is to take full advantage of the skill they bring to school (fluency in an important world language) by recognising its value in the curriculum and by offering instruction with Spanish as the medium.

There is presently considerable experimentation in bilingual education, and perhaps the best pattern cannot be identified at this time. Typically these programmes offer instruction in the language and literacy of both Spanish and English and also use both languages as tools for further instruction in the other subjects of the school curriculum. The idea of bilingual education has worked well else-where, when both languages are culturally viable, and the prospect is attractive in the American south-west for an improved educational opportunity that should help to salvage some of the current loss in the school-age Mexican-American community. If this effort is successful, perhaps the idea can be applied to some of the American Indian communities, which share many of the same problems.

The other development, E.S.L. for native speakers of English, is a slight exaggeration. This refers to language instruction inspired by E.S.L. models for students who speak a non-standard variety of English. Typically these are students who are disadvantaged by a weak cultural background and few opportunities for a varied linguistic or cultural experience, coming from homes where the means or the interest to provide the means of complementing and supporting the formal education provided by the schools is lacking.

To remedy this situation is a tall order, and there is little assurance that 'English as a second language' can be modified to 'standard English as a second dialect' in a way that will help meet the needs and solve the problems of this group. In common with the bilingual situation, some sort of 'bidialectal' solution will have to be designed, one that will offer the advantages of control of some variety of speech approaching the standard language, while still maintaining the speech of the home and preserving a favourable self-concept. But mastery of the standard language is indispensable to further education as well as to acceptance by a wider segment of the community. It will be fascinating to watch the progress of this educational effort.

Most language teachers are aware that there are very many problems to be solved if language teaching is to attain a respectable level of efficiency in the schools. The yield per hour of instruction under present conditions is nowhere near what it should be, and the means of improving teaching efficiency must be found. It is trite to repeat the clichés about how much smaller the world is growing, but certainly it is true that international communication has never been more important in the history of mankind. We cannot afford anything less than maximum efficiency in exchanging our thoughts across cultural and linguistic boundaries. This means that more people will have to learn more languages than ever before.

A correlated search for better answers to the problems of teaching is urgent. Fortunately the present academic and administrative climate is favourable to basic and applied research, and language teaching should benefit from this interest. There are many problems that should have better answers. Given the observation that languages, both first and second, are learned very efficiently in 'natural' circumstances, that two or three or even more languages can be learned simultaneously if each has a separately defined role in the life of the student, teachers should be highly dissatisfied that they cannot come anywhere near duplicating these achievements in a formal classroom. We need to know much more about incentives, about means of realistically assigning roles to languages. If it turns out to be physically impossible to reproduce the conditions that provide for 'natural' learning, we need to have an idea of what the most attractive alternatives are.

Much time is wasted in language classrooms. We must identify the activities that fruitlessly consume class time in order to eliminate them. A better understanding of the language learning mechanism (whatever it is) would very likely help us to exploit its potential. We know that some students are better learners than others, and some research has been done on the characteristics of language learning. We can also observe that some teachers are better than others. It might be productive to identify the traits and skills that prove to be effective in a teacher – to better recruit and train the teacher corps.

Certainly there is room for experimentation and reasoned innovation in our classrooms. Care should be exercised not to dissipate interest and talent by needlessly replicating work already done, and efforts should be made to assure sufficient control, so that identification of significant variables can be made and the possibility of the Hawthorne effect can be controlled, but beyond that almost any classroom can be experimental.

Another area that can well be supported is the development of more imaginative teaching materials. It is not common to find teachers who can do the detailed planning that goes into a lesson sequence. Nor should they; their function is better described as interpretative. The teacher should be skilled in presenting lesson material, with enough sophistication to understand learning problems and the ability to take full advantage of the opportunities that arise in every classroom that simply cannot be planned or programmed into a course. This is the artistry of teaching, and the text, if well designed, can provide the setting in which the teacher has opportunity and latitude to perform.

Teachers should look to their professional organisations, local, national and international, to provide help and support in their professional activities. There are journals to report the latest research and experimentation, which should be the seed-bed of new ideas that can be discussed and tried. Better solutions must be found, and if the profession does not actively pursue these solutions, then who?

We all have a stake in better schools and better teaching. If we are to find excellence, we must be intolerant of mediocrity, open to new suggestions, and active in the pursuit of ideas that promise improvement. Professional support really means individual support, co-operation with one's colleagues, and a healthy respect for those scholars whose research seems most promising. Better teaching is far too important to leave to chance.

Second language teaching has improved notably in the last thirty years. But there is still a long road to traverse. With good will and co-operation from the full profession the momentum can be maintained and we can look forward to continued improvement, perhaps, with luck, even a breakthrough.

7 Programmed Instruction

G. O. M. Leith

INTRODUCTION

Programmed learning burst on the world some fifteen years ago as a set of techniques to revolutionise education. In many areas of industry and communications automation was already bringing about great improvements in efficiency. Education, alone, seemed incapable of responding to the accelerated pace of the electronics era. Programmed learning arrived in time to give the traditional conceptions of education a new image in terms of 'mechanisation', 'improved productivity', 'target populations' – a whole new jargon akin to that of advertising campaigns and production management. Before long we began to hear of teachers as 'managers' and of schools and universities as education 'plant'.

At the same time another revolution was taking place in which traditional curricula and teaching methods were being transformed. This was the curriculum reform movement, which undertook to eliminate from syllabuses all those aspects of traditional teaching which had accumulated unsystematically over many years and could no longer be justified as coherent elements of systematic knowledge. The restructuring of mathematics and science, changes in languages teaching and so on also involved radical reforms in pedagogy based on the work of innovative teachers and of such men as Jean Piaget, whose findings about the development of the human intellect have vast implications for the contents and methods of teaching. In brief the new wave was an organised application of heuristic or personal discovery and direct, oral methods in classroom instruction.

These two revolutions for a number of years have apparently been opposed. They had in common three ideas which many teachers accepted as justifiable. The first was that education in the past had often been practised with limited and unanalysed aims. The second point was that the emphasis in teaching/learning situations was often too much on teaching – whereas it is the children's or students' learning which is the goal of education. The third common theme was the importance of catering for individuals rather than classes. In other ways, however, the two movements were difficult to reconcile. Thus programmed learning, based on principles of animal conditioning, put forward methods for achieving *control over* students' behaviour, developed materials which were extremely formal and didactic and seemed to oblige learners to adopt an accepting attitude to what they were learning, rather than inspiring a spirit of inquiry. Moreover, almost without exception, children were all provided with exactly the same pathways to an educational goal. In other words, in practice, programming was perceived as the antithesis of methods which aimed to promote creativity. It was almost exclusively textual, at a time when there was increased emphasis on personal experience, and the use of many media and sensory channels. Finally, its emphasis on individuality took the form of working by oneself in a way which excluded social interaction and all forms of group activities.

Recent advances in programmed learning have, however, not only shown that reconciliation is possible but given a new perspective to progressive education.

MODELS OF PROGRAMMED LEARNING

Three models of programming were put forward in the fifties. The first of these, historically, had been formulated in the 1920s. Sidney L. Pressey developed a method of instruction which depended on giving immediate knowledge of results for each item of a multiple choice test (54).* By means of early teaching machine devices, learners were able to try all the alternatives until an item was passed. Indeed, one machine was geared to cumulate all the items which had been incorrectly attempted for further practice at the end. These self-correcting tests were associated with conventional teaching, and if given regularly, added to the learning achieved by students to a significant degree. It was also found that learning was even more greatly enhanced if, besides immediate knowledge of results (correct or incorrect), students were provided with reasons for being right or

* Figures in parentheses refer to works listed in the Bibliography, pp. 268-72.

wrong (9). This approach was given the name 'adjunctive programming'.

It is B. F. Skinner's name, however, which has become most closely identified with programmed learning. He saw the school situation as an opportunity to extend his principles of animal learning into practical human affairs (58).

In Skinner's view, learning takes place when an animal or human makes a response which is *reinforced*. Reinforcement is an event after the response such as getting a morsel of food (when hungry) or being given knowledge of correct performance (in human learning). Skinner has shown that complex performances can be built up in animals by a process of successive approximations to the goal performance. Thus a pigeon, which can already peck, can be induced to peck one shape on a wall rather than another and can be brought to walk in a figure-of-eight, play ping-pong with another pigeon, etc. This is done by reinforcing each movement which is a step to the goal and by omitting to reinforce movements other than these. Hence, complex behaviour can be programmed by defining the performance to be achieved, analysing a series of approximations and steps to the goal which starts at something which can already be done, and then reinforcing the sequence of responses required (59).

Skinner, examining school learning situations, found that, whereas his animals were actively involved in making responses which contributed to their learning, children were not for the most part engaged in making frequent, relevant responses – in other words they were listening or watching. They were reinforced infrequently, in fact most of the reinforcements tended to be 'aversive' – 'don't do that', 'stop talking', 'pay attention'. To make things worse, the teacher conducted lessons at a pace which was too slow for some and too fast for others, often missing out important steps or using steps in the exposition which were too big for pupils to follow. Table 1 illustrates this point from an experiment comparing the effectiveness of a good teacher with that of a programme (27). The students were 16-17 years old and the teacher had based his lessons on the programme.

Pupils learning from the programme were almost all in favour of learning at their own individual pace and of the small progressive steps of the programme.

In short, classroom teaching was criticised for not giving enough opportunity for active participation, not giving enough reinforce-

TABLE 1. Questionnaire Item Completed by Students at the End of a Lecture Course

In listening to the lectures did you:	Percentage responding
Often miss points?	30
Sometimes miss points?	7
Find the pace just right?	43
Sometimes feel he was explaining too slowly?	3
Often feel you could be learning faster?	17

ment, having a pace set by the teacher, and for telescoping instruction so that many points are given insufficient weight and practice.

A number of studies, outside programmed learning, have given independent testimony to these points. Thus it has been shown that learning spellings (38) and German–English vocabulary (69) is less successful or ineffective if pupils do not themselves practise all the responses required, with reinforcement. Meddleton (46) compared Schonell's arithmetic practice materials, which were systematically arranged after extensive studies on the validation of his diagnostic arithmetic tests, with teacher-prepared lessons, in several primary schools. Not only were children more successful in retaining their knowledge of number combinations if they used Schonell materials, it was also established that, unaided, teachers paid little or no attention to many number bonds – in particular those which have been shown to give difficulty. The point can also be made by referring to the way in which lecturers – experts in their field – make many assumptions about what can be understood by an audience. By analogy, they have laid the foundations, built up the structure of their knowledge and dismantled the scaffolding. What they present to the audience is the finished building – the foundations are out of sight and pupils may never be informed about the props which are needed during construction. Teachers might also try giving the 'same' lesson three times and, from recordings, notice which points have been telescoped or omitted.

The techniques of programming which were devised by Skinner can be outlined as follows:

1. Determine precisely the objectives of the teaching.
2. Analyse the teaching material into small steps.
3. Order these into a progressive sequence.
4. Ensure that each learning point is exercised in the form of a response *composed* by the learner and written down.

5. Prevent the learner from making errors by making steps smaller or by giving hints which guide responses (prompts).
6. Provide immediate reinforcement – i.e. give the correct answer as a check.
7. Try out the materials with pupils who can do what is required of them at the start but not later.
8. Note the steps at which they make mistakes in order to
9. Revise the programme to eliminate mistakes.

The resulting programme is given to pupils to work through at their own pace – each programme having been prepared and tested with particular groups of learners typical of those who will later use the programme.

The programme below has been written to illustrate Skinner's techniques. It is self-contained. The objectives are given at the end. Readers should conceal the answers at the right of the page until they have attempted to compose them.

The Concept of the Susu

1. In many societies a person traces his lineage through his male ancestors. An individual's line of . . . . . is through his . . . . . .   descent, father

2. Some societies, however, think that inheritance is not through the male line but through the . . . . . line.   female

3. The islanders of Dobu, near New Guinea, inherit from a male relative on the female side. He is not the father but the . . . . .'s brother.   mother's

4. A man's heir is not his own son but his . . . . .'s son.   sister's

5. If a man wants an heir it is not his wife he urges to bear him a son but his . . . . . .   sister

6. On Dobu the basic kinship group is called

the *susu*. It consists of all those people who
can trace their descent from the same . . . . .
ancestor.   female

7. A man and his sister and his sister's children
   belong to the same . . . . . .   susu

8. A person's mother and grandmother belong
   to the same susu. The grandfather belongs to
   the same / a different susu.   different

Objectives of the Programme on the Susu

1. Students will select correctly, from a three-generation family
   tree, the individuals belonging to one susu.
2. They will state what relationship a man has to the children of a
   marriage after he and his wife are divorced. (Transfer problem)
3. Students will choose the correct alternative from the following
   selection.
       Which of the following belong to the same susu?*
   (*a*) A man and his daughter's son.
   (*b*) A woman and her brother's son.
   (*c*) Both of the above, (*a*) and (*b*).
   (*d*) Neither of the above, (*a*) and (*b*).

Each numbered section is called a *frame*. It will have been noticed
that in many frames the correct response is guided by the form of the
sentence, by opposites, etc., but that, towards the end of a sequence,
such prompts or cues are removed. Gradual removal of prompts is
referred to as 'fading' or 'vanishing', and evidence has been brought
forward that this may be an effective technique (2).

The topic of kinship in social anthropology is unfamiliar to most
people. Many prospective programme users have examined programmes on topics which they know intimately and have found
them trivial and tedious. A more valid test is to put oneself in the
position of a novice (the pupil) in order to assess the method.

Programmes arranged in this form are called *linear* programmes
because their sequence follows one line. Another approach offers
alternative routes and is referred to as *branching*.

* The correct answer is given on p. 159.

The branching technique was developed by N. Crowder (71) in opposition to Skinner. His method is based on a different model which is influenced by cybernetics and communications theory. He argued that learners need not take such small steps as those employed by Skinner. His programmes, therefore, present a fairly large 'chunk' of information, grasp of which is tested by means of a multiple choice question. Incorrect choices lead the pupils to 'remedial branch lines' in order to clarify the teaching points, explain them more simply, in smaller steps, or give further practice. Correct choice leads to the next large 'chunk' of exposition or may even enable students to jump explanatory points which they have shown they understand already. Skill in choosing alternatives which expose misunderstanding is required or, better still, trials designed to discover the kinds of mistakes which are made (55).

A brief section of a branching programme is given to illustrate the description of Crowder's methods. The style of writing advocated is conversational and even chatty. Errors may even be occasioned in this system, which claims to take account of individual differences through the provision of branches. It is almost exclusively textual in form, as are the adjunct and linear methods.

Kinship and Residence

1. In some societies a woman who marries goes to live among her husband's relatives. In others the husband lives with the wife's kin. On Dobu, the practice is for husband and wife to live alternate years in each other's villages. There are two facts of importance:
   (i) People are divided into two classes: the villagers and the outsiders. It is not permitted for two outsiders from the *same* village to stay simultaneously in another village.
   (ii) The only people allowed to enter one's house are members of the same susu, one's spouse and the children.

   How will the man living in his wife's village feel?
   (*a*) At home and have many friends.   Go to Frame 2
   (*b*) Isolated and cut off socially.   Go to Frame 5
   (*c*) It will depend on the individual.   Go to Frame 6

2. Your answer: 'A man living in his wife's village will feel at

home and have many friends.' I'm afraid you have chosen wrongly. Let's look closely at the situation. There is no one else from his *own* village. All the other outsiders are strangers to him. He cannot visit anyone else's home and only his wife's susu (his in-laws) can come into the house he shares with his wife. He would therefore feel cut off socially.

When his wife comes to live in his village how would she feel?
(*a*) The neighbours are friendly.   Go to Frame 4
(*b*) The neighbours are unfriendly.   Go to Frame 5

5.* Your choice: 'A man living in his wife's village will feel isolated and cut off socially.' You are right, of course. Similarly a woman living in her husband's village will feel isolated. The social system operates so that the man has no friends from his own village, cannot go to anyone else's home or have people other than his in-laws under the roof of his wife's house. Now a wife in her own village (or a husband in his) has a rich social life including a good deal of flirtation and infidelity with less closely related kinsfolk. Whatever insults are suffered by a spouse, when an outsider, are repaid with interest when the pair changes residence.

Which of the following practices to you think is common?
(*a*) Duelling or fighting between the injured party
    and the offenders.   Frame 12
(*b*) Casting of spells and sorcery.   Frame 10
(*c*) Suicide.   Frame 9
(*d*) Divorce.   Frame 8

Using a teaching machine the student presses a button corresponding to a letter. In a textbook the pages are 'scrambled' so that he cannot find the correct answer page until he has chosen the correct answer.

TEACHING MACHINES

From the outset programmed learning has been associated with teaching machines – the connotations of this phrase provoking

* Several remedial frames have been omitted.

resistance to programming among many teachers. Early teaching machines include those designed by Pressey. Skinner's linear programmes were first printed on 'discs' which were rotated, a section at a time, to expose a frame in a window. After filling in a space in the response aperture a lever could be pressed* which removed the response and showed the correct answer. Another movement revealed a second frame and so on. Many devices of this kind were designed using continuous rolls of paper, single sheets or cards, the aim being to have a brief, incomplete exposition of between ten and twenty words (apparently a carry-over from Skinner's first programmes) and a way of preventing the learner from seeing the answer until his response was made. Some linear programmes used multiple choice responses and machines with piano key or press-button controls.

A few linear machines and almost all branching machines employed film strip and optical projection instead of paper. A branching programme needs a means of transporting the film to and fro to reach branching sequences. Thus machines are devices for presenting frames (turning 'pages') and preventing learners from looking ahead at the answers (49). There were one or two developments of self-adapting equipment which worked like a computer to adjust the learning task to the learner's pattern of errors and success, and more will be said about this in a later section.

It should be said that it was assumed at this time that programmed learning was *verbal* learning and most examples of programmes were textual, i.e. printed words. Not unexpectedly, therefore, it was suggested that programmes might be presented in book form with suitable textual arrangements to avoid giving away the answers. A variety of forms grew up – consecutive frames being placed on bands and being read through the book, returning to read the second band and so on until the book had to be turned upside down and read through again. This was in order to print the answers on following pages. Other programmes used a more conventional form and printed answers alongside the next frame, but suggested the use of a cardboard strip to conceal them. 'Cheating' became a major source of worry. Nevertheless a vast number of programmes have been published in book form. It has, in fact, turned out that the original

---

* Readers will notice that just as railway carriages were first made in the shape of coaches, this teaching machine is essentially a Skinner box – an apparatus for studying learning in rats.

emphasis on teaching machines was unnecessary. A survey of studies comparing machine- and book-presented programmes shows that mechanical page-turners play a very limited role in learning (Table 2) (65).

TABLE 2. Studies Comparing the Use of Teaching Machine with Textbook Presented Programmes

Machine better	Textbook better	No difference	Total
2	1	20	23

OBJECTIVES OF EDUCATION

Before going further with the discussion, the notion of objectives must be considered. Perhaps the most important feature of programming has been its highlighting of the idea that, in order to improve a course of teaching, we must have a precise formulation of its aims in terms of learner *performance*. Aims are more often expressed either in terms of syllabus content ('doing fractions') or hoped-for states of mind ('understanding logarithms', 'appreciating poetry'). Such statements do not permit evaluation of the success of teaching. Indeed it is often said that many lessons and courses could not be given more definite goals.

Programmed learning assimilated the ideas of specifying objectives from a movement begun in the thirties by Ralph Tyler (68), who criticised classroom teaching for its lack of defined objectives. He insisted that a teacher should be clear about what kind of things his pupils should be able to do (which they could not previously do) as a result of his teaching. This entails formulating means of assessing competence and mastery, i.e. tests of achievement of the teaching aims. Not only do such measures inform the teacher of his relative success, they also indicate areas of a course which may be inadequately mastered – thus pointing the way to improvements in the design and content of the curriculum. Incidentally, if frequent tests are given with knowledge of results to the pupils it becomes possible to modify course materials, as learning proceeds, by amplifying sections which are poorly learned. The result is then close to programming.

As soon as one begins to analyse teaching objectives in this way, what to teach and how to teach it becomes much clearer. Thus

F

objectives will be framed in terms of teaching: specific information (either for recognition or recall); routines and procedures (in standard cases or a variety of situations); concepts (either for definition or use); principles (for verbatim recall or application in problem-solving situations); restatement of comparisons or unrehearsed evaluation and judgement, The task has been immensely aided by such publications as *The Measurement of Understanding* (50) and *Taxonomy of Educational Objectives* (7). In defining objectives in terms of what learners will be able to do – how we would determine whether a person 'understands' logarithms, etc. – we may arrive at a list of performance criteria which gives sufficient evidence of mastery. We can also go further and determine what prior things our pupils will have to be able to do before they reach the final goal, and what objectives are prior to that and so on. That is, in order to carry out long division with remainders, pupils will have to be able to operate with exactly divisible numbers, estimate, do short division, subtract, add, etc. These subordinate objectives represent components of the total task. Working out successively what must be learned before each stage of knowledge helps to ensure that nothing is left out and that the sequence of tasks is properly arranged. The objectives of a programme to teach conversion of the present British currency to the new decimal coinage are given as illustration (39). The final objective states that learners will be able to:

6. Assess the value in new currency of sums of money in mixed coinage (e.g. a person may present both old and new coins to make a purchase).

Before they can do this they will have to be able to:

5. Give the nearest approximation for £ s d in decimal currency when there is no exact equivalent.

An earlier stage requires them to be able to:

4. Translate present coinage into decimal currency equivalents swiftly (and the reverse) when conversion is exact.

And before this they must be able to:

3. Set out the new notation, read it fluently and make calculations in decimal notation.

This entails previous ability to:

2. Compose sums of money in the new coinage with the smallest number of coins.

The earliest stage involves that:

1. Learners will identify coins in the new currency and give their

face values from visual (or tactile) cues other than figures and
words.

In this example it can be seen that (6) depends on (5) and each of the
others on the earlier ones to permit the smooth execution of the
final objective. It ought to be observed that these objectives are
broader than those actually used to guide preparation of the programme, but specification of the details at this point would obscure
the notion of drawing out successively from the final objective(s)
every successive stage involved. Greater detail is obtained by inquiring
what would show mastery of stage 5, etc., and this in turn suggests
the kind of *activities* in learning which will bring about the achievement.

It is often objected that many of the outcomes of education are so
intangible that they could not be specified as objectives, i.e. stated in
measurable form. This is, however, either to make a mistake about
the nature of measurement or an acknowledgement that there are
things which people learn that make no detectable difference to
them. It is sufficient to point out that it is possible to tell the difference between one who has acquired standards of culture such as
evaluating artistic creations, conducting rational discussions, etc.,
and one who has not. If such recognition is possible then the bases of
the judgement can be analysed and set out as what differentiates the
cultivated and uncultivated person. The purposes of discussion
lessons in English may be put forward as being too insubstantial to
formulate in measurable form. Exactly this problem arose in
attempting to assess whether programming could contribute to the
aims of discussion (45). An experiment was carried out in which
classes of secondary school children were divided into groups
which received programmed instruction or 'live' teaching in discussion lessons. A programme on a controversial topic (capital punishment) was prepared in branching style so that whatever a pupil's
original opinion he was led through a sequence which also gave him
information and arguments leaning towards a counter-view. The
same points and factual data were presented by a teacher to one part
of each class while the others read the programme. After this introduction the groups (half-classes) engaged in discussions which were
recorded and later played back to a panel of judges who assessed, on a
check-list, the degree of participation of the children (whether many
contributed to the discussion or only a few), the extent of the
teacher's intervention, the use of relevant information and support-

ing argument. Without knowing which group was which the judges consistently gave favourable assessments to the groups which had read the programme. They were, therefore, able to recognise and rate the achievement of objectives of discussion lessons.

One could itemise other objectives in terms of ability to entertain ideas and examine their consequences (without being committed to one side or another), to present new perspectives on conflicting issues, etc. If things which people do who have acquired skills, ideas, understandings or abilities can be identified, they can be formulated in objective terms and their attainment assessed. Even so ineffable a skill as recognising a good cigar has been analysed successfully with great savings to the manufacturer (51). The firm was enabled to train staff for the job rapidly (is spite of those who feel it takes a life-time's experience) and to reduce the number of smokable cigars previously rejected and also the number of bad ones which previously were permitted to go through.

ARRANGING THE SEQUENCE OF STEPS

At first, in programmed learning, the order of steps was arranged intuitively with care to avoid omissions, supplemented by the results of trials with samples of learners whose errors would indicate that there was a gap. Later a more formalised method was designed which reduced the need for a special flair. This method is known as the *Ruleg* system because the first step is to list all the rules (relatively general statements) and examples (e.g.s) in the topic to be analysed (15). All the rules are written out along the top and down the side of a large sheet of squared paper or matrix and each rule is examined for its relationship with the other rules. A relationship known as 'association' has been used by many programmers. This turns out to mean that a rule contains the same key term as another. Rules which are associated can be denoted in the matrix by colouring a square at the intersection of the vertical and horizontal lines they are on. In this way blocks of coloured squares designate concept areas and breaks in the diagonal line show discontinuities. A gap occurs if a rule is out of order or something is missing or the end of a sequence has been reached. Simple rules help to find how to make the rearrangement (63).

This technique, which seemed at the time to be beneficial and to aid the structuring of instructional materials, has unfortunately been damaging in the long run, as have other rule-of-thumb procedures, e.g. for writing frames. This system has placed the major emphasis on verbal subject matter analysis with the result that *syllabuses* have been structured in detail, rather than the learning processes required to reach objectives. An experiment carried out in Sweden demonstrates the fault (61). Arts students were taught principles of physics by one of two methods. The first, called the traditional, lecture–demonstration method, presented students with an account of the principles followed by a demonstration of a phenomenon which illustrated the laws. The second (modern or problem-solving method) gave the demonstration first as a puzzling phenomenon which students would not be able to account for but which the principles (given next) would enable them to explain. The students, then, had exactly the same materials of instruction but given in different orders. The next step in the experiment was to give two tests. One required solution of a new problem which also came under the principles taught. Only 20 per cent of the lecture–demonstration group was successful, whereas 65 per cent of the modern group solved the problem correctly. The other test was of recall of principles. Here the traditional method students were successful and the modern group failed. The point is that two groups of objectives were assessed – one involving application of the principles in a new situation, the other being verbatim recall. Each method was successful in the attainment of a different objective but not both. Exactly the same subject matter was given to the two experimental groups but in different orders.

In two experiments in which two related subtopics, one of them being more difficult and unfamiliar than the other, were taught, the order of subtopics was varied. Contrary to most views, which hold that the easier and more familiar topic should be presented first, it was the opposite order which was the more successful (35, 40).

Experiments like these show the rule-of-thumb matrix approach to arranging sequences to be of limited value. It is not subject matter but learning which needs to be ordered. We must pay attention not only to what is taught but to how it is learned if we are to be sure of providing learning situations which lead to our objectives.

A final criticism may be made. The matrix becomes enormously unwieldy beyond about 30 rules. It can however be computerised.

This was done by two of the writer's colleagues, who reproduced a similar order to one made up independently using pencil and paper. They were able to do this by making the vocabulary of the rules consistent and picking out common words and phrases.

The resulting ordered sequence is in fact an impoverished network. Using another method of analysis (variously called PERT analysis, network analysis or critical path analysis) they found not one order but several optimal paths. Choice of which to adopt rested not on mechanical but on educational grounds (26).

The strategy explained in the previous section, in which subordinate objectives are successively unpacked from the final one, is similar to critical path analysis and is much more likely to give a valid sequence. The Swedish experiment can be examined in this light. If the objectives involve solving problems of a particular kind, analysis of the subordinate objectives would disclose a need for opportunity to solve similar problems, etc. The traditional method did not involve problem-solving as a learning task.

TASK ANALYSIS

The models of programming presented earlier are, in fact, far too restrictive. Thus on Skinner's view every set of learning tasks can be submitted to his small step analysis with constructed responses, made overtly (e.g. writing words or drawing diagrams, rather than thinking the answer but making no witnessable response), with prompts to prevent errors and knowledge of results as reinforcement. Crowder appears to believe that telling people (in large steps) and having them choose alternative possible answers to problems, with remediation for errors, is superior to this.

Unfortunately there is not a single type of solution for all the different kinds of educational problems which exist. Hence one kind of programme writing and general purpose teaching machines will not do. We have to let the problems point to the methods of solution.

Over a number of years the writer has been making an experimental analysis of the kinds of learning processes which can be identified as forming the basis of school learning.

The following categories of learning activities could each be analysed further. Instead the broad classifications are set out together with points on how to facilitate learning at each stage or level. In general earlier categories of learning are involved in or subsumed under later ones, e.g. a large number of particular associations must have been learned before a concept can be achieved. Hypothetico-deductive inference (problem-solving) requires the availability of a large number of concepts.

Learning to Distinguish between Stimuli

Even for adults there are many situations where, before learning, the difference between cues (stimuli or signals) is unclear. Think of listening to a *strange* foreign language. The native speaker seems, at first, to be uttering gibberish. American cars seem all alike to a European who has not been long in the U.S.A. Cytological specimens which are being screened for the presence of cancer are initially hard to sort into categories. Arabic script looks like marks made by a fly after walking through a pool of ink.

There are a number of ways to improve learning. Thus differences can be highlighted to make elements stand out and distinctive names may be given – together with knowledge of results during practice. Emphatic cues should, of course, be faded (11, 60, 62).

Learning Novel Responses

Adults have already learned most of the responses they will need, but foreign languages contain new sounds, children learn to whistle, etc. There are responses which are new at some time in life. There are also the limits of some responses to be learned – e.g. how far a school ruler may be bent before it snaps (30). Such things as new sounds may be shaped, i.e. successive approximations drawn out. Often advice on how to make the response is helpful. Feedback, e.g. matching response to a standard, is necessary.

Response Integration

Having learned the responses and having them available, one may have to assemble them in new ways. Thus the stock of names encountered by a schoolteacher contains the same elements in different arrangements from one year to another. Last year there was Brenda Jones and Alan Smith – this year Alan Jones and Brenda Smith, etc. Very often integrations must be learned by dint of repetition – though mnemonics and other linking methods can help. The difficulty is that conflict and confusion often arise. One method of programming, known as *mathetics*, presents all confusable elements together, with mnemonics or mediating links designed to facilitate initial learning as a schema (19).

Association or 'Hook-up'

If one has learned to distinguish between things and has learned all their names, they will also have to be linked together, correctly. Suppose a new teacher has learned to distinguish between the faces of children in a class (they are Eskimo children) and to utter Eskimo names correctly, he still has to relate each name to an individual. Sometimes the two things are best learned separately and then linked together, as when discriminations have to be learned and novel responses acquired. If neither presents difficulty, the things to be associated may be learned together. Systematic practice and use of 'mediators' or 'links' (think of anatomy: humerus – funny bone) are the appropriate methods (28).

Trial-and-Error Learning

In seeking the correct response in a situation one may have to run through many responses until one of them is noted as successful. Knowledge of results is of course important. This learning situation may, however, be inefficient and frustrating.

Learning-Set Formation or Learning How to Learn

The American psychologist Harlow discovered that if trial-and-error learning situations were made into a series, containing many similar problems, animals and humans, after at first choosing correctly by chance, begin to make correct choices as if by 'insight'.

In other words they learn not merely the solution to a particular problem but *how to solve* any such problem (21). This new level of learning is related to the variety of problems experienced and also to how well each has been mastered. We could say that they have 'got the hang of it'. That this is a structural organisation is shown by the fact that reversing the response which is correct in the experiments (e.g. if choices are left or right the formerly correct response 'choose the one on the right' is reversed to 'choose the one on the left') is only briefly upsetting and the whole system of responding is changed. An example in practical life is switching from 'drive on the left' to 'drive on the right'.

In learning-set formation what seems needed is a range of problem situations, each of which has been individually mastered. Learning-set formation is almost certainly the basis of fundamental notions like the concept of conservation of number. Young children judge number and quantity on the basis of global patterns. Thus a group of things which is spread out will be judged as having more than one which is clustered together. The emergence of a learning-set at this stage involves children learning to pay heed to some features of the situation (the number of things, or their one-to-one matchability) rather than size, spread-out-ness, etc.

Forming Concepts

A concept can be thought of as a class of 'things' all having some common quality. If a person knows a concept he is expected to be able to pick out instances of the same concept and distinguish them from similar things which do not belong to the class. He might, in addition, be expected to formulate the concept, e.g. as a verbal definition. This gives the clue to how concepts are learned. Unless the learner has opportunity to discover the things which are distinguishing properties of the concept, he can at best learn to respond with a list of words. Given that he already has a set of related concepts, a new one can be explained verbally – but the experience of sorting out what belongs and does not belong must at some stage be obtained. Thus we can have two kinds of apprehension of concepts: knowing *how* to recognise e.g. mammals, and knowing *that* 'mammals are warm-blooded animals which suckle their young'. The ability to recognise e.g. the italicised words in '*What saved it* was *how it was*

F 2

written' as noun clauses is different from being able to define the latter as being replaceable by nouns. To invent examples such as these needs at least 'know-how' and probably 'knowledge that' as well. A further example is that most people have a good idea of the meaning of 'sister', i.e. they know how to determine if someone has this relationship to anyone. Fewer people could give a formal definition of the concept.* (Not: 'It's like when you have a brother', etc.) Note that being able to say this definition is unlikely to be of practical use. Again, it must be clear that being able to state the definition of number (the class of all classes equivalent to a given class) is no substitute for experiences of matching, seriating, etc., in forming the concept of number in young children.

Hence, learning concepts is facilitated by giving opportunity to sort out the basis of the concept with immediate knowledge of results. Formulating the concept either by getting pupils to make the abstraction or to apply it is a further stage. A wide range of practice is important.

Concept Integration

Concepts may become interrelated in many ways to form logical or contingent groupings, networks and hierarchies. Thus amphibia are creatures which *both* breathe with lungs as adults *and* spend the first part of their lives under water; an aeroplane travels through the air by means of *either* propeller-driven, turbine *or* jet engines. The concept of conservation of momentum *subsumes* the concepts of mass and of velocity. Velocity *includes* concepts such as direction and speed. The set of concepts known as the Renaissance happens to include political and economic evolutions in Florence and their relationship to patronage of artists.

Whether the principles which relate concepts together, e.g. the conservation of momentum, are best acquired by discovery or by direct instruction in the principles, is still a controversial issue (3, 8). No doubt teachers will want to choose methods by reference to the objectives they seem to serve, as in the Swedish experiment referred to above. On the other hand, recent findings about personality and discovery or reception learning make it difficult to be dogmatic. (See p. 190.) Perhaps it should be urged that methods be validated in

* Female sibling.

each situation until more knowledge is gained about styles of learning and strategies of instruction.

Even so, it can be pointed out that when concepts become linked under a superordinate idea there is a tendency for distinctions and clear limits to blur until the whole cluster becomes a vague, general notion. Furthermore, there is a general tendency for established systems of concepts to assimilate related but different systems so that the latter become distorted to fit well-known categories (assimilation by distortion) (22). Schoolboy howlers are instances of this. If existing categories are modified and reorganised to take account of the new ideas, we may be said to have 'accommodated' to them.

In teaching two systems, one of which fits already existing conceptual categories (and thus can be assimilated), while the other presents novel arrangements of concepts (and therefore requires accommodation), there is often difficulty in learning the second. The susu kinship system is a case of the latter. It has been shown that the novel organisation should be taught before the familiar, with a perspective-giving view relating them (40). The same finding was made in teaching two systems of conventions for projective drawings (35).

This is to point out that failure to learn and retain complex material often results from processes of interference and 'simplification', which can, however, be overcome. The use of overall perspectives to mediate conflicting sets of ideas, provision of reviews and summaries at the end of each subsection, and ordering of topics in a sequence organised to reduce conflict (not necessarily the logical order) have all been found helpful (32). Incidentally, several experiments show that after learning successive levels of a hierarchy of concepts in order to achieve a terminal performance, students very often forget earlier learned material which was needed to build up to the final objective (17). (The scaffolding, no longer needed to support the building, is not retained.

Hypothetico-deductive Inference (Problem-Solving)

Among the aims of teaching are that schoolchildren and students in higher education should come to be able to apply the knowledge and principles they have learned to new situations, solve novel problems, find new approaches, methods and explanations, and be able to test and evaluate them against criteria they have learned to judge as relevant, or have invented.

While particular kinds of problems can be solved by following rules (e.g. 'troubleshooting' in electronic equipment, for which there are strategies for successively eliminating sectors of the equipment until the fault is located), the cases we usually think of do not belong to closed systems. It seems likely that practice in problem-solving over a sufficiently wide range of cases is needed to improve these abilities. Of course, a condition of successful problem-solving is that the learner is well endowed with relevant conceptual knowledge and experience, but this, by itself, is not enough. Hence it is important that students should be able to retrieve previous knowledge readily and have many interconnecting links between ideas. This is probably better accomplished by previous training in which concepts are discovered, interrelationships between principles are sorted out and a readiness to search is fostered in the student, rather than by the learning of given rules and explanations (8).

The idea of seeking to prevent errors by prompting and guidance does not seem appropriate here, any more than in learning-set formation, though knowledge of results in some form (e.g. failure of a test of a hypothesis) is needed (57).

USE OF THE TAXONOMY OF LEARNING PROCESSES

A few examples will be given to suggest how this analysis of learning can be helpful in deciding what and how to teach a number of things. The problem of training children in reading readiness skills was tackled by identifying processes which need practice (23). Thus discrimination between shapes, especially reversed and inverted forms, and left to right orientation were picked out. A programme was written which presented, at first, easily distinguishable rotations of animal shapes, went on to harder ones, geometrical forms and words. The order was decided empirically. To get children to look from left to right a system of colour cues was developed (again, the most noticeable colour was found in practical trials) which focused children's attention first on the left, then the middle and the right. These cues were transferred to writing the shapes of letters and finally were faded. Principles of learning-set formation, it will be seen, were also used in preparing this programme.

A programme on the most frequently misspelled words was given many prompts to prevent errors in response integration as well as mediating rules and a high degree of repetition and redundancy, together with overt responding (47). Conflicting cases were taught in relation to each other. A shorter version and use of the programme with fewer or no overt responses were much less effective (33, 42).

A programme aimed at the ability to calculate in any number base system taught mastery of a variety of different bases and involved conflict to be overcome so as to attain a higher order concept rather than knowledge of independent sets of rules (34). Teaching the ability to make up all combinations and formulate and test hypothetical inferences was carried out by requiring students to make the entries in cross-classification tables and by providing case histories of experiments with hints where necessary for them to form a hypothesis and later suggest amendments. Covert responses were found to be better than overt ones (4).

The form in which the concept of the susu would be prepared, in preference to either small step linear or branching methods, is given to illustrate how complex covert responses can be employed to foster thinking and to overcome conflict.

The Concept of the Susu

On the island of Dobu, near New Guinea, the basic kinship pattern is that of the susu. A susu consists of all those people who are related by descent on the mother's side. Thus a woman and her children belong to the same susu. So also do her brothers and sisters, her mother and maternal aunts and uncles, but not her father or her husband. Descent and inheritance are counted only in the female line. A man inherits property from his mother's brother not from his father.

Which of these belong to the same susu?

(*a*) A man and his daughter's son.

(*b*) A woman and her brother's son.

(*a*): (*b*): Both: Neither.*

* Neither.

ADVANCES IN PROGRAMMED LEARNING

The advances in programmed learning can be reviewed by contrast with the formulae for programming which were advanced by pioneers in the field.

Programmed learning involves a progressive series of small instructional steps. Size of step is nowadays governed by the nature of the task and the abilities of the learners. In general the largest possible steps are prepared and made smaller if they prove to be too big during trials.

Learners should make overt constructed responses, i.e. compose their answers and write them down. The type of task should determine what kind of response is required. It has been shown that response learning and integration benefit from overt responding but that concept integration may be hindered if pupils have to write or draw responses rather than think them (covert responding). Such tasks as learning spelling are helped by writing words (42), whereas learning probability (12-year-olds) (36), co-ordinate geometry (14- and 15-year-olds) (37) and the structure of genetic materials (18-year-olds) (4) are learned more successfully if pupils compose their responses mentally. Responses, by the way, may be such acts as selecting, comparing and contrasting, matching, ranking, co-ordinating, extrapolating, inferring, etc., as well as filling in blank spaces.

Making errors should be prevented, e.g. by giving prompts. Whether the making of errors hinders or helps learning depends on what is being learned and the learner. Thus rote learning is more successful if errors are avoided, while concept attainment need not preclude mistakes – they may even be necessary for learning (13, 57).

Branching programmes cater for individual differences by giving remedial teaching to those who make errors. Several experimental inquiries suggest that the conventional branching programme may have all its remedial sequences removed without reducing the amount learned (6, 12, 41).

Programmed learning is essentially verbal learning. This view is unnecessarily restricting. Many programmes have employed non-verbal materials to enhance learning. Concepts of volume and density were taught by arranging sets of objects for comparison of size, weight, etc., by placing cubes made of different alloys into holes designed to fit them, using displacement vessels, and so on. The movement of molecules in teaching osmosis was simulated by shaking trays of ball bearings of different sizes separated by a barrier with holes in it. The relationship between time-signature in music and duration of notes was programmed with tape-recorded music for junior school children. Learning the new decimal currency was achieved by tape-recorded instruction, coins to handle and a group game. Audio-visual as well as tactile experiences are given wherever they are clearly effective (48).

Programmed learning is essentially at the learner's own pace. It was probably this 'law' of programming which held back the use of audio-visual methods for so long. A number of years before Skinner's methods were launched groups of research workers had been evaluating methods of teaching by film (44). They had come to the conclusion that learning from films was helped: (*a*) by having frequent opportunities for responding (overtly for poorly educated learners, covertly for those with appropriate background); (*b*) by providing immediate knowledge of results; (*c*) by employing structuring methods which helped to prevent confusion and interference; (*d*) by trying out early versions to find where modifications were needed. There were even experiments on the amount of prompting or guidance which should be given to prevent errors in responding (25). What caught attention in programmed learning, however, was the idea of individual self-paced instruction.

It has now been made clear, however, that children and adults can learn effectively from programmed materials presented simultaneously to a class. Some of the work done employed textual programmes, either in book or machine form or projected by means of closed circuit television, slides, etc. (10). When no clear differences were observed at different levels of education and in several subject matters the way was clear to produce audio-visual programmes for group use.

Programmed film and television lessons are quite clearly superior to conventionally produced film and television (16, 64). Audio-visual programmes have often been found to be at least as good as individual programmed texts (or better), while it appears to make no difference whether learners look and listen at their own pace or go along at a predetermined pace (31, 66).

The following examples will illustrate the point more emphatically.

A university course in economics had been given for several years by C.C.T.V. and improved 'intuitively'. A further revision was made after careful examination of objectives, and another television course was prepared by programmed learning methods. On comparison the programmed course was superior (64).

Another project programmed lessons in elementary mathematics and physics for 12-year-old children, without reference to the medium to be used. The materials were adapted for presentation by television, tape recorder with slides (or transparencies) and programmed text. All versions included practical work kits for carrying out experiments, etc. Children learned in groups having a wide range of intelligence. Greater attainments and transfer were achieved from the group-paced lessons than from the self-paced programme. In one of the two series the differences were significant. Both above and below average children learned better in the group-paced situation (31).

These results are by no means unique. On the other hand there is some evidence that audio-programming is not always the best approach. For example, great care must be taken to ensure that the learner's attention is focused on the task and that all the material (e.g. the diagrams, pictures or moving film) is relevant and causes no confusion or distraction (39). Difficulties of this kind are normally detected during validation trials, but sometimes they may arise from outside conditions such as whether pupils are seated correctly in relation to the screen and whether headphones are used or not.

In programmed learning the individual learns on his own. Self-pacing has the implication of individual learning. The idea of children being isolated from each other (often in booths) does not, however, appeal to all teachers. The benefits of social interaction can, however, be used to good effect in co-operative programmed learning. An example of this was the preparation of a programme for use by teams of four junior school children who learned about magnetism with the help of practical apparatus. The same programme could also be given to individuals. The groups of four contained bright, average and dull children (I.Q. range 701–20).

The average gains in knowledge of the teams were much higher than those of the individual learners, who made poor scores if they were below average in intelligence and moderate ones if they were bright. Both above and below average intelligence children working in teams achieved the same level of gains. In other words team-work was better for both the more and less able children (53).

A further experiment with junior school children grouped boys or girls into pairs. Some pairs were at the same level of ability, others had above and below average children working together. There was a further set of children learning individually. The task was to learn the principles of levers and balances and each pair (and individual) had a metre rule balanced on a stand with weights and sandbags to give concrete embodiment to the principles. In addition there were sets of verbal instructions and workbooks. In this experiment team-work was shown to be superior to individual work and mixed ability pairs obtained highest scores, both the able and less able children having equal amounts of learning as well as transfer (application to completely new situations).

An explanation can be given for these and the similar results of a series of follow-up studies in terms of social interaction. Children working in mixed ability pairs verbalise what they are doing in this situation. The brighter children expound and the less bright are obliged to explain. The high ability child working alone sees what responses to make, intuitively, without consolidating his learning. Below average children, though they help each other, do not do so as well as in the heterogeneous ability pair. Two bright children together find intuitive solutions in parallel or alternatively (1).

A Russian account of conceptual learning also throws light on the findings. On this view (akin to Piaget's) a learner must pass through stages of manipulation, verbalisation and abstraction. Before he can *internalise* the concepts he must deal with them externally. Thus it is important to provide concrete models of the structure of concepts for manipulation (e.g. Cuisenaire Rods, Dienes Multibase Arithmetical Blocks). Structural diagrams will serve, instead, for some purposes. Problems should be solved with the help of the structured apparatus with some kind of verbalisation or overt use of symbols (speaking or writing). After a period of practice internalisation is achieved (there may be a time when words as symbols are whispered) (18). Group interaction in solving problems with the help of self-correcting practical apparatus obviously fits this model. An example of this is the double balance which can be used for teaching addition and subtraction of positive and negative numbers in algebraic equations (52). The mathematical balance is a physical model of an equation. On each side of the balance are two smaller balances labelled + and −. By putting weights in the pans of the scale individuals or groups can discover and verify the values in an equation, can find out what happens in transformations, etc., discussing and testing differences in points of view being part of the system of learning.

Programmed learning eliminates individual differences in achievement. This proposition is not well established. A number of early experiments provided results showing that the influence of intelligence (which is usually correlated with attainments in school) was reduced in learning from programmes. It was therefore suggested that pupils of lower than average ability would be able to reach the same levels of knowledge and understanding as more able students, though they would take longer. Findings which show that ability differences were not reduced by programmed instruction are criticised, by those who hold the optimistic view, on the ground that the programme was inadequately prepared or that earlier learning was inadequately mastered (because it was not programmed). At present, there is little likelihood of settling the issue, which is indeed about whether intellectual functions can be improved by educational procedures.

These theorists can be criticised, however, for taking the view that the only important way in which scholastic learners differ is in intelligence and that a single form of instruction is appropriate for everyone.

As teachers are well aware, children differ in their approaches to learning in many ways, and one of the marks of a successful teacher is his ability to discover how to adapt instruction to different kinds of learners. It is beginning to become clear, for example, that people who differ in temperament may have different styles of learning.

In one experiment a course in genetics was programmed in two different ways. One of these presented a complex family tree and asked college of education students to work out a principle for the inheritance of a particular characteristic. After receiving a hint they were given an ambiguous answer and were shown complications which made a simple solution impossible. The course was conducted by requiring hypotheses to be formulated and tested. Much of the time the students were uncertain and were given evidence to contradict their hypotheses. Towards the end, of course, the theoretical principles had been discovered and verified as consistent (discovery).

The other approach involved problem-solving but was carefully structured to give rise to no uncertainty and was highly supportive (direct instruction).

The two versions were validated with unselected students, and when they were found to give the same degree of learning were used with a sample of over two hundred students. Most of them were ignorant of this aspect of biology. The factors investigated in the study were two dimensions of personality – general anxiety and introversion/extroversion. It was found, on tests consisting mainly of application-to-novel-situations problems, that the discovery and direct methods had the same results if personality were ignored. Extroverted students, however, were more successful with the discovery approach while introverts were better if they used the direct instruction programme. Whichever method was used, anxious students were poorer than non-anxious ones (29).

Comprehensive school pupils using different versions of a programme in modern mathematics have shown a similar trend. In junior school, however, though personality and method of learning are related, it may be that anxiety (rather than extroversion) influences styles of learning, since anxious pupils were found to be better than non-anxious ones when given highly structured and prompted materials to learn from, while randomly arranged, unprompted problems, designed to give rise to many ambiguities and errors, helped non-anxious pupils to learn but not those above the average in degree of anxiety (29). An American study has also found that clearly structured teaching is helpful to more anxious children while less anxious ones are able to tolerate and profit from situations which initially may be ambiguous (e.g. phonics and 'look-and-say' methods of teaching reading) (20).

One further study which related ability and personality to methods of programmed instruction may give a lead in considering individual differences in learning (39). The learners were adult clerical workers and executives whose task was to achieve mastery of the new decimal currency system of coinage to be introduced in Britain in 1971. They were divided into groups above and below the average in intelligence and then given one of three methods of programmed instruction. One method was listening to tape-recorded instruction.

Another presented the same material in the form of a programmed text. The third method consisted of a brief text followed by test items and the correct answers (adjunct programme). The results are shown in the table below (Table 3).

TABLE 3. Average Percentage Attained by Above and Below Average Learners Given Three Different Methods of Programmed Instruction

	Methods		
	Audio programme	Text programme	Adjunct programme
Above median I.Q.	90·8	84·0	82·8
Below median I.Q.	77·8	65·0	51·2

The method which helped learners most at both ability levels was the audio programme. There was a slight correlation between test scores and personality which did not reach statistical significance. The ability levels of the text programme group were, however, significantly different though there was no relationship with personality. The adjunct programme was the least supporting of these learning situations – there was no guidance except for knowledge of results and there was no analysis into steps. The bright students were only slightly worse than with the other methods but the less able ones were very much the poorest in scores. There was also a strong correlation between extroversion and scores (0·75) and between emotional stability (anxiety) and scores ($-0·85$), i.e. the more unstable attained low scores while stable subjects scored high.

While no general principles relating methods of instruction, styles of learning, ability and personality can yet be formulated it seems clear that some ways of teaching offer insufficient flexibility and opportunity for sorting things out for particular types of learners, while other types are confused and uncertain unless teaching is clear-cut and carefully arranged. At the same time stress may interfere with either kind of learning. We need to find out therefore, what the optimal amount of difficulty and tension may be for different kinds of students so that strain can be reduced for some, e.g. by audio-visual or small step instruction, and for others the degree of challenge can be increased either by presenting a greater span of logically coherent material or by a more 'stretching' set of problems.

Programmed learning and learning by discovery are incompatible. Illustrations have already been given of programmed learning situations which involve discovery, e.g. in the last section. The incompatibility is between a particular view of programming and an attitude towards 'discovery'. This term does not, unfortunately, denote a clearly defined approach to teaching, as reference to the taxonomy of learning activities will show. Thus 'discovery' may refer to discrimination, trial-and-error learning, learning-set formation, concept attainment or hypothetico-deductive inference (problem-solving). We must also distinguish between guided and unguided discovery – the extent to which attempts at discovery are given feedback and, if unprofitable lines of inquiry are being followed, whether hints are given to redirect thinking.

The approach to programming advocated in this chapter starts from objectives and works out methods which are best capable of achieving them. If engaging in personal hypothesis testing should be required then the programme will incorporate such activities. Much of the programmer's ingenuity will be applied to finding means which do not extend the resources of a school. He may, for example, believe that a computer would help, but if this is not available to him he must find other ways of providing flexible or adaptive learning situations – e.g. he might use other students as monitors of performance or a teacher.

The physics problem used by Szekely (1950), referred to earlier, was programmed by having students frame a solution, match it with a list and look up the comments attached (5). If the solution put forward was inappropriate its consequences were outlined and the student tried again until his search was narrowed to fruitful hypothesis. This can, of course, be done more deftly by setting up a computer to monitor student performance, keep track of the types of errors and bring forward hints, reminders and remedial or fill-out instruction (14).

The role of the teacher. Many experiments have compared the attainments of children learning either from programmes or from teachers, thus posing a problem in terms of 'Which is the better?' This is to make a mistake about the design of teaching systems, in which the questions are 'What are the elements of the system and how should they be interrelated?' While teachers and programmers alone seem about equivalent for the attainment of specific subject matter objectives, far better success has been achieved when teachers play a part in an overall design of learning situations. Three groups of 14-year-old children in urban English-speaking schools in West Malaysia undertook an experiment in which matched teachers taught a course in geography in 'co-operation' with a programme, by programme only, or by teacher only. The integrated method of teaching was very significantly better than the other two, which were equivalent in attainment (43).

In another experiment four methods of programming were compared. The basic frames of a skip-branching programme and the branching programme obtained the same results. A linear small step programme was better. Best of all treatments was this programme with the basic branching frames as reviews following each section. One set of children also had a teacher to follow up and integrate the programmed instruction in groups of sixty to a class. All four programme methods reached the level of the linear programme with reviews when a teacher took part. There were great savings in time for some groups as an additional gain (41).

In East Germany large-scale experiments have varied methods of programme use and teacher co-operation. A method in which teachers are free to reinforce and complement the programme has been most successful (56).

Another illustration comes from the British Royal Navy, which has developed a technique known as 'integrated programmed instruction'. Instructors are made responsible for the progress of their individual students and give one tutorial or teaching session for about every three sessions by programme – though they also give individual advice, etc., during these sessions. Instructors have been able to double the number of students, e.g. from twenty-five to fifty, and at the same time reduce failure virtually to zero and increase average attainments over instructor-led or programme-only groups (70).

In the U.S.A. Kersh has endorsed the point that teachers who are well acquainted with the materials can enhance carefully validated programmes which employ tapes, feedback devices, displays, etc., by using their skills as teachers to intervene, substitute, add or suppress examples, and provide extra variety and enrichment (45).

DESIGN AND EVALUATION OF LEARNING SYSTEMS

The attitude of many of the early programmers seems to have been to replace 'conventional instruction' by programmes. In doing this

they expected a great many other changes to follow. Only those who
are acquainted with the implications of lock-step teaching in North
America can fully understand the zeal of those who wanted to sweep
away the frustrations of not being allowed to go at one's own pace.
The writer's eight-year-old son, to quote one of the frustrations, had
to rub out pages of sums because he ventured to go further than
required, until he learned to sit out the lesson in boredom. Furthermore, children who do not achieve high enough marks in many
places have to remain for another year in the same grade and repeat
exactly the same work at the same rate. This is one reason why so
much stress was placed on the importance of self-paced learning.

Nevertheless, though in programmed learning there was immediate feedback, active responding, etc., very often the style of instruction was that of text and workbook based classroom instruction. In
fact, programmes very often got to be tacked on to the familiar
system. What changed things was a view of teaching/learning
processes as a whole – as an integrated set of parts and functions all
related to each other, providing feedback and evaluation about the
operation of the parts in relation to each other and their mutual
adaptation. Furthermore this organism can be conceived to steer
itself along a course towards its objectives, taking account of drift and
even modifying its final target.

Now of course human beings (children, students, teachers) are
major elements in this system. But this new perspective permits one
to view programmes, television teaching, team teaching or the
Dalton Plan not as 'the only, best method', but as techniques and
resources available for a planned learning environment. It should be
said at once that planning does not rule out opportunities for
spontaneity. Indeed, approaches to programming the teaching of
creativity build them in (67).

A highly successful project in the U.S.A.,* with the help of the
teachers, has designed sets of materials which carry children forward towards educational goals. Some of the materials and learning
situations may involve 'concrete' apparatus, other versions for
different children are more abstract. Children help themselves to the
things they need after they demonstrate how they are learning a
particular skill, concept, etc.

Though the general idea of diagnostic testing and choosing

* Directed by Dr Robert Glaser of Pittsburgh University.

appropriate patterns of learning for individual children is widely familiar in Britain, there has been nothing so ambitiously programmed and so constantly evaluated and modified. Moreover, the functions of teachers have changed in this system. They are not dispensers of knowledge but play a much greater role in advising, guiding and appraising, feeding back into the system ideas to make it work better, co-operating more with each other and with the outside world. While this sounds in many ways like a lot of primary schools, the scale of the enterprise, the amount of programming and the continuous adaptation to feedback involve vastly more systematic team-work and sensitivity to individuals than is possible without such an overall, long-term, integrated viewpoint.

At Memorial University, in response to an expected intake of 900 first-year psychology students, the course has been redesigned as a series of programmed units.* Materials (e.g. reports of research, perspectives on scientific method, laboratory work) are provided. Evaluations of learning indicate if a student needs supplementary material (e.g. audio-visual, group session, individual tutorial supplements) before he is ready to go on to the next unit. The objectives are much more demanding than having factual knowledge – requiring, rather, application, evaluation and the solution of problems. Not only has this complete reorganisation of the conditions of learning eased the strains of the lecture system when it is stretched to its limits, it has boosted success rates, diminished failures, enhanced students' morale and has revealed over and over again places where further improvements can be made. It has made use of existing resources and given a participating role to many students who find they can modify the system, can achieve a status as temporary teachers (of other students) and, at senior and postgraduate levels, can act as programmers, diagnosticians, etc. The writer has found that senior students, given training in methods of programming such as mathetics, are extremely apt at preparing materials at their own stage of education which will help their successors (this work, of course, helping them too).

This is the present perspective of programmed learning. It is beginning to be taken for granted that it is the total learning environment which must be programmed: objectives set; learning processes analysed; learning situations (materials, partners, types of

* By Dr Arthur Sullivan.

activities) prepared; social organisation (teacher-led or teacher-directed) determined; media chosen; and methods of feedback decided upon. When this is taken for granted – when 'Programmed Learning' is no longer spoken of – the revolution in education will have succeeded.

Part Three

MODERN TRENDS IN SUPPORT DISCIPLINES

In this final section we consider the extent to which research is causing us to modify our concept of intelligence; what social psychologists working with small groups can contribute to classroom organisation, and to what extent automation (or more properly, cybernetics) is effecting changes in the procedures used by teachers.

Although few psychologists would be foolhardy enough to take a definitive stand on the meaning of intelligence for the educator, there is little doubt that the experience of the 1960s has forced us to re-examine the idea of intelligence as a largely unchanging and inherited factor in cognitive endowment. Environmentalists who have maintained that tests measure the performance level of intelligence rather than its potential and who point to a partnership between heredity and social context in human development have the support of most teachers. Teaching itself would be an impossible task if one did not believe that human behaviour was modifiable and that – given a proper understanding of the developmental process – one could promote new behaviour patterns. In fact, it is basically this belief that underlies the promotion of education in underdeveloped countries such as Kenya and minority communities such as the American Negroes. The quarrel of the decade has taken place more at the pragmatic level. Just how far are intelligence tests reliable indices of later performance? To many educators it seems something of a quibble to say that they measure potential, and that the concept of performance introduces factors such as motivation, opportunity or personality variables. What predictive value do these tests have, and to what extent can one measure intelligence at any particular school age with the reasonable assurance that no wide variation will later occur? Or again, have we, in fact, any evidence that intellecutal function can be developed by appropriate educational procedures? Arthur Jensen, an American authority on intelligence, cast considerable doubt on the ideas of those of his fellow workers who held environmentalist views and thereby rendered suspicious much of the work being done by educators working among the culturally deprived. But the problem remains, of course, as to whether an intelligence test devised for middle-class White American pupils is valid when used for slum Negro children. We appear to be at a most interesting moment of development in this field, and the findings of geneticists in regard to DNA and RNA still further diversify the contemporary debate.

The separation of creative intelligence from academic intelligence, the possibility that some people may be 'slow developers' and the way in which intellect and emotion interact to provide valuable diagnostic clues to the clinician are further facets that require clarification as research proceeds. The study of intelligence has been a career-long interest of Professor John F. Lavach, who has himself contributed to the American literature of this subject and who is able, through his professional organisation, to remain closely in touch with contemporary developments. In addition to providing an incisive survey of this specialist field, he identifies its growing points and evaluates some of the more important trends. Since so much depends on the predictive reliability of these tests, parents, educators and students will find this knowledgeable survey a useful introduction to more extensive reading.

The pressure on classrooms during the 1960s has fixed the ratio of pupils to teachers above what many of us consider to be the proper limit if effective teaching – as distinct from uncontrolled instruction or 'telling' – is to be achieved. Teaching, in fact, might well be defined as a management art *in which learning experiences are organised. The modern teacher of science is accustomed to breaking down large classes into* small work groups *in his laboratory, and of arranging his work in such a way that it involves the active participation of 'work-bench' groups. Certainly, this requires a different organisational approach to conventional teaching, but there is nothing to prevent teachers in the primary school and those who teach the humanities in secondary schools from organising their work in much the same way. To an extent active learning groups of five or seven must generate a new educational strategy. It immediately breaks with the conventional active-teacher/ passive-class principle that seems almost inevitable when the teacher is regarded as only doing his job when he is giving information. It also changes the implications of 'discipline' – since it soon becomes apparent that actively engaged pupils are seldom disciplinary problems, and only so when they are (in a wider sense) behavioural problems in need of clinical attention. Furthermore, the peer group at work, subject to motivated direction and built-in checks and controls, is a co-operative rather than a competitive group, and many of the aggressions implicit in authoritarian educational procedures disappear. The work done by Herbert Thelen at Chicago and (at an earlier stage of his career) by Matthew Miles of Columbia, pointed to a number of exciting lines that the classroom teacher could develop.*

It became increasingly clear during the 1960s that university and secondary school students were asking more of their lecturers and teachers than mere information giving. They realised – even though many teachers were unaware of it – the effect that emotion has on teaching, and more particularly the effect that positive or negative attitudes towards the teacher may have on the student learning process. The inhibitory effect of emotional conditions such as anger, fear or anxiety on the cognitive process has been demonstrated in innumerable research projects. The concept of teacher authority is giving way, at the higher level of the secondary school and certainly at the college and university level, to teacher credibility. *But the learning group, whilst involving class and teacher, is – in so far as the class is concerned – a* group *rather than an* individual *experience, and Mr R. K. Muir adroitly outlines the internal network of relationships and stress dynamics that characterises the structure of a classroom group, and which so considerably contributes to – or inhibits, as the case may be – the learning process. Group study was the concern of education long before medical men began to take an interest in it for psychiatric purposes, and although the contributions of men such as Bion do indeed throw light onto group behaviour of a special and interesting kind, educational concern is more closely allied to Moreno and the social scientists who followed him. Mr Muir has made an extended study of small group problems and their effect on the educational process, and his work will appeal to teachers particularly because it moves through theory to the practical everyday problems.*

The time may well come when teachers, like medical men and nurses, admit as assistants qualified helpers to relieve them of much of the drudgery of their work. And one of the big drudgeries that nobody can sensibly deny is that of the daily correction of piles of exercise books. No teacher would object to correcting work in a tutorial situation, but any teacher with a heavy timetable and overcrowded classes is justified in feeling occasionally submerged. One way out is to have teacher auxilliaries – perhaps retired or married teachers – who will, by taking up some of the clerical load, relieve the practising teacher for his real job: teaching. If many universities are able to fee out script marking, it is difficult to see why it should be any the less dignified in secondary schools or primary schools.

There is, of course, another possibility, which a cyberneticist such as Dr Gordon Pask would be the first to suggest. Why not use machines?

This suggestion raises doubts in the minds of many teachers, who subconsciously may see in automation in the classroom the gradual obsolescence of the teacher himself. But even with closed circuit television – a most useful teaching aid – the presence of the teacher is essential. C.C.T.V. is, after all, a one-way *communication system. The student cannot get feedback from it, nor can it check his response behaviour. Far from invalidating the teacher, it makes his presence as a resource person and as an organiser all the more necessary. There will probably always be a certain amount of intercontinental jealousy, more especially between Americans and European specialists in the younger disciplines. Dr Pask is one of those British authorities whose reputation is widely acknowledged in the United States. His own work in cybernetics has been that of a leader in the field, but, as the reader will find for himself, he has the great virtue of simplicity. When Professor Schonland was at the head of Britain's atomic research he once told scientists that they needed to be bilingual. They needed to be able not only to speak the language of science but to be able to translate their scientific knowledge into ordinary speech without loss of essential meaning. Many said they could not do this. Schonland added, 'But anyone who really knows what he is talking about will succeed.' The reader will agree that Dr Pask knows what he is talking about.*

8 The Meaning and Use of Intelligence in Modern Education

John F. Lavach

THE NATURE OF INTELLIGENCE

A survey of recent psychological and educational literature reveals a general consensus that intelligence is something which does exist, but there are divergent opinions concerning some key aspects such as its definition, origin and measurement. Noted psychologist H. J. Eysenck, for example, states that descriptions of intelligence have been undergoing change ever since Galton first attempted to relate the measurement of sensory processes to intelligence, and Cattell delved into intellectual measurement by examining reaction time data on his human subjects (1).*

Terman proposed that intelligence is the ability to carry on abstract thinking (2), while others have suggested that intelligence is what intelligence tests measure (3). Such partial definitions or descriptions are abundant, but in the final analysis it appears that intelligence must be regarded as a rather loosely defined and frequently ambiguous construct. It is not something definite or concrete – not a thing. It is a descriptive term, like personality, applied to certain relatively stable and enduring behaviours, usually associated with the educative or schooling process.

Munn contends that intelligence is the variability and flexibility with which an organism adjusts to its environment (4). This description applies to the various species of the animal kingdom as well as to the individual members within the human race. From primitive animals to man, the most striking difference in intelligent animal behaviour becomes evident in the area of symbol manipulation, or symbolic learning. Further examination of intelligence at the human level reveals more subtle differences, particularly in linguistic facility.

* Bibliographical references to this chapter will be found on pp. 272-6.

G

Here it becomes readily apparent that learners do indeed vary in their capacity to learn.

In 1905 Alfred Binet, the French psychologist, devised and administered a series of mental ability tests to children of the Paris schools. Predicated on the assumption that intelligence is a general ability to learn or profit from instruction or experience, Binet felt that the difference between people of equal intelligence found in differing occupational settings was not intelligence itself, but, rather, a function of psychological or experiential variables such as motivation, interest or previous learning. In considering intelligence to be a unitary trait, Binet computed a single mathematical score which represented an individual's average performance on a series of tasks. Binet's 1911 revision resulted in an intelligence test which was used to identify children, aged from 2 to 18, who, according to their score, would probably not profit from exposure to the traditional curriculum of the Paris schools. Questions dealing with home life, community and school experiences were constructed and surveyed in areas in which, theoretically, every child had had an equal opportunity to gain experience. By computing the number of items the student answered correctly, Binet arrived at what he concluded to be an estimate of the developmental rate for each child. Relating this figure to his standardisation sample, he was able to calculate the mental age of his subject, obtain an indication of the subject's previous intellectual development, and predict future intellectual facility (5).

William Stern, a German psychologist, also embracing the unitary trait view of intelligence, like Binet, suggested that mental and chronological age could be expressed as a ratio – an intelligence quotient or I.Q. (6). With Stanford University's Lewis Terman's adoption and subsequent popularisation of the I.Q. in the 1916 revision of the Binet intelligence scale for use in the United States (which thus came to be called the Stanford–Binet intelligence Scale), the formula $M.A./C.A. \times 100 = I.Q.$ became widely accepted in educational and psychological research. Terman, also oriented towards the general view of intelligence, believed, like Binet, that intelligence was basically a general ability to do abstract thinking in any area (7).

Charles Spearman, an English mathematician, challenged the general unitary concept of intelligence and postulated a two-factor theory. To him, g, a general factor, was necessary for all situations or activities; but s, a specific factor, applicable only in situations requiring it, also existed (8). Cattell amplified Spearman's views by proposing his fluid and crystallised intelligence theory. To Cattell, fluid intelligence was a general innate adaptability which did not depend upon prior learning. Crystallised intelligence, however, required for cognitive tasks, was crystallised from early learning and was, therefore, environmentally determined (9).

Edward L. Thorndike provided support for these dissenting multifactor views in proposing a three-factor theory of intelligence in which a person's mental ability was viewed along three dimensions: mechanical, social and abstract intelligence (10). Thorndike argued that a person could be characterised as being of high abstract intelligence but simultaneously be low in social or mechanical intelligence. Similarly, another individual could be described as high in social intelligence and low in mechanical intelligence.

Factor theories of intelligence are based on statistical analysis of intelligence test items, and range from Spearman's two factors to Guilford's 120 factors (11). One of the most popular, however, is Louis Thurstone's primary mental abilities theory, which provides a measure of such factors as verbal meaning, number, reasoning, spatial relations, word fluency and memory. Thurstone considers these factors to be essential for intellectual functioning. But even Thurstone found his primary factors to be intercorrelated, suggesting the existence of some underlying general factor – perhaps reasoning. Therefore factorial explanations such as these may be further subdivided into those which presume that these factors operate as unrelated abilities and those which presume that these varied abilities are in some way related to some underlying common factor.

GENETIC, ENVIRONMENTAL AND INTERACTIONAL EXPLANATIONS

In addition to the disagreement concerning the nature of intelligence there is the concern of researchers over the source of intelligence, i.e. its genetic and/or environmental origin, limitations and potentiality. Various schools of thought have been represented in this controversy and numerous studies have been conducted in order to determine what role heredity and environment play in the development of intelligence.

Adherents to the genetic orientation propose a physiological explanation – one which postulates that the carriers of hereditary traits, the genes, control physiological and anatomical development. Particularly important in this explanation is the development of the central nervous system, associated with intelligent behaviour. Geneticists have shown that certain physical disabilities and specific abnormal biochemical conditions can be inherited (12). Therefore an individual's intelligence could also be viewed as genetically determined and relatively fixed by heredity, thus controlling the extent to which the nervous system, and subsequent intellectual facility, may be modified by the environment.

Support for this genetic orientation is provided by Burt, who, in administering individual intelligence tests to groups of children, discovered correlations ranging from 0·92 for identical twins reared together, and 0·84 for identical twins reared apart, to 0·25 for unrelated children reared apart (13). The high correlation between I.Q. scores obtained for identical twins reared together lends support to the hereditary argument. Having come from the same fertilised ovum (egg), identical twins have the same genetic make-up. Such twins if reared together in the same household would have almost identical environments, although it is recognised that no two environments can really be exactly alike. As indicated, Burt found a significant correlation between I.Q. scores for such twins. Identical twins reared apart, however, have different environments. Therefore in such studies it seems logical to conclude that any difference in intellectual development can be ascribed to heredity or environment by considering heredity to be the variable held constant and testing the significance of environmental differences. Burt's study indicates that I.Q. scores of identical twins reared in diverse environments are still significantly correlated with each other, lending further support to the genetic determination of intelligence. Burt also points out that the correlation between the intelligence of foster parents and foster children is not as high as between these same children and their natural, biological parents.

But the environmentalist point of view is not without its disciples. Based on the assumption that everyone, with the exception of the mentally defective, is born with a wide latitude of intellectual and biological potentiality, the environmentalists argue that man never reaches his intellectual potential. Learning plays a significant role in this viewpoint. Newman, Freeman and Holzinger examined I.Q. scores of nineteen pairs of identical twins reared apart. Results of their study showed that on the dimensions of I.Q. and quantity of education a clear relationship may be seen. A twin reared in an educationally sterile environment could be expected, it was observed, to score as much as 20 I.Q. points below his counterpart reared in a rich educational setting (14). Skeels and Skodak provide additional support for the argument in reporting that when children are adopted into a home judged intellectually superior to that into which they were born, when tested at six months and again at five years, they exhibit an approximately 35-point increase in I.Q. over their biological mothers (15).

A significant longitudinal study has been conducted by Skeels in which thirteen institutionalised mentally retarded children received the attention and care of mother surrogates. A control group of twelve similarly mentally retarded children received no such care. Two years later the experimental group's intelligence measured 28·5 I.Q. points above their original starting point, while the control group had dropped 26·2 I.Q. points during the same time period. Skeel's follow-up studies indicate that the two groups grew further and further apart in their intellectual development. All members of the control group remained wards of the state, while the experimental group made significant intellectual gains and societal contributions (16).

Reymert and Hinton similarly report that children placed in foster homes for a period of four years gained on the average 6 I.Q. points if placed before the age of six, while those placed in similar situations after the age of six made no such significant gains (17). Bayley's findings also support this viewpoint when she points out that children and their parents exhibit greater I.Q. similarities as the temporal factor in their continued association is increased (18). Studies such as these support Honzik's contention that environmental factors significantly affect intellectual development (19).

Contemporary psychologists such as Hunt support the view that intelligence is a function of both heredity and environment and that the effect of taking either independently is an unnecessary and meaningless dichotomy. Combs suggests that a person's intelligence is a function of his quality of perception and is therefore dependent upon his experiences. To Combs, it is essential that a person be exposed to a rich environment in which he may constantly re-evaluate his goals, values and self-concept (20). This approach to intelligence seems to support the findings of the Skeels study and is, furthermore, in accord with current theories which agree that from a neurological point of view experience occupies a key role.

It appears that the interactional relationship between heredity and environment is a meaningful explanation leading to the conclusion that heredity sets a broad genetic limitation on intellectual, and certainly other, development, but that one's environment permits or inhibits the realisation or actualisation of this intellectual or developmental potential. The importance of the environment to intellectual development is a variable which should be of particular interest to educators, psychologists and those concerned with the process of education. The significance of environmental factors and their relationship to intelligence cause us to reflect upon intelligence as a culturally defined concept. What is judged to be intelligent behaviour in one culture need not be judged the same in a different culture. Low scores on intelligence tests are related to a general inability of the person to perform well on learning tasks, particularly of an academic or scholastic nature. But Eells argues that intelligence tests are unfair to certain socio-economic classes. He maintains that tests are culturally biased when they measure areas which all socio-economic groups have not had an equal opportunity to experience and, therefore, do not give a true picture of the person's intelligence (21).

CULTURAL FACTORS AND THE MEASUREMENT OF INTELLIGENCE

In studies of cultural deprivation, evidence is accumulating which points to the importance of early, and particularly pre-school, experiences for efficient and effective intellectual development. Deprivation of early learning not only interferes with the development of learning capacity, but depressed learning capacity seems to go hand in hand with depressed I.Q. scores. One characteristic of such early experiential deprivation is an intellectual handicap which is most difficult, if not impossible, to overcome. Dreger and Miller suggest that the differences frequently observed between races in the intellectual area are really a problem of environmental restriction and that early restriction does exert a serious impairment on future performance, while early enrichment has an opposite effect (22).

Difficult to define, and equally difficult to explain, intelligence presents still a third problem when it comes to measurement. Intelligence tests are frequently categorised into individual or group tests. Individual intelligence scales, such as the 1960 revision of the Stanford–Binet, the Wechsler Adult Intelligence Scale or the Wechsler Intelligence Scale for Children, will, in the hands of a competent trained psychologist, provide a good indication of a subject's verbal as well as non-verbal capabilities, permitting a reliable diagnosis and prognosis of intellectual functioning. Because of this verbal emphasis of intelligence tests, other more specialised clinical instruments are available for working with infants, the blind and deaf, as well as the environmentally, culturally or linguistically disadvantaged.

Group intelligence tests are administered when a general estimate of the subjects' ability will suffice. If, however, the group test score is inconsistent with the subject's performance, as indicated by grades or other criteria, an individual corroborative test may be administered to provide a more reliable and accurate measure. Intelligence test scores have been most useful in predicting academic aptitude. Edwards and Kirby, for example, report a correlation of 0·50 in their study of the relationship between I.Q. and general academic achievement, 0·44 between I.Q. and reading ability, and 0·45 for I.Q. and arithmetic ability (23). Similarly, it has been reported that Australian boys taking an achievement examination and tests of mental ability have a correlation of 0·40 between the two instruments and 0·40 between the examination and academic achievement (24). With general academic achievement, reading, arithmentic and similar abilities representing some of those commonly used to describe the intelligent person, I.Q. tests do, it appears, correlate with traits people generally consider the intelligent person to possess; for example, the ability to solve problems relatively rapidly, verbal and numerical ability, and the ability to reason and to benefit from experience.

Contemporary intelligence tests, as well as Binet's original work, seem to be most effective in predicting academic or school success, or in predicting learning of primarily verbal and quantitative skills. Several decades of intelligence testing have failed to produce what might be termed a culture-free test; that is, a test which could be used to measure innate intelligence unaffected by environment. It has not been possible to separate what a person has learned from any specific genetic endowment which may be regarded as innate intelligence.

In attempting to circumvent this problem, researchers are investigating avenues of psychological inquiry in an effort to obtain a measurement of mental ability not dependent upon environmental factors. Kunce points to a recent study of the performance of Alaskan natives on a maze learning task. (Maze learning studies are frequently conducted with human subjects in order to examine aspects of intellectual functioning not dependent upon environmental influence.) Kunce reported that subjects in his study demonstrated an ability to learn the maze as efficiently as those subjects tested in the continental United States (25). Recognising, however, that intelligence and its measurement are difficult to separate from environmental factors, Vernon, in discussing the administration of tests to East African children, stresses the importance of the test items being constructed and formulated by psychologists of that culture. This is essential if the material is of a verbal and/or pictorial nature (26).

Intelligence test scores, when taken for a large population, are found to be distributed, as are other aspects of human development, in a normal pattern, statistically represented as the bell-shaped curve. A small percentage of the population falls into the extremely intelligent or extremely dull range, while the majority falls into a category designated average. For example, on the Stanford–Binet test, 50 per cent of the White American population falls between the I.Q. range of 90 to 110. 28 per cent falls between the 80 to 90 and 110 to 120 range, with 14 per cent falling into each bracket. Intelligence quotients of between 70 and 80 and 120 to 130 account for 14 per cent, while those persons scoring between 60 to 70 and 130 to 140 represent about 6 per cent. The remaining 2 per cent are located in the less than 60 and more than 140 I.Q. range (27). Psychologists in the past frequently labelled such categories with terms such as idiot, genius, etc., but recently there has been a trend away from such categorising.

The stability of I.Q. scores has been of great interest to educators, for if I.Q. can be shown to be a relatively stable measure then we should be able to predict the future level of performance in terms of capacity to learn. This would be more effective than relying on judgement alone. Honzik, Macfarlane and Allen examined the intellectual development of children aged 6 to 18, using the 1916 Stanford–Binet, 1937 Stanford–Binet and the Wechsler–Bellvue Intelligence Test at 6 to 7, 8 to 15, and 18 respectively. The correlation between scores taken at 6 and 18 was 0·62, a relatively high figure. Between ages 6 to 18, 40 per cent of the sample varied less than 15 points, and 60 per cent changed less than 20 points, indicating that the I.Q. is indeed a relatively stable measure, particularly after the age of six (28). Bayley similarly studied 555 subjects in the Berkeley Growth Study, testing subjects at 16, 18, 21, 26 and 36. She noted an increase in verbal knowledge and no decrement in I.Q. over the time period (29). Owens reports another study of 96 subjects tested with the Army Alpha, in 1919, 1950 and again in 1961. The average age of the subjects was 61 at the 1961 testing. From 1950 to 1961, I.Q. scores were reported to have remained relatively constant, with changes being statistically insignificant (30).

Measurement of I.Q. prior to the age of six, however, is not as reliable, and it is not until school age and after that a stable measure may be obtained (31). Bayley has shown that measurement of infant I.Q. is not particularly useful for predicting future intelligence (32). The correlation between infant intelligence measures, which are primarily motor ones, and later behaviour, which emphasises verbal ability and conceptualisation, is understandably low.

In studies of the stability of I.Q., dramatic changes in score are sometimes observed. Subjects demonstrating such dramatic score changes, investigators postulate, may have been exposed to environments in which there was some extreme variation resulting in deviations not only along the intellectual, but along other dimensions as well. Analysis of longitudinal studies seems to indicate that children with deviant I.Q. score increments or decrements are expressing either hereditary tendencies or environmental variables which, it is hypothesised, may account for the deviation (33). Similarly, both cross-sectional and longitudinal studies of 'deprived environments' reveal that children reared under these conditions test lower than their non-deprived counterparts, and continue to drop in I.Q. (34).

Several studies have attempted to relate intelligence to other human characteristics. One of the most notable was the Lewis Terman longitudinal study beginning in the early 1920s and currently continuing with a sample of over 1500 subjects representing I.Q.s of 140 and above. Terman reported that contrary to popular belief the mentally superior subjects in his sample were not only intellectually superior, but were judged physically superior as well. Their grade placement was approximately 14 per cent accelerated and their average academic achievement was about 44 per cent accelerated, as compared to their age peer group. Representatives of the sample exhibited diverse interests, were judged to be of high moral character, had a 90 per cent college entrance rate with 90 per cent of these subsequently graduating, were active professionally, and by the age of 30 were receiving annual incomes in excess of twice the national norm. Similarly, subjects had a statistically significant lower suicide rate than their peers, were less frequently victims of mental illness, and maintained a divorce rate below that found in their native state (35).

Yamamoto reported that among fifth-grade children those judged to be more creative and/or intelligent were more apt to be nominated by their classmates as 'friends' and less often as 'non-friends' by their less creative and/or intelligent peers. A further refutation of the claim that subjects of superior intelligence tend to be more troubled with physical ailments comes from India, where Varma conducted a study of the aetiology of headaches. The investigators reported that no intelligence factors were found to be correlated in cases of reported headaches due to vascular disorders, tension, hysteria, neuralgia, schizophrenia and combined causes (36).

Baller, Charles and Miller reported a study at the opposite end of the intellectual continuum. The subjects, 206 children with I.Q.s below 70, were tested at the ages of 20, 40 and again during their mid-fifties. The investigators stated that within this group all had made below average school progress, 6 per cent were institutionalised, only a half of those married were living with their spouses, and 80 per cent were usually employed, with 60 to 70 per cent reported as being fully self-supporting. Therefore research seems to indicate a positive correlation of human traits.

DEPRESSED INTELLECTUAL FUNCTIONING

Depressed intellectual functioning is theoretically easier to comprehend when mental growth is viewed from a developmental point of view, typically characterised by a positively accelerating growth curve which rises rapidly during infancy and early childhood, slows down through middle and late childhood, and continues at a reduced rate of acceleration through adolescence. In line with this, Bloom postulates that by the age of four, children develop 50 per cent of their adult intellectual potential; between 5 and 8, 30 per cent more is added; and from 8 to maturity, the remaining 20 per cent is gained (37). Harms, in discussing adolescent development, suggests that intellect matures at about 5, emotion at about 9, and other characteristics such as motivation during puberty (38). This later characteristic, motivation, is gaining recognition in studies of intelligence. Several research studies describe the elementary school child or adolescent who tests high on an I.Q. measure, but whose academic achievement seems to be uncorrelated with his learning potential. Gordon, in a study of kindergarten children and their teachers in the United States, revealed that teachers in his sample frequently overestimated the intelligence of the positive attitude, fast responding child, while underestimating and judging inferior those children who expressed negative attitudes and who took a longer period of time to become acclimated to a task despite their intelligence (39).

Haywood, in examining the prediction of scholastic achievement on the basis of I.Q., suggests that other factors play an important role, with motivation being particularly important. Haywood found that students described as overachievers are more motivated by inherent factors or intrinsic aspects of a task, while underachievers are more motivated by extrinsic factors or variables not inherent in the task, such as pressure exerted by the teacher, grades or other extraneous variables (40).

MODERN INTERPRETATIONS OF INTELLIGENCE AND INTELLECTUAL DEVELOPMENT

Several modern psychologists have deviated from the traditional path in examining intelligence. Current thinking, reflected by such investigators as Piaget, Bruner and Guilford, maintains that there is more to intelligence than that which is measured by our traditional tests. New avenues of inquiry are being opened, new tests are being constructed, and previously untapped areas such as creative thinking are being explored.

Dissatisfaction with traditional tests of intelligence centres around the idea that these instruments are primarily concerned with what Russell has termed 'product thinking' rather than the intellectual process (41). This may be partially explained by examining the history of intelligence testing, which is characterised by a preoccupation with the more readily measured product aspects of intellectual functioning as opposed to what constitutes the processes involved.

Recently there has been an active interest in the work and methodology of the Swiss psychologist Jean Piaget and his followers, the Geneva School. Piaget has studied the development of thinking by working with individual children, asking them questions, providing descriptions of their behaviour, and speculating concerning their development. Although a more subjective approach to psychological inquiry, Piaget's theories and methodology are currently gaining adherents in the United States.

Piaget, author of over thirty books and hundreds of articles, many of which have been translated from the French language, postulates that development of understanding and intellectual ability is accomplished as a child passes through a series of stages determined by heredity or environment. Stage I, with six sensory motor substages, encompasses the period from birth to about two years of age. Stage II begins at this point and continues until the child is about 10 or 11. Stage III commences and continues through adolescence. Piaget contends that a child's ability to understand is a function of his sequentially experiencing these three stages, during which the child's own exploration of the environment and logical interpretation plays a key role and each step becomes a foundation for the next (42).

During Stage I, the sensory motor stage, the child explores his environment through his senses and establishes an elementary relationship between himself and the external physical world. The child at this stage is capable of primitive reasoning and the formation of basic mental images, although his reasoning ability differs from that of an adult (43).

Stage II finds a child's development characterised by the expansion of symbolic behaviour, with rapid increases in language facility during what Piaget terms the preoperational stage. At about 7, the child becomes adept at conceptualisation and establishes a basic understanding of concrete logical operations which permits him mentally to carry on thought problems without being tied to objects of reality. This stage continues until about 11 or 12 (44).

Stage III commences at this time and continues through early adolescence, resulting in a stabilised thought system in which hypotheses may be logically formed and consequences of action deduced by the adolescent. At this point the adolescent is capable of adult reasoning, which includes the inauguration of future plans and actions and the formation of ideals (45).

The question which educators and psychologists are asking is what is the possibility of either skipping certain stages or accelerating the process? Will properly devised instructional procedures result in the earlier acquisition of a desired response? Hunt contends that the more new things an infant is exposed to through his senses, the greater will be his capacity of coping with the environment (46). Much research has focused on Stage II, during which, Piaget asserts, basic principles of conservation develop. This is the understanding on the part of a child that despite apparent changes in the features of an object, there has been no change in the object itself (47). For example, before the age of six or seven, a child will report that the quantity of a fluid poured into a tall thin container is more than the same quantity poured into a short stout container. The child's decision at this developmental stage is based upon the visual level of the fluid, not upon a rational interpretation of the problem. Furthermore, it is not until about the age of two that children begin to develop an understanding that objects no longer present to the senses are still in existence (48). Smedslund studied the acceleration of the development of weight conservation and discovered that if children received instruction related to this prior to reaching the appropriate developmental stage, the concept of weight conservation was not retained. For those children who had reached this stage, the concept persisted (49). Whowill, in another study, however, demonstrated that conservation development could be accelerated with training (50). So the question of what kinds of experiences, and the proper time for experiencing them, remains unknown.

Traditional views of the development of the child's intellect are being challenged. Researchers are discovering, as Piaget has suggested, that the child appears to perceive differently from an adult. He is dependent on purposeful or 'why' thinking, and is unable, owing to his intellectual immaturity and self-centredness, to put himself in

another's place or see things from a different point of view (51).
Piaget implies that perhaps our teaching at the early elementary
school level is above the children in being too abstract and based on
adult reasoning and logic. This point of view is supported in research
which shows that children between 6 and 7 are capable of solving
word problems if objects are available to represent the symbols, but
these same children are unable to handle similar but purely verbal
tasks (52).

While Piaget's concern is with the development of thinking processes and the importance of sequential stages, other psychologists
have also been working in the area of problem-solving and creative
thinking. In the United States, Harvard psychologist Jerome
Bruner has been responsible for introducing American researchers to
Piaget and his methodology, and has formulated many theories
of his own concerning the development of human problem-solving
abilities.

Bruner contends that people develop what he terms techniques for
intellectual functioning and it is these which are important in
problem-solving behaviour (53). Action, imagery and language are
the techniques to which he refers, and it is through these that we
come to understand our environment. On Bruner's view the
environment is represented mentally through three developmental
modes: enactive, iconic and symbolic, which unfold in much the same
manner as Piaget's three stages. Enactive representation is the
registration of past events through motor activity, such as those
learned in muscular responses. Iconic representation refers to the
mental organisation of perceptions and images, while symbolic
representation deals with words or numbers (54).

For both Bruner and Piaget the development of language occupies
a significant place in the evolution of intellectual ability. Bruner
places little emphasis on innate ability, and believes that for a person
to derive the most from his environment he must efficiently organise
and manipulate information in a grouping or conceptualising procedure whereby new information is classified according to its similarities or differences to information previously learned.

If a learner is to profit from experience he must be able to categor-
ise vast, unmanageable quantities of information into a usable,
orderly pattern to which he may then respond (55). Bruner argues
that for a person to be most efficient and effective in dealing with
problem-solving, emphasis should be placed on discovery in

learning, so that problem-solving behaviours will be learned and generalised to new situations, rather than on accumulating more and more cumbersome and useless factual information (56). In this way, problem-solving is learned and stereotyped, rigid thinking is reduced.

THE IMPLICATIONS OF RECENT BIOLOGICAL RESEARCH

While current theories of intelligence are being explored, attention is also being directed to recent neurological and biochemical research, including the study of the effects of various drugs on brain function Rosenzweig and Leiman indicate in a recent report that within the last few years alone several international symposia have been conducted in order to explore the subject and its potentiality (57). Studies of learning and subsequent biochemical changes within the brain have led investigators to examine the effect of specific drugs on learning, retention and behaviour.

The injection of puromycin, an antibiotic, for example, directly into specific areas of the brain of mice by Flexner, Flexner and Stellar resulted in the elimination of a previously learned avoidance habit acquired in a simple maze (58). This and similar experiments are being conducted to explore Swedish neuro-biologist Hyden's hypothesis that the modification of a biochemical compound, ribonucleic acid (RNA), in the brain appears to have a function in the synthesis of specific protein substances. Such protein, it appears is influential in memory functioning (59). It was discovered that puromycin prevents the synthesis of protein by RNA, with the result that there is interference with memory function.

Agranoff, at the University of Michigan, reports similar research in which puromycin is injected into the brain of a goldfish. While the drug does not interfere with initial learning, it appears to inhibit memory. Injected before, during and after training sessions, the drug produces different reactions. Administered before training, puromycin results in the goldfish forgetting what it had learned a few days ago, but it does not interfere with the original acquisition of the response. Injected seconds after training, the drug causes complete and immediate destruction of memory. Injection of the substance an hour after training has no apparent effect on the animal's behaviour (60). Researchers examining these and other findings suggest that in the early stages memory is very sensitive to extraneous stimulation such as drugs; but once established, memory becomes stronger. Some are advancing the theory that short-term memory is electro-neurological and therefore sensitive to stimulation, while long-term memory is more stable because of its complex biochemical nature (61).

McGaugh, at the University of California, has discovered that drugs such as strychnine facilitate maze learning in mice, particularly in intellectually inferior mice. His injection of strychnine, administered fifteen minutes before or after learning, facilitates the acquisition of the desired response (62).

Although the studies reported deal with animals, most researchers agree that in the near future findings will be applied to man. Already, Plotnikoff of Abbots Laboratories reports that pemoline and magnesium hydroxide increase learning efficiency and enhance memory in the presenile aged (63). In another study, Gilgash examined the effect of thirty days of treatment with glutamic acid on the intellectual activity of mentally retarded males. On the Wechsler Adult Intelligence Scale, subjects treated with glutamic acid made statistically significant gains in I.Q. over a control group. When tested again at ninety days, the subjects maintained a statistically significant gain (64).

Still another avenue of investigation lies in the follow-up studies to McConnell's work with the flatworm *planaria*. McConnell and his associates fed ground-up, trained *planaria* to experimentally naïve worms. When the researchers tested the *planaria* who had cannibalised the trained worms, they discovered that the ability to learn was transferred to the naïve group, who performed the task in a significantly shorter period of time. RNA was assumed to be responsible for the memory transfer process (65).

Still another area of research has centred around examination of the nervous system of animals exposed to an enriched and stimulating environment. Such exposure results in modified brain anatomy. Rats exposed to environments with a variety of activities such as exercise wheels, games and toys, when given a learning task, outperform their non-stimulated counterparts. Furthermore, the cerebral cortex, probably responsible for complex learning in such stimulated animals, increases about 6 per cent in size and thickness and is found to contain more RNA than that of non-stimulated rats (66).

Although these findings have been questioned, this and similar investigations in laboratories throughout the world have resulted in the accumulation of information concerning the existence of a memory transfer mechanism (67). If such a mechanism is discovered the educational implications will be unlimited. It may be that the most significant discoveries will come from the neuro-biological and biochemical laboratories as they study anatomical and physiological aspects of intelligence and explore the meaning of Hyden's question, 'Do we think because we have a brain, or do we have a brain because we think?' (68).

9 The Influence of Group Research on Educational Practice

R. K. Muir

Experienced teachers frequently express scorn for the views of specialists in fields closely related to teaching, like child psychology and group research. They reject the findings and recommendations of these specialists as largely irrelevant to their own experience in the classroom. While possibly allowing themselves to be influenced by the specialists, they adopt what they feel is a practical approach to the class and to the schoolchild, founded on native common sense and sensible intuitions. Even when they pay lipservice to the findings of these social scientists, they are unsure of their practical application to the school class.

Teachers are exhorted to act in accordance with the dictates of many academic disciplines like psychology, philosophy and sociology, as well as the academic disciplines which attach to the content of the school curriculum, like mathematics, history and so on. They are therefore used to bowing to other academic disciplines, and are easily made to feel it is a dereliction in their duty that they do not immediately apply the 'latest methods and ideas' established by research to their teaching. The specialists on their part are easily irritated by the teachers' neglect of their speciality and imply that teachers are inflexible or plainly too unintelligent to use the facts of research.

These attitudes arise because it is not realised by either teachers or researchers that there is no logical connection between the facts of research, the value interpretations placed on these facts, and the subsequent actions taken by teachers in the classroom. In discussing the influence of group research on educational practice, therefore, it is necessary to start by examining how they can be logically related.

This is a philosophic problem, and will be tackled from the point of view of analytic philosophy that there is no logical connection between a statement of fact and a statement of value. It may be stated for a fact, and it often is, that a democratic approach to a classroom group is best. This is confusing the actual facts and our attitude towards them. It may be a fact that a classroom group which decides upon an activity to be performed derives a great deal of satisfaction from the activity, and shows this satisfaction in word and deed. To judge that this procedure is the best, is, however, a value judgement placed on the facts, without regard for other facts which also may be relevant. It may be the firm conviction of a second person that classroom groups work most happily when they have firm direction, know the limits of the demands to be made upon them, and are kept quiet and orderly by an interesting presentation of material by the teacher. When they are allowed to choose for themselves they become noisy. A second value judgement is made that democracy does not work in the classroom, and this judgement, too, is based on a selection of facts.

It is possible to have one set of facts about the functioning of a classroom and to have two or more value judgements about these facts. A simple example would be the fact of children talking about the work they are doing. One judgement may be that this is an educationally sound practice, supported by the facts that children interact to teach each other, and help clarify each other's ideas, when they are allowed to talk. Another judgement may be that talking must not be allowed and in support of the judgement is cited the fact that talking is disturbing to other classes and to the teacher, and that illicit behaviour may be cloaked by it. The judgement is expressed that pupils will learn much better by receiving material first-hand from the most knowledgeable person, the teacher, instead of seeking for it among themselves.

The facts of group research do not logically determine the value judgements made on them by teachers and by the researchers themselves. It is not that teachers do not understand the facts, although the research experts may facilely believe this to be the case. The problem is that there is no logical connection between facts and value judgements, and, further, no logical connection between both and classroom practice.

Two values which will possibly be accepted by most teachers are the following:

(a) It is good for mental hygiene and for the emotional satisfaction of the members of a group to create integrated groups.

(*b*) It is good for encouraging high standards of excellence, individual attainment and creativity to establish competitive conditions.

Both these value judgements can be supported by facts, obtainable by experimentation. The facts may be indubitable, but that does not assist the teacher in deciding whether to arrange for experiences which integrate the participants, or for those which set the group members testing themselves against each other. Facts need not necessarily solve the dilemma of what values to hold, or of what educational practices to follow. But it will be easier to make sound decisions if facts are known, and some of the facts of group research are of great importance for the teacher.

The relationship between the facts and values and educational practice can be distinguished by a discussion of what must surely be the most often-quoted series of experiments on groups. The data of these experiments are always used to support an argument that certain teacher behaviours are better than others, because teacher behaviour affects children in certain ways. The experiments in question are those done by Lippitt and White, under the influence of Kurt Lewin. Reports of these are included in Cartwright and Zander (1960) and in Maccoby *et al.* (1958).*

Lippitt and White studied four groups of five ten-year-old children, the members of which had been matched on teacher ratings of social behaviour, observations of social behaviour in the playground, a sociometric test, intelligence, physical development and socioeconomic background. Each group engaged in hobby activities in their leisure time spent at youth clubs under the direction of adult leaders. Three kinds of leadership were exercised, authoritarian, democratic and laissez-faire. In order that the personality effects of the leaders could be controlled, all the leaders were trained to adopt each of the three leadership styles, and changed the style in turn as they went from one group to another. Likewise, each group experienced a different leadership style with each new leader. The three leadership styles were carefully defined. In the authoritarian style all decisions were made by the leader, work was closely controlled in step-by-step fashion and the leader insisted on individual work. In the democratic style groups were allowed to make decisions about the work to be done and to allocate it among themselves with the help and guidance of the leader. The leader was

---

* Bibliographical references to this chapter will be found on pp. 276-8.

closely associated with the group effort. The laissez-faire leader left the group entirely to its own devices.

The behaviour of the groups showed clear differences for the three leadership styles. Authoritarian leadership resulted in one case in an aggressive reaction. In other cases the groups did a lot of work, but they did not find the work as satisfying as when they were working under a democratic leader. Democratic leadership resulted in less work than was done by submissive groups under authoritarian leadership, but it resulted in greater satisfaction to the members of the group.

This set of relationships was found for a specified set of conditions, with one condition (leadership style) being systematically changed. If one of the other variables were to be changed (for example, the age or the number of the participants, or the work they were doing), the relationship would possibly change. The experiment would require dozens of repetitions, with one variable being changed systematically, then another, and then another, till all combinations had been tested. It is one of the difficulties of this kind of experimentation that it is impossible to give a result which will be general for all cases.

Although the Lippit and White study has aspects which teachers will find interesting, and although it may tentatively be concluded that pupil behaviour is a response to that of teachers, the experiment does not prove that democratic control by teachers is better than authoritarian control. This is a value judgement which has been placed on the facts by commentators on the research, and by many who have since used the facts of the experiment to justify supporting democratic practices in the classroom. The value judgement is expressed that the social satisfaction experienced by the group is the most important outcome of the group process, and the facts show that social satisfaction is related to democratic leader control. The facts also show that submissive groups with authoritarian leaders produce the greatest quantity of work. If amount of work output were to be substituted as the value aimed at, it must be claimed that authoritarian leadership is best, provided the group is submissive.

Experiments on the organisation of groups into co-operative or competitive ones also illustrate the problem under discussion. Morton Deutsch (1949, 1954) showed that tasks requiring co-operation resulted in high group cohesiveness, while competitive tasks broke it down. He used university psychology students in his experiments. The groups were engaged in discussion of case histories. Some groups were told that their grades depended on the quality of the group effort, and therefore each individual was marked according to the overall group contribution to the discussion. In other groups competitive conditions were created by marking individuals on each member's personal contribution, and making good marks dependent on outshining the other members of the class.

The different groups of students behaved in completely different ways. In the co-operative groups there was an attempt to integrate all the members and to show friendliness and consideration; in the competitive groups individuals tried to dominate. Deutsch evaluated the ideas of the co-operative groups as being better than those of the competitive ones.

Studies on the use of group work in the classroom have also been inclined to reach the conclusion that better evaluation of problems and more emotionally satisfying working conditions result from co-operative group work. Richardson (1948), Hallworth (1952), Rasmussen (1956) and Muller and Biggs (1958) all found evidence for a better response to a group task when the group was well integrated.

On the other hand, it has been found that this result is dependent on certain conditions. The nature of the task must require co-operation, the size of the group must be such as to make co-operation possible, and the group must receive adequate direction in their task. Phillips and D'Amico (1956), using fourth-grade children, found that competition did not break down the integration of the groups provided there was not a great deal of inequality in the chances of success at the task set.

Apart from the fact that there are equivocal results in this experimentation, it must again be noted that the facts of a relationship between variables in the group and the group's behaviour have been interpreted in the light of judgements that cohesive or integrated groups are socially satisfying and therefore of value; and that the group experience gives a superior facility for handling particular problems, especially of a social kind, and is therefore of value.

There is another argument that can be put forward, however, to the effect that the end-results of co-operative group experience are not the only valuable ones. Our society is based on individual enterprise, on the uniqueness of the individual, on individual creativity and talent. Does a training in co-operation, then, not result merely in conformity and a deadening of individual initiative and unique thinking? Therefore, is it not better to insist upon individual competition in the classroom? The argument between the two points of view is an argument about values, logically unconnected with the facts of group research. The argument may be resolved by trying to gain different desirable ends by a variety of practices in teaching. It should now, however, be plainly evident that it is very difficult to establish any clear logical relationship between the facts of group research, the values placed on the group experience, and educational practice.

The facts of group research need to be looked at not in terms of ethical imperatives about how teachers should behave in the classroom. Unfortunately too many commentators on education have promptly used factual data to derive just such ethical imperatives. Group research provides a body of factual data on the basis of which teachers can hope to understand group processes, predict outcomes of particular behaviours and choose between different educational programmes to realise different goals more surely.

The amount of research work on groups is voluminous. Psychologists, social psychologists, psychiatrists, sociologists and researchers in the field of business management and of complex organisations have all experimented with group variables. Variables in the group situation have been related to the group's performance and behaviour in hundreds of experimental investigations. These investigations have been concerned with establishing what the variables are, what appropriate measures of the variables exist, and how the variables are related.

Centres of interest have developed in the study of groups, with different workers pursuing research in what could be called different traditions of thinking. As teaching is an interdisciplinary exercise, it will not be difficult for teachers to borrow ideas from all these traditions, but Borgatta (1960) is rightly of the opinion that the disparate nature of the traditions has impeded group research.

Three centres of interest which are pertinent are the following:

(*a*) The study of small groups by those working in the 'group dynamics' tradition.

(*b*) The study of groups by theorists in the field of complex organisations.

(*c*) The use of sociometry to study groups.

Each will be discussed in turn.

THE 'GROUP DYNAMICS' APPROACH TO THE STUDY OF GROUPS AND THE THEORY OF SMALL GROUPS

One centre of interest is that which has formed round the work of Kurt Lewin. He popularised the term 'group dynamics', which he first used in a lecture in 1944. The emphasis in this work has been on topology and field forces, and the groups studied have usually been small. The work has been associated first with the Massachusetts Institute of Technology and later with the University of Michigan. Thousands of studies have been done, many of them reported in the journal *Human Relations*, which has been the chief vehicle for making the work known. Well-known workers in the field have been Lippitt, White, Festinger, Schachter, Polansky, Cartwright, Zander, Deutsch, Hurwitz, Horwitz, Bach and Back.

The emphasis in this work is on topology and field forces. Lewin uses as the basic tool for analysis a representation of the group and its setting as a 'social field'. He draws analogies between the social field and a physical field of gravity, and employs 'social forces' and 'resultants of social forces' in the same way as the physicist uses field forces. These social forces can be associated with individuals, subgroups or any number of groups in a system. Among others, he uses as examples of social forces such disparate factors as the desire of the privileged in a discriminatory society to retain their privilege and the raising of production under incentive salary schemes. He regards these as dynamic social entities, capable of being analysed scientifically as objective variables in a study of groups. The basic means to this end is to represent a social situation as a 'social field'. He says of this that

> ... the social happening is viewed as occurring in, and being the result of, a totality of co-existing social entities, such as groups, subgroups, members, barriers, channels of communications, etc. One of the fundamental characteristics of this field is the relative position of the entities which are parts of the field. This relative position represents the structure of the group and its ecological setting. It expresses also the basic possibilities of locomotion within the field.
>
> What happens within such a field depends upon the distribution of forces throughout the field. Prediction presupposes the ability to determine for the various points of the field the strength and directions of the resultant forces. (Lewin (1947) p. 14.)

He recognises the necessity for studying the whole field, or in other words the total social setting, in studying any problem in group life. He allows, however, for some demarcation of the field when studying specific properties of a group, and he employs the term *phase space* in doing so. He also describes the idea of a stable social state as being a 'quasi-stationary' process, with social forces and their resultants at or around a particular level of equilibrium. Any change or fluctuation in the social process will change the level of equilibrium, and the direction and strength of the social forces operating.

Lewin, therefore, analyses groups not in terms of the individuals composing them or of their other constituent elements, but in terms of properties of the group, for which he employs constructs like social force, phase space, and equilibrium in quasi-stationary process. In other words, he analyses groups and changes in groups in terms of their dynamics.

Other researchers on small groups, notably Hare, Borgatta, Bales and Homans, have used the concept of social interaction in groups as a tool for analysis. They have been concerned with what could be called input variables and their effect on the output of the group or the group's performance and behaviour. Examples of input variables have been individual personalities and abilities of group members, number of members, behaviour of leaders, and kinds of task performed by the group. The effect of a variable on the group's output has been studied by systematically changing the variable. One of the difficulties of this experimental design has been that while relationships between inputs and outputs have been demonstrated for changing conditions, it has still not been possible to predict a generalised relationship between input variables and output ones. While a relationship can be shown for one set of conditions, and systematically changing one variable may yield consistent results, there are nevertheless several other variables which can also be changed. And with a change in one of these other variables the relationship may disappear.

McGrath and Altman (1966) reviewed a sample of 250 studies in this field, with the object of integrating these studies into a system. It was hoped to see what group variables had been related with consistent results, and what gaps existed in research. On the basis of the classification system they developed, they then looked at a number of studies in the area of the effectiveness of the performance of small groups, and finally classified over a thousand studies in their system.

Variables, measures of variables and relationships between variables were examined. It was proposed that data could be described in terms of six parameters. A description of their complex procedure in categorising the variables used in small group research cannot be given here, but what is important for the present discussion is that their attempt to integrate small group research revealed six distinct but interdependent systems of data, which they suggested were conceptually related to one another.

Their six classes of variables are:
1. Properties of group members.
2. Properties of the group.
3. Conditions imposed on the group.
4. Interaction process.
5. Subjective measures of member and group performance.
6. Objective measures of member and group performance.

The authors of this classification list a large number of concerns in each class. Under Class 1 are the many individual personality and ability characteristics of the group members, as well as individual attitudes and values. Included here are also positions of the group members – social position, task and physical position in the group. Under Class 2 are group capabilities and abilities, group experience and structural properties of a group. Class 3 concerns social conditions imposed on the group, and listed under this class are influence and conformity pressures, induced social conditions, task and operating conditions in the group, including the stimulus properties of the task, feedback and reinforcement conditions and induced task conditions. Class 4 includes interaction process, content of interaction, patterns of interaction and outcomes of interaction between the variables. Some inputs in the group situation interact with other variables in different ways. For example, boys may behave differently from girls in the same situation or older boys differently from younger boys, and so on. Classes 5 and 6 are primarily concerned with measurement of the group's performance. In Class 5 the individual, subjective assessment of group members and task performance is included. Objective measures of group members and task performance are classified under Class 6.

Included in this classification are the elements of a simpler classification suggested by Borgatta (1960) as a result of a review of the research, and based on perceptive judgement rather than on the sophisticated technique devised by McGrath and Altman. Borgatta proposed that the variables of research with small groups were concerned with persons, tasks and group performance, and that there was interdependence between these kinds of variables. It will be seen that both Borgatta and McGrath and Altman suggest that the study of groups involves relationships between persons and tasks. The latter pair of researchers suggested an additional category of group properties, involving interpersonal relationships and structural properties.

McGrath and Altman arrived at a series of generalisations based on the many studies they examined. Many of these were concerned with relationships between persons, their personalities, attitudes or abilities, and performance on a task in the group. Some of the results are trite: those with highest ability perform best. They found that relating individual personality characteristics like authoritarianism, individual attitudes, personality traits of leadership and so on to group task performance yielded equivocal results. They concluded that the study of individual personality variables has not yielded a consistent pattern of results, possibly because the variables are too complex and measures of variables not valid or reliable. Stogdill (1948) suggested much the same in respect of studies of leadership. He demonstrated that the study of individual traits as part of the study of leadership was a barren pursuit – and that the focus should be placed on group processes. McGrath and Altman likewise present evidence to justify concentrating on characteristics of a group, such as its structure, rather than on individual characteristics.

One relationship which is established in small group research in the group dynamics tradition is that high status position in a group results not only in greater authority and leadership in the group, but also in higher task satisfaction and involvement. Fruitful results have been obtained in relating size of group to group performance and behaviour, and the communication studies by Bavelas and others successfully related group variables.

A series of communication studies was begun by Bavelas (1948, 1950) and continued by many other workers, especially Shaw (1954a, b, c, 1956, 1958, and Shaw and Rothschild 1956, 1957), who has systematically worked over this area. A very useful review of this work is given by Glanzer and Glaser (1961).

These studies all sample the structure of groups by establishing a network of communications between persons in groups. Structure is used as an independent variable and is manipulated by allowing or disallowing communication channels between members of small groups. Invariably the setting is a laboratory one in which communication channels can be opened or blocked. Bavelas started by asking the simple questions: What effect does the structure of the group have upon its efficiency? What effect does position in the group have upon the subject's morale and upon group satisfaction? Subsequent work showed that the answer to the first question differs according to the kind of task. The answer to the second question appears to be that the greatest satisfaction is given to those subjects in the group who occupy central positions in it. Variables, like the number of persons in the group, the pattern of communication allowed and the task variable, have been systematically changed and tested in many possible combinations.

This account cannot include a detailed examination of the many topics in this kind of research which are relevant to the teacher, but some idea has been given of the predictive powers which are achieved by careful, systematic examination of variables. Variables which are of particular interest to the teacher are leadership, interaction between the leader and the group, and group factors like cohesion, group norms and group goals. Some generalisations for teachers and schools which can be made from studies are:

(a) The behaviour of the group is a response to the teacher's behaviour, and the teacher's behaviour is a response to that of the group.

(b) Both good and bad behaviour are strengthened by group membership. Change in behaviour is achieved more easily in a whole group than in an isolated individual.

(c) Reluctance to learn may be due to the fact that teachers are attempting to break down powerful group organisations among the pupils. Teachers cannot ignore the group norms of the pupils.

(d) The more communication there is between teachers and pupils, the more likely it will be that pupils accept the teacher's norms.

(e) The organisation of the group will influence task efficiency and conditions for learning in the group.

In seeking for predictive scientific control in groups it has been found that individual personality variables have not been consistently related to group functioning. From the teacher's point of view, it would seem profitable to put the focus on group processes rather

than on individual personality traits. The teacher has little contact
with individual pupils in a class group, and these come fleetingly
and usually outside the classroom. For the most part the teacher is
dealing with a group of pupils, usually up to thirty in number, and
sometimes more. In keeping control over as many as thirty persons
at a time, the opportunity of treating each pupil as a unique individual is lost.

Fleming makes this point when she states that '. . . the teacher has
never to do with an individual child in the sense of an entity with
fixed attributes unfolding in comparative independence of the
treatment he receives but always with a child within a group'
(Fleming, 1955). This is not a denial of the importance of the
individual. On the contrary, an understanding of the classroom
group will result in the creation of conditions satisfying to each
individual.

The foregoing account of group dynamics has emphasised the
objective experimental approach. There is, however, another important branch of the work which has considerable significance for
teaching. This is the work on T-groups. T is short for training, and
the purpose of the group is to give its members a training in interpersonal relations, and a subjective experience of the dynamics of the
group. By participating in the T-group, members become aware of
the motivations for their behaviour towards other people, and of the
needs they themselves and others seek to gratify in group membership.

A frequently adopted approach is to leave the training group in an
unstructured leaderless situation. After the members have set about
structuring the situation for themselves, a leader takes over to give
the group an insight into the reasons for the various behaviours of
the members. The skill of the leader in interpreting the many events
in interpersonal relationships in the group is crucial for the success of
the experience. He uses many problem-solving situations, and techniques like role-playing, in order to illustrate what are usually problems in human relationships. The experiences afforded by T-group
training are valuable for all people who are in control of others, and
whose handling of human situations will make for happiness or
unhappiness of others. The techique has been extensively used in
industry with persons in managerial positions and in personnel
work. It has been used in teacher training with great success, and it
should be used more widely than it is.

The T-group approach has been developed by the National Training Laboratory in Group Development at Bethel, Maine, U.S.A. The Tavistock Institute in London has also done much to exploit the usefulness of the approach. For those interested in its application to teacher training, the work of Bion (1961), Thelen (1954, 1960) and Oeser (1960) is important.

THE STUDY OF GROUPS BY THEORISTS IN THE FIELD OF COMPLEX ORGANISATIONS

The approaches used by workers in this field were first established by the Mayo study at the Hawthorne Works of the Western Electric Company just over forty years ago. Most of these studies were undertaken to improve productivity in business and industrial concerns, or to create harmonious working conditions in other large-scale organisations, like hospitals, prisons and the civil service.

The school could be regarded as another such complex organisation, and a very fruitful field for research would be testing in the school setting some of the hypotheses formed for complex organisations. A consideration of this work gives teachers some idea of how the school operates as a system to either promote or inhibit good learning. The studies which have been chosen for discussion are chiefly concerned with relating the structure of the organisation to the behaviours of individuals in it. Because little work has been done on the school as an organisation, studies in other settings have been included as well. They have been chosen to give teachers an idea of their place in a system and how the system affects both their own behaviour and that of their pupils. It must again be stated that the studies are not discussed in order to give teachers moral prescriptions about how to teach. They should serve to provide teachers with further factual information on which they can base their decisions, and better decisions should be possible in the light of the facts.

Tannenbaum (1961) investigated the relationship between the structure of voluntary organisations (the Leagues of Women Voters in the U.S.A.) and their effectiveness. Two aspects of structure were considered as follows: the hierarchical distribution of control between president, board members and ordinary members, and the total amount of control exercised at each level. It was found that those groups in which members felt that they had a large measure of control, and in which the total amount of control exercised was high, were significantly more effective. Smith and Tannenbaum (1965) then attempted to relate the president's co-ordinating behaviour to effectiveness. While high member activity and high leader co-ordination produced the most effective groups, the relationship between high and low member activity and high and low leader co-ordination and effectiveness remained unclear. The researchers were of the opinion that the co-ordination function of the leader was distinct from the structural variables used in the experiment, but was complementary to it. Together, the co-ordinating function of the leader and the pattern of control account for a significant part of the effectiveness of the voluntary organisation.

Blau and Scott (1963) report a study on the effects of group structures on individual bahaviour. The problem was to determine whether action in a group was undertaken as a result of individual attitudes in the group to which the individual belonged. The structural effect of the group was isolated in a study of twelve teams of social workers engaged in work for a welfare agency. Each worker was rated individually on attitude to raising assistance for clients. A group was similarly rated to produce a group attitude score for willingness to raise assistance for clients. The data showed that regardless of individual scores, members of groups with high group attitude scores were more likely to render extra services to their clients than members of groups with low group attitude scores. Attitude scores were the measurements used and it has been shown that the prevailing attitude of the group has an effect on individual behaviour in the group, independent of individual attitudes.

Among a very small number of studies done on the school as an organisation, there is one done by Orth, Professor of Business Management at the Harvard Business School. Orth pointed out that every class group becomes a separately structured system within the whole system, and the persons in the class group exist in a number of social systems. At the Business School the dormitory or the fraternity, athletics or social activities can each provide a system of structural relationships.

Orth found two kinds of structure which developed in two class sections, A and E, of a year's intake to the School. He called the one an internal cohesive structure, and this was marked by a development of close social relationships, avoidance of competition and pride in the group's success in sporting and social events. The orientation of the class was social, and towards close, friendly relationships between students. In the other group this pervasive friendliness did not develop, but the group concentrated their attention on the task in front of them. They spent their time and effort coping with the pressures of the academic programme (at the Business School these pressures are very strong), and stressed the individuality and independence of members. This structure Orth chose to call an external adaptive structure.

It is not surprising that different norms developed in the two sections, and these norms were associated with different behaviours, both in and out of the classroom. Orth showed which norms were common to both sections, and how norms relating to work activities and to social activities differed between them. In regard to work activities, Section A wanted a practical rather than an academic focus in the work; no one person should dominate the discussion; another's point should not be refuted; knowledge gained outside the School and not the common property of all should not be brought into discussions; viewpoints should be conservative; no one person should try to shine in the group at the expense of the rest. In Section E, however, the norms were to take work seriously, to bring in outside knowledge if it advanced the work; to refute another's point, but to do it politely; to develop unusual 'off-beat' ideas; to insist on the relevance of the discussion and to shine individually. Similarly, there were differences in the friendship norms and behaviour of the two sections.

That particular structures have particular effects is well shown in work on the classification of organisations. Etzioni (1961) provides a good example of such a classification, with a lot of empirical evidence to back it, based on what he calls *compliance*. He defines the term as the relationship between the power employed by superiors to control subordinates and the response of subordinates to this power. Power is a structural category of analysis, in that power determines the pattern of relationships between persons. Three kinds of power and their distribution in organisations are analysed as follows: coercive power (control by threat of painful punishment); remunerative power (control by monetary reward); and normative power (control by allocating esteem according to the organisation's norms). The response is concerned with motivations of subordinates, rather than with structural power relationships between superiors and subordinates, and Etzioni speaks of the involvement of the subordinate in the system, which can be great or small, negative or positive. He lists three kinds of involvement: alienative (a highly negative kind of involvement), moral (positive involvement) and calculative (involvement which is neither highly positive nor negative, but for motives of gain or interest).

Compliance is the relationship between a person who exercises power and one who responds. With three kinds of power and three kinds of involvement, Etzioni's typology of compliance relations caters for nine kinds of compliance, as follows:

	Kinds of Involvement		
Kinds of Power	Alienative	Calculative	Moral
Coercive	1	2	3
Remunerative	4	5	6
Normative	7	8	9

Etzioni suggests that the most frequent types of compliance are 1, 5 and 9, and these he calls congruent relationships. The first and last of these would be the categories of importance to the study of the school as an organisation.

Etzioni relates the structure of compliance to other structural elements in a complex organisation. He finds that three systems of norms in an organisation (he calls them goals) can be related to the compliance types 1, 5 and 9 above, and that when norms and compliance structure are congruent the organisation works on a high level of effectiveness; when norms and compliance structures are not congruent effectiveness is reduced. The norm for compliance structure 1 is order; for 5 it is an economic one and for 9 the norm is concerned with the group's culture. He shows further that the structure of the elite in an organisation is consistent with the type of compliance structure in the organisation. The integration of participants into the organisation is also looked at in terms of consensus with the norms of the organisation, communication in the organisation and socialisation. The last-mentioned concept is one of learning to adopt suitable behaviours in accord with the person's position in the group on the part of the participant, and bringing new participants into line with its norms on the part of the organisation. Etzioni suggests that integration of persons into the group is different for the three compliance structures he postulates. In addition, he considers recruitment to the organisation, its scope and pervasive-

H

ness (defined as the range of activities for which the organisation sets norms), as well as cohesion.

It has already been stated that very little of this work has been done in the classroom, and Etzioni seldom refers to the school. Much of what he says, however, about compliance of the first kind (coercive power and alienative response) is very important for understanding what has gone wrong in schools of the 'blackboard jungle' type. Webb (1962) analysed Black school, and showed clearly that the structure of the school was as much responsible for the unpleasant conditions for learning as was the unstimulating home background of the pupils. Partridge (1966) and Hargreaves (1967) have also succeeded in showing how the structure of school classes affects the behaviour of both teacher and pupils.

This account of the study of complex organisations has served to point out that teachers and pupils have a position in the social system of the school. The effectiveness of the teaching will depend on the way in which all the persons in the system interact to perform the many tasks involved. Both teachers' and pupils' behaviour are interdependent, and a knowledge of the nature of this interdependent, relationship will give teachers more certain grounds for choosing particular behaviours in the classroom, and avoiding others.

THE USE OF SOCIOMETRY TO STUDY GROUPS

Both traditions in group research discussed thus far have used sociometry as a technique for measuring group structure, so sociometry is not entirely a separate tradition in group research. But its use can be identified with some workers rather than others, and it can most easily be described in a separate section.

A description of sociometry is required in this discussion of the influence of group research on educational practice, firstly, because it is employed so frequently in group research. Secondly, and more importantly, the discussion is required because sociometry holds out excellent possibilities for providing teachers with a useful tool for studying their own classroom groups. The emphasis in this discussion has been that group research provides teachers with facts on the basis of which they can make their choices about educational practice.

Sociometry can provide the teacher with a whole range of useful facts.

The sociometric approach was first suggested by J. L. Moreno in the early years of this century. His ideas were published in *Who Shall Survive?* in 1934, and subsequently in a revised and enlarged edition of the work in 1953.

Moreno (1953) gave a definition of the sociometric test as follows:

The sociometric test consists in an individual choosing his associates for any group of which he is or might become a member. The choice is made on the basis of definite criteria and the resulting pattern of choices is examined to provide an objective measure of the structure of the group.

In her definition of the sociometric test Northway (1953) did not stress the manner in which the technique functioned, but rather the results which could be obtained from it. 'A sociometric test', she wrote, 'is a means for determining the degree to which individuals are accepted in a group, for discovering the realtionships which exist among these individuals and for disclosing the structure of the group itself.'

These are very far-reaching claims indeed, and should be qualified. The test is most ingenious in its simplicity. Each member of the group is given a criterion or criteria of association on which to make a choice of other members of the group. The criterion could be, for example, 'Suppose you were to move to another classroom, which boys and girls from this classroom would you like best to go with you?' This is typical of the conditional question used for the sociometric test. The number of choices can be as few as one or unlimited in number, depending on the design of the test. The seeming simplicity of the test hides the complexity of analytic procedures required to interpret the results, and care must be taken not to make unwarranted claims on the basis of the results.

The data collected by administering a sociometric test are such information as the number of times each member has received a choice, the number of different members choosing a member, the range of choices a member may make of other members, and patterns of choice to and from members, like mutual choices (A chooses B and B chooses A) or chains of choices (A chooses B who chooses C who chooses D).

These are all objective measures which are useful in determining the structure of the choice relationships in a group. The 'structure' of the group is the sum total to choice patterns, the distribution of choices, and the configuration of choices which identify cliques in the group. Data are provided to put all the members of the group into positions, first on the basis of the number of choices they received (choice status), but secondly and more importantly to place members in a position in the network of choices – to show which pupils are closely linked by choices.

The analysis of the data can be fairly simply done by using what is called a sociomatrix and developing sociograms from the sociomatrix. Northway (1953) gives a very clear account of such procedures. On the other hand, some very complicated and sophisticated techniques have been developed. Proctor and Loomis (1951) gives a very good description of indices which can be formed from the data. Katz (1947), Festinger (1949) and other workers have developed the application of matrix algebra to sociometric data, and a very good summary of these complicated approaches is given by Glanzer and Glaser (1959).

Very useful accounts of the application of sociometry to the school class are given by Gronlund (1959), an American author, and by Evans (1962), who relates the work to the British school. These sources will provide the teacher with a variety of ways in which sociometry has been used in research on the classroom, of which only a brief indication can be given here.

Sociometric studies show that classrooms contain 'stars' and 'isolates', and they reveal interpersonal realtionships in cliques and cleavages. Some studies show that teachers are frequently quite inaccurate about estimating the amount of influence wielded by pupils among their fellow-pupils, as revealed in the sociometric test, and are unaware of basic cleavages between groups in the class. Sociometric studies of classes have also been used to answer questions about the best use of groups for teaching; and in investigations of streaming, group cohesion, and so on. The danger with much of the latter work, though, is the one which has been pointed out several times already. Researchers are too ready to base a value judgement about how to teach on the basis of the research. The sociometric test remains, however, the best of the available measurements of classroom structure. With due regard for its limitations and a proper attention to how to use it, the test has many possibilities for use in research on the classroom and the school.

SUMMARY

The teacher works in an environment in which many interdependent variables are continually at play. If the teacher is to be able to manipulate the environment, to be able to predict behaviour, to be able to create the optimum conditions for learning, the teacher needs to understand how the variables of the group situation are related.

Three centres of interest in group research have been discussed to discover what possibilities there are in group research for giving the teacher such understanding. Group dynamics, the study of complex organisations and sociometry have been examined to show what procedures each follows to discover the facts about group variables. Cautions have been sounded about two factors in particular: the danger of generalising from a specific relationship, and the danger of ignoring that there is no necessary logical connection between the facts of research, the values for education and the practice of education in the classroom. With these precautions in mind, some of the facts of group research were then considered, because these are the facts which the teacher must take into account for decision-making.

10 Teaching Machines

Gordon Pask

INTRODUCTION

What is meant by 'teaching' or 'training'? For the present purpose I shall adopt the view that teaching (or training, for these words will be used interchangeably) consists in the control of a learning process. This is a cybernetic point of view (1,2).* Nowadays, it does not represent an altogether idiosyncratic position and will serve well as a base from which to discuss the philosophy of teaching and various types of functionally distinct teaching machines and programmes.

Mechanisation

If teaching *is* the control of learning, then it might be mechanised. That is not say that it *must* be mechanised or that mechanisation is either economic or practically advantageous. But it might be mechanised in so far as a control procedure is a prescription for what to do at each step in a process; frequently (in the case of feedback control) a prescription that is contingent upon evidence regarding the current state of the process. The controller which executes the prescriptive strategy may be a human being who carries out some algorithm or it may be an artefact, made in the metal, which does the same thing. In other cases again, the function of executing the control strategy may be relegated to the student himself in so far as he adheres to certain rules and interprets the contents of a programmed book. The important thing, in all these cases, is that a strategy exists. For, if it does, then the control procedure of teaching is well specified and open to evaluation and discussion. It may contain random elements (refer to a table of random numbers or throw a dice); it may call for intuitive judgements (if the student is fatigued, do A, if not, do B); it may be more conveniently instrumented in a human manner than

* Figures in parentheses refer to works listed in the Bibliography, pp. 278-82.

by a machine (recognise a pattern rather than go into some classification routine). But all of these formal loopholes are quite insignificant compared to the overriding fact that, given a potentially mechanisable strategy, we know what we are doing, whereas without it we do not.

Models

The control strategy is either founded upon or makes use of a *prescriptive* model. But it also relies upon a *descriptive* model for the learning process in the student. No engineer would design a plant controller without having a model to represent the working of the plant, its likely random perturbations and so on. By the same token no teacher should embark upon the exercise of his profession without a model for the student's learning process. There are many sorts of learning model of course and it is by no means obvious that the most rigorously specified mathematical models are always the best. On the whole, they are too restricted in scope, unless they are entirely intractable. For example, it is perfectly reasonable to countenance the intuitive 'model' entertained by an experienced teacher, provided that he can use it, at any stage in the teaching process, to answer the question 'Why did you do what you just did?' For practical purposes, it is often convenient to use models betwixt and between these extremes; non-numerical structural constructs such as behaviouristic models based on conditioning theory or error factor theory and computer-programmed 'artificial intelligence' learning models which have their roots in cognitive psychology.

The Form of a Teaching System

What *sort* of system is a teaching system? Well, it depends upon the sort of model that is employed. For instance, given a behaviouristic model, it turns out to be an operant conditioning system not altogether unlike the experimental set-up in an animal laboratory. However, this is an insufficiently general paradigm and I wish to contend that a proper representation of the control system involved in teaching is a tutorial conversation. It should be emphasised that the conversation may be either esoteric or mundane in calibre; the conduct of a history or a logic tutorial involving a professor and an individual student is a conversation; so, also, is the interaction between a well-versed instructor and a trainee who is learning a skill in the workshop.

The operant conditioning set-up and a variety of other experimental situations are special cases of conversations; but they are limiting cases, and the mechanisation of a conversation in the full-blooded sense is a fairly complicated business. It would be premature to claim that any mechanised (or, in principle, mechanisable) teaching system *has*, as yet, achieved full conversational status. But this ideal has been approached quite closely and future developments are likely to improve the approximation. In my own laboratory the conversational paradigm has always been explicit. We have tried to stimulate tutorial conversations as closely as possible in the belief that these constitute the most effective known teaching systems; we have tried to mechanise them because effective real life tutors are in such short supply that one of them cannot be assigned to each student. As a premium, it sometimes happens that the mechanised system is less expensive to run than a real life tutorial.

Subject Matter

Then there is the question of what is taught; what skill or subject matter. Since the types of skill and subject matter are legion, it is tempting to introduce classification schemes of one sort or another. Thus it seems reasonable to distinguish between teaching a *skill* and inculcating *knowledge*; similarly to demarcate intellectual skills (theorem-proving, being generally creative, adding up sums or making historical inferences) from perceptual-motor skills (driving motor cars, running races, using typewriters or recognising patterns). In much the same vein it is customary to classify teaching procedures according to the constraints imposed upon them by the nature of the skill or subject matter; for example, knowledge (of the most primitive sort, a list of facts or concepts) must be instilled by a sequential process. This is because of a property inherent in lists. We might or might not *like* to teach dates and tables in some other way (all at once, for example; impressing them as an image on the mind). The fact is we cannot do so, at any rate so long as we adhere to verbal, written or iconic communication. By the same token, you cannot teach someone to control an aircraft or even a motor car sequentially. You can give him the rules of driving or flying, of course, and provide him with a sequential algorithm. But that is quite a different matter. 'Learning to fly' and 'learning to drive' both necessarily entail contact with the pertinent situation as a whole.

Since we need a framework to talk within, we shall make distinctions of this sort; 'intellectual' versus 'perceptual-motor' or 'knowledge' versus 'skill' or 'sequential' versus 'parallel' ('as a whole', 'all at once'). At the same time, it is crucial to the argument that we recognise how artificial and nebulous they are. So far as I am aware, there is *no* skill which is *not* based on knowledge; conversely, it is hard to conceive of knowledge that exists independently; all knowledge is tied to a skill in the sense that it is useful in achieving some goal and (apparently, at any rate) in the sense that it is registered as part and parcel of a goal-directed system. To be even more emphatic, I do not believe it is possible to 'learn facts' without a goal or goals, the achievement of which is contingent upon knowledge of these facts.*

Taking the other distinction, there does not seem to be all that much difference between the learning processes involved in the acquisition of intellectual and perceptual-motor skills (this is not to suggest that intellectual learning can be reduced to simple conditioning and association; on the contrary, a detailed scrutiny of perceptual-motor learning reveals the whole gamut of mental processes commonly placed in the domain of complex thinking).

Machines

Having said all this, it is hardly necessary to stress that the hardware of a teaching machine is unimportant compared to the software (the teaching programme in a sequentially acting device or the programmatic organisation in the case of a parallel acting training machine). As noted at the outset, the essential issue is whether or not teaching *can* be mechanised; not whether or not it *is*. Nevertheless, it is always convenient to have a machine, and the administration of a programme may even be impracticable without one. Apart from the

---

* Of course, the goals may be spurious, like the majority of goals stated implicitly or explicitly in laboratory learning experiments, or they may be goals generated by the student himself.

H 2

teaching function as such, it is usually possible to connect up recording devices which provide the data needed for programme assessment, adaptation and revision.

Since the available hardware is by no means standardised, very little will be said about the appearance or the detailed operation of specific machines. However, the discussion is based upon the machinery capable of administering certain types of programme. It starts with simple and special purpose machines and passes to computer-based teaching systems. After digressing to describe a particular programming technique, we deal with skill-training machines and return (with some lessons learned in that area) to a further review of he educational field.

SEQUENTIAL TEACHING MACHINES

Sequentially operating machines can be roughly classified as devices that administer *linear* programmes, devices that administer *branching* programmes and computer-based systems able to do either or to perform more elaborate tricks.

Linear Programme Machines

The simplest and most familiar teaching machines administer linear teaching programmes. Functionally, they can be replaced by programmed texts, flash cards or the like, though, convenience apart, there is some motivational advantage in having a piece of machinery in front of the student. The sequence of operations carried out by the machine is as follows:

1. Some descriptive or explanatory material is presented, in writing or pictorially, as 'frame' or 'item' number n, in a linear sequence. The presentation is accomplished by projecting the material from a microfilm onto a screen, by exposing one page or one card, by starting a tape recorder that conveys a verbal message (the latter expedient is uncommon: most commercially available machines are restricted to visual presentation).

2. A question is asked about the material in frame n. This poses a problem.

3. The student tries to solve the problem or respond to the questioning stimulus either (i) by *constructing* a written response (filled in within a blank space on the frame itself, a note-pad or an auxiliary tape) or (ii) by selecting one of several multiple choice alternatives, usually by pressing a button corresponding to the chosen alternative. Generally, the student is allowed to respond at his own pace, but occasionally a mild form of time constraint is imposed to prevent dawdling or downright inattention to the material.

4. The student indicates that he has completed his response by pulling a lever or pushing a button.

5. The machine presents the correct response to frame n in such a way that the student can compare his actual response with the correct response.

6. The student is asked to contemplate the difference, if any, between the actual and the correct response and to remedy any misconceptions that led to this deviation.

7. The student indicates, for example by pressing a button, that his comparison is complete and that he has taken the necessary steps to put his mental house in order.

8. The machine moves frame n, the nth response and the correct nth response from view and exposes frame $n+1$ in the programme.

Machines of this sort and the techniques that go with them have been used and developed by Pressey (3), Skinner (4, 5), Holland (6), Glasser (7), Markle (8), Gilbert (9), and many others (10). The programming procedure is based upon the idea that behaviour can be shaped according to the principles of operant conditioning and upon the side assumption that knowledge or skill can be built up sequentially in steps (corresponding, roughly, to the frames in the linear programme). Since the programme *is* linear (frame n is always followed by frame $n+1$) there is also a supposition that one good sequence of presentation of the material can be chosen for *all* individuals in a target population.

The basic precepts of operant conditioning hold that operants* are established by contingent reinforcement and that a successful response is inherently reinforcing. Hence, linear programmes are generally written to secure an expected correct response percentage

* Responses that the organism emits, possibly contingent upon a class of stimulus situations or discriminating stimuli.

in the order of 80 or 90 per cent. Apart from the establishment of correct operants, there are four main processes involved in the fundamental learning model: (1) chaining of responses into sequences wherein the response to an item evokes the discriminating stimulus eliciting the next response;* (2) the development of higher level reinforcers; (3) discrimination, whereby responses become more selective; and finally (4) generalisation, whereby responses are made to classes of similar stimuli.

Using a 'classical' technique, the programmer specifies a terminal behaviour he would like the student to exhibit (commonly he designs a post-test to determine whether or not this terminal behaviour is achieved) and writes a sequence of frames $1 \ldots n$, $n + 1 \ldots N$ to shape the student's current behaviour so that the terminal behaviour is approximated. The subject matter is thus broken down into segments and the size of the segment that goes into a frame depends upon the expected value of the student's operant span, i.e. the size of gap he is able to fill in answering one of the questions whilst having an 80 or 90 per cent probability of being right. Some of the frames, interpolated at suitable points in the sequence, are intended to instrument chaining operations, others to carry out discriminations, others to induce generalisations. To secure these ends, the programmer has a repertoire of standard tricks at his disposal which refer to the minutiae of the conditioning process. Perhaps the most important are (*a*) the provision of cueing or 'prompting' information which partially specifies the correct response, and (*b*) the converse operating of stimulus 'fading'. By the provision or withdrawal of cues, it is possible to adjust the correct response probability with respect to a given type of material. Of course, the self-paced presentation allows the individual student to adjust his load within quite wide limits. He can go rapidly through the frames he finds simple and slowly through the difficult ones.

In fact, the same procedures are justifiable (for certain types of material) with respect to a cybernetic model in which teaching is assumed to establish goal-directed or problem-solving systems in the student's mind. However, the jargon is modified. The corrective signal (comparison of the actual response and the correct response) provides 'knowledge of results' information rather than reinforcement, and the external goal achievement test implied by the provi-

---

* The discriminating stimulus signals an occasion on which the response may be reinforced. It thus also serves as a conditioned reinforcing event.

sion of the corrective knowledge of results becomes internalised as learning proceeds. Cueing information partially solves the problems posed by the stimuli and may reduce the overall goal to subgoals. However, it is not at all obvious, from a cybernetic point of view, that the subject matter should be split up into the small constituents necessary to achieve a very high correct response probability, and the method has to be augmented by the introduction of goal statements (before each block of frames) that enunciate the nature and organisation of the subgoals instructed in that block.

The 'classical' technique has recently been supplemented by a more systematic behavioural method called *mathetics*, chiefly developed by Gilbert (9) and his associates. As before, a terminal behaviour is stated, but this is systematically transformed into a 'synthetic prescription' that states how the student's current behaviour is to be modified in order to attain the terminal criteria. The basic units of the programme are no longer frames but 'exercises', and the small step concept is de-emphasised or even discarded. The exercise brings about a specific behavioural change, and it entails instructing, cueing and observing stimuli over and above the discriminating stimulus that elicits the main or 'mastery' response. In other words, each exercise is a pattern of behaviour-changing operations; typically, it involves a sequence of frames in which a mastery response is demonstrated, prompted (or cued) and released. Further, in the construction of an exercise, the programme writer takes systematic account of the symbolic representation of the subject matter (the theory behind the behaviour). Probably mathetics is the best developed and most elegant programming technique. However, we shall do no more than mention it, because (1) many of the responses are covert rather than overt: only the mastery response need be overt; and (2) as a result of this it is not obvious that well-written mathetics programmes should be administered by any sort of machine. On the whole they are better suited to book administration.

Whichever model is adopted, it is evident that the linear programme is a feedforward control process* in which the onus for the intimate control of learning is placed firmly on the subject's

* In other words, the programme instructions control learning in so far as they are based upon a predictive model for how the student will react to them. It follows that the learning model used in linear programme design must be complete and, if possible, firmly validated.

shoulders. (This comment applies, very strongly, to the mathetics programmes.) The decisions made by the machine are trivial or non-existent. The subject is responsible for pacing the trials and he acts both as comparator and corrective agent. True, a feedback signal is *received* by way of knowledge of results information, but it is *used*, in comparison and correction, by the *student* and *not* by the machine. (The programme sets up conditions for internal, student-mediated feedback, but it does not itself exert feedback control over the learning process.)

It will be clear that not every sequence of frames constitutes a programme. To qualify for this title, it must be possible for the programmer to say what each frame is intended to do and why (with reference to the criterial or terminal behaviour) it has been introduced at a given point (i.e. frames should 'establish the conditioned response i' or 'make the discrimination j' or whatever). Further, any worthwhile programme must be adapted to suit a target population of students. With this object in view, the original programme is submitted to tests, revised and modified and fully retested until it satisfies empirical criteria of efficiency.

Branching Programmes

Branching programmes (commonly, though not necessarily, administered by a teaching machine) are instruments capable of mediating feedback control over the learning process.* The distinction between linear and branching programmes is illustrated in Fig. 1, where (I) represents the arrangement of frames (nodes in the network) for a linear programme and (II), (III), (IV) and (V) correspond to various types of branching sequence.

Suppose, for example, the student finds himself (on trial n in a teaching process) at frame i in Fig. 1 (II) (it will be evident from the figure that being located at frame i on trial n depends upon a previous path through the network, i.e. the student *could* have reached frame j on trial n). The following operations are performed by the teaching machine or the student: (1) As in the case of a linear programme, the frame i material is presented. (2) A question is asked about frame i.

---

* Because of this the learning model employed in constructing a branching programme can be much less specific than the model for a linear programme addressed to the same subject matter and student population.

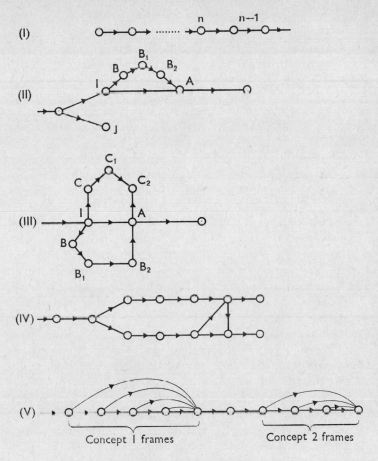

FIG. 1. Forms of Programme

(3) The student is required to respond either constructively or selectively. (4) The response is evaluated. If the response is selective and mechanised (for example, button selection) then it is evaluated by the machine relative to some criterion. In the least elaborate case the evaluation consists in a comparison between the response made and a set of responses which, the programmer has predicted, *might* have been made. This set certainly *contains* the correct response. But it may also contain response possibilities which, if they *are* selected,

indicate the existence of misconceptions about the material in frame i. (5) As in the linear case, the machine presents the student with the correct response to trial number n (frame number i). (6) The machine uses a built-in decision rule to determine which frame (A or B in Fig. 1 (II) should be displayed at trial $n + 1$. The input to this decision rule is the evaluation of (4) above. (7) The student is asked to contemplate the correct response information and (if necessary) to use it in modifying his concept of the material in frame i (trial n). When he has considered the matter sufficiently, the student indicates that he is ready to receive the next frame (by pressing a button or in some comparable fashion). (8) The teaching machine selects the next frame, A or B, depending upon the evaluation of (4) and the decision rule of (6) and presents it to the student.

Clearly steps 4, 6 and 8 mediate *external* feedback control based upon an evaluation function and a decision rule that are chosen by the programmer. In many commercially available machines the forms of the evaluation and the decision rule are restricted, but in principle this need not be so. On the other hand, steps 5 and 7 mediate the *internal* corrective feedback which is present even in a linear system.

If the response is constructed rather than selected, the machine is unable to interpret it. Consequently in these circumstances it is usual to hand over the evaluation and the decision to the student. In fact we give the student certain rules (saying how to weigh up his constructed response relative to the correct response) and certain directives (if you feel that your evaluation is a, go to A, if b, go to B). The student himself selects the next frame by pressing buttons or just by turning to the appropriate page. The important point is that in doing so we have, as it were, isolated a subsystem of the student as a supervisor and controller of his own education, using the rules and directives that are given. This may or may not be a good thing to do, depending upon the student and the subject matter. The technique certainly does impose a real cognitive burden; it can prove tedious from the student's point of view and the rules may be difficult to obey.

Several different sorts or programme network may be appropriate according to the intention behind the decision rules. The case we have just considered (Fig. 1 (II)) is a network structure containing a mainstream linear programme with remedial loops. In the simplest possible conditions the response to frame i is evaluated as right or wrong and a decision is made to select A (for presentation at trial $n+1$) if the nth response (to frame i) is right; to select B if it is wrong. Frame A is part of the main stream of instruction; in a linear programme it would be the next item after frame i. Frame B, on the other hand, is the start of a remedial loop B, B_1, B_2 which contains frames intended to iron out the misconceptions about frame i which are manifested by the evaluation 'wrong'. The student is returned to the main instructional stream at frame A only when he has shown evidence that his misconceptions are put right. Clearly, if the evaluation and the decision rules are more elaborate, the remedial action can be more discriminating and the programme structure may, with advantage, be more detailed. For example, in Fig. 1 (III) there are two different sorts of remedial loop – B, B_1, B_2 and C, C_1, C_2 – one of which is selected when the subject is 'wrong' at frame i; *which* one depending upon *how* he is wrong. Clearly, the use of remedial loops is akin to a cueing procedure extended over several frames. Because it *is* extended, it can be a controlled cueing procedure.

The evaluation and decision process can also be used as a mental testing facility to determine what sort of individual each student is and to prescribe essentially different forms of instruction for different sorts of individual. The relevant programme network is shown in Fig. 1 (IV), where the first part of the structure serves as a test sequence for sorting students into classes and the remainder serves to administer several more or less linearly arranged courses contingent upon class membership. Two comments are in order at this point: (1) it is usual (as in Fig. 1 (IV)) to provide retest facilities for reassigning a student from time to time, and (2) the 'more or less linear' sequences of frames may, in fact, contain 'remedial loops' (as in Fig. 1 (II) or Fig. 1 (III)).

Perhaps the simplest type of programme network is the *skip linear* form of Fig. 1 (v). It is, however, practically important and features in the scheme of the section below headed 'Programming Operations'. Basically it consists in a linear programme addressed to the inculcation of a given concept. From time to time a test of concept mastery is made, and if the concept has been mastered, then the student is directed to skip over the remaining frames dealing with this concept. Hence the name skip linear.

The first branching programmes were written by Crowder (11), who also designed the first teaching machines to administer them. Many people have subsequently been active in this field: Galanter (12), Lumsdaine (13), and Stolhurow (14), to mention only a few of them (15).

Since the branching programme is a more versatile instrument than the linear programme, it allows for much more latitude in the choice of model. Behaviouristic models are perfectly applicable; so are communication models, cybernetic models and cognitive models. One scheme is detailed later in the chapter.

A Comment on Optimality and the Choice of Models

Occasionally, it is possible to have sufficient confidence in a model to specify a control (or teaching) strategy that is optimum with *respect* to that model and to argue, because of this, that it *really* is an optimum strategy. For example, in paired associate learning, and perhaps in analogous real life situations such as vocabulary learning, a single element stimulus sampling stochastic learning model* appears to describe what goes on quite adequately. Now it is possible to use the statistical technique of 'dynamic programming' (not to be confused with 'teaching machine programming' or even computer programming) in order to work out a statistically optimum control strategy (which prescribes an optimum order and frequency of presentation of the items to be learned). Matheson (17) has recently done so, and his calculations lead to a strategy which is known, on empirical grounds, to be good.† However, the fact is that if we accept the stochastic learning model as an account of what goes on in the student's head, then Matheson's procedure is the best (not just a good procedure).

Now the single element stochastic learning model, though *adequate*, is certainly not a *complete* representation of what goes on in vocabulary learning; for example, it leaves out a whole lot of conceptual and interaction effects that are known to occur. But it might, of course, be augmented or developed, and the dynamic programming technique might be applied to the more elaborate structure. The real difficulty is that the mathematics of the more elaborate

---

* A specific and well-known type of stochastic learning model. For an account of it, see Estes (16).

† Comparable work has been done by Smallwood (18).

models are utterly intractable; though we might, in principle, look for optimum solutions, they could hardly be computed in practice. As a result (especially in more complex learning situations), we are often faced with the dilemma of choosing between a mathematically manipulable bit of arrant oversimplification or an essentially non-numerical model that has more pretension to reality. One very real issue is finding a way to deal with the well-attested and often all important higher level processes of learning; for example, the acquisition of learning-set (learning to learn how to solve a class of problems), positive transfer and interference effects, concept transformation and innovation. Broadly, too, it must be recognised that although the teaching programme is a sequential instrument, neither knowledge nor skill is mentally registered in a linear array. Bits of knowledge and bits of skill are multiply accessed as though their images were embedded in some multidimensional complex. Someone, I cannot recall whom, put the matter beautifully: 'Mental organisation', he said, 'is more like a polymer or the microstructure of a living cell than the record in a computer memory.' Since the words are from my own memory, I may have misquoted the unknown gentleman. That just goes to show what a tricky, dynamic, parallel acting system the mind really is.

It is extraordinarily difficult to model systems of this sort. So practical teaching problems are often dealt with by rather ad hoc expedients like 'spiral programming' (the programme is written to revisit similar topics for the purpose of subsequent generalisation, and to revisit confusable topics for the purpose of discrimination).

If we are to be more 'scientific' than this, some compromise is needed between versatility and mathematical elegance. Surely each practitioner will choose a model to suit his predilections. One possibility is a cybernetic learning model of a type outlined below under 'Programming Operations'. Though basically non-numerical, it is precise enough to yield computer programmes representing the learning process in the context of specific tasks. Often the overall model provides sufficient guidance for intelligent programming (the section on 'Programming Operations' goes no further than this). Occasionally it is worthwhile writing a computer programme that gives a rigorous formulation of the model but, it should be emphasised, offers no mathematically respectable solution to problems like finding an optimum strategy.

A Note on Response Information

It will be evident from the discussion so far that the subject is required to respond for two quite distinct purposes: (1) so that he can be provided with knowledge of results on the basis of which he can remedy misconceptions by 'internal' feedback (maybe it does reinforce him as well); (2) so that the teaching system can gain information about the subject's state of mind, the 'external' side of the coin.

Objective 1 is passably well served by the conventional gambit of forcing the subject to make a definite assertion (a constructed or selected response) which is subsequently criticised and possibly modified. However, that is not a particularly efficient way of aiming for objective 2. Real subjects are frequently in a state of doubt about what response to submit, and it would be altogether more efficient if the teaching system could somehow sample the subject's degree of belief in the several alternatives. There are serious difficulties in getting people to make veridical estimates of their degree of belief. Fortunately, many of these have been overcome by a technique called admissible probability measurement, pioneered, in the psychological context, by Shuford (19) and his colleagues. The subject is invited to engage in a game-like situation, and the game is scored in a special way. Each move made by the subject consists in a probability statement about a set of possible response alternatives. For example, given the question: 'The Prime Minister in 1968 is (A) Wilson, (B) Disraeli, (C) Gladstone, (D) Macmillan', the subject assigns numbers such as A = 70 per cent, B = 5 per cent, C = 25 per cent, D = 0 per cent, which purport to express his degree of belief in A, B, C and D. Any set of numbers that adds up to 100 per cent will count as a probability statement. But the scoring scheme is such that the subject can only maximise his score if the numbers reflect his *real* degree of belief.*

Since an adequate scoring scheme is available (one of the admissible probability measurement schemes), it only remains to persuade the subject to output statements of the required type (such that the numbers add up to 100 per cent). Various devices have been used

---

* Notice that for *most* scoring schemes, the mathematical expectation of score would be maximised by setting A = 100 per cent, B = 0 per cent, C = 0 per cent, D = 0 per cent even though the real degrees of belief were A = 70 per cent, B = 5 per cent, C = 25 per cent, D = 0 per cent.

for this purpose; in my own laboratory, for example, we employ a gimcrack array of potentiometers and meters. By far the most elegant arrangement has been devised by Baker (20). It depends upon the C.R.-tube display of a computer and a light pen facility.

In Baker's system, each of the multiple choice alternatives is displayed on the C.R.-tube screen together with a histogram bar. At the outset, all the bars have equal length, that is, $A - 25$ per cent, $B = 25$ per cent, $C = 25$ per cent, $D = 25$ per cent. The student is invited to adjust the lengths of the bars, using his light pen, so that they represent his degrees of belief in A, B, C, D. Thus, for example, he lengthens bar A. When he does so, the computer adjusts the remaining lengths so that $A + B + C + D = 100$ per cent. The student plays around in this way until he is satisfied with the distribution, and at that moment he presses a button which submits the prevailing numbers (bar lengths) as his probability statement. This information may (as below) be automatically incorporated into a learning model.

Computer-Assisted Instruction

If the decision rules (or the evaluation functions) are at all weighty, it is difficult to handle them with special purpose teaching machines. We have already commented upon the limitations imposed by many of the commercially available devices. These are not due to ignorance, incompetence or bad design. They are there as a compromise (usually a good one) between the conflicting demands of an economically viable device and the ideal vehicle for all kinds of branching programme.

One way out of the difficulty is to make on-line use of a general purpose computer linked to special peripheral equipment that displays auditory or visual material and receives the student's response. Even a modest computing machine can easily handle any practicably sized decision rule. It can also accumulate measures and statistics over the previous performance of the student and use these, rather than the immediate evaluation alone, as the input to a decision rule. The computer is, in addition, able to accommodate a learning model, such as one of the cybernetic models mentioned a moment ago, and, if explicitly employed, this becomes part and parcel of the prescriptive decision rule.

Finally, in a computerised system, it is possible to carry out on-line adaptation,* using information derived from a single student or from the group who have interacted with the system in the past. In its simplest form, adaptation amounts to modifying parameters of the decision rules (for example, the threshold of error for which remedial action is instigated). In its most elaborate form, it consists in modifying (indeed, in on-line building up) the learning model. Hence computer-assisted instruction makes it practicable to use a new and powerful type of teaching system: an *adaptive* system in which the teaching machine learns about the student's oddities and modifies the teaching programme to encompass them. It should be stressed, however, that the computer only makes the adaptive system practicable. You *can* carry out adaptive teaching with special purpose equipment. Indeed, in the case of skill instruction, a great deal of adaptive teaching has been done with special purpose equipment.

Several sorts of peripheral equipment are used in computer-assisted instruction (hereafter abbreviated to C.A.I.). At one extreme the student–machine interface is provided by a standard teletypewriter used in the 'conversational' mode of TELCOMP (or some similar language where the machine can type out a statement or a question, ask for the student's response and comment upon it). For many purposes, the resulting discourse (though logically adequate) is too cumbersome and perceptually impoverished; for example, it is hard to teach history this way and well nigh impossible to teach a subject like structural organic chemistry or the organisation of enzyme systems in biochemistry that calls for graphical representations which condense a great deal of written material.

One of the first systems to get away from the teletypewriter was PLATO at the University of Illinois (21). Here the student console includes a C.R.-tube that may either display written statements (such as questions with gaps to fill in) or material derived from a random access slide library controlled by the computer. The student's response is obtained via a typewriter-like keyboard but, depending upon the question format, it may be either a selective response ('press A, B, C or D according to the alternative you favour') or a constructed response ('type in the name of the Prime Minister' or 'complete the equation by filling in the gap'). In the latter case, the system is able to look for relevant features of the response and to neglect others; for

---

* As distinct from off-line adaptation, to which any competent programme is subject before it is finalised.

example, it can accept any one of a list of synonyms as the *same* response, it can disregard any of a list of common misspellings of a word, it can look for the salient connective in a logical expression.

The programme format can be of various types; for example, it may be made identical with the sequencing already described for a typical branching programme. Usually something a little more complicated is employed. The student is provided with additional function keys labelled 'Aha!' or 'Judge', etc., which allow him to return to the main material from a branch, to ask for evaluation, to embark upon a remedial or explanatory branching routine at will, and so on.

Similar facilities* are made available in the I.B.M. 1500 system, which is in use at Stanford University and elsewhere (22). The 1500 console has a C.R.-tube display and an independent local slide projector which is controlled by command signals from the central computer, but which serves also as an auxiliary 'memory'. The student's response is registered either on a teletypewriter keyboard (as in the PLATO system, function keys are provided as well as alpha-numeric keys) or by a light pen (for pointing at and operating upon the C.R.-tube display). Much the same is true of other hardware configurations, for example, the system used at Sheffield by Kay and Sime (24).

Currently the most sophisticated and comprehensive C.A.I. system is in use at HumRRO. The display and response facilities are broader than those described above (for example, there is a special type of image projector allowing for superimposition, and there is an electronic tablet input). More importantly the designers of this system, Kopstein and Seidel (25, 26) have introduced several conceptual innovations. Amongst other things, they are (1) explicitly introducing a structural representation of the subject matter and an on-line learning model into the software of the system, and (2) instrumenting the admissible probability measurement procedures described in the previous sections of this chapter. The probability measurement information forms a controlling input to the learning model and the system decision rules.

Several other investigators have designed systems of comparable

---

* The S.D.C. CLASS System (23) is something of an exception in this respect It has a special purpose interface including a controlled image projector and a limited response board. Further, in CLASS, communication is maintained, through the machinery, with a real life teacher.

sophistication, notably Donnio (27) in France, Landa (28) and his colleagues in Russia (32), and Atkinson (29), Licklider (30) and Uttal (31) in the U.S.A. However, so far as I know, these are not yet fully operational.*

PROGRAMMING OPERATIONS

Before going any further, let us pause to collect some of the loose ideas (like goals, concepts and levels of abstraction), by detailing a method for programme writing. This method is based upon a model and it has been used for writing both industrial and academic programmes administered by simple teaching machines. With some (rather obvious) elaboration it is a useful tool in the C.A.I. domain as well.

Outline of a Programming Model

Students learn to *do* something; in particular, to *solve* some class of problems (for example, the problems of logic, of mathematics, of history, of computer programming or of motor car driving). Since it is possible to show that any problem-solving system (human or otherwise) is a 'goal-directed system' or, in a rather abstract sense, a 'control system', it is legitimate to translate the foregoing remarks into the more general statement that a job or field of accomplishment is characterised by a task goal (abbreviated as T-goal). To say that someone can achieve a given T-goal (for example, dealing with connectives in logic) implies that he has a mental organisation with the form of a T-goal directed system.

Such a system is also a concept, using the word in a fairly rigorous sense.† Thus the concept of orange squares is a goal-directed system with the goal of recognising and naming an orange square whenever such an object appears in the environment or the imagination.

* When this article was written, in 1969.

† The word 'concept' is also used in the sense of a description of a goal-directed unit. This is a perfectly legitimate usage and is compatible with the system outlined below if appropriate renamings and substitutions are made. However, the usage of 'concept' to designate a *class* without a statement of *how* class membership is determined or of the universe of discourse in which it is determined would not be compatible with the present system.

Similarly the concept of motor car driving is the array of goal-directed systems involved in the performance of this skill and it may, theoretically, be viewed as a single very elaborate goal-directed system.

As suggested by the last example or, for that matter, by a contemplation of a field such as logic, a large T-goal is usually the name for an equivalence class of pertinent T-goals. Thus the student may be able to recognise the connective in a given class of logical expressions (but in what size of class?) or to construct a logical expression given a connective and certain variables or propositions (but which, or is it both?) or to do other relevant tricks (but which tricks are relevant?). In teaching we usually determine these matters by specifying a criterion test for terminal behaviour in which the T-goal system C, is put to work and counted as competent in so far as it can pass the test (i.e. in so far as the student with C in his psyche can pass the test). As a matter of fact we may also require the student to exhibit his *understanding*, either by describing the system with T-goal C or by demonstrating the availability of *many* different systems attaining goal C.

Since students learn without being taught, it is necessary to postulate some mechanisms that operate upon the repertoire of goal-directed systems. The present idea is that these other mechanisms are also goal-directed (problem-solving) systems but that they exist at a higher level of control or organisation (*not* to be confused with a higher level of abstraction). Designating the levels of control as L^0, L^1..., the L^1 processes operate upon a domain of L^0 goal-directed systems to concatenate them, to abstract them, and in various other ways, but always in order to repair manifest deficiencies in the L^0 repertoire. This idea is diagrammed in Fig. 2, where the L^0 box contains a repertoire of T-goal directed systems addressed to problems posed by the environment and the L^1 box contains the goal-directed systems to do with learning. Box L^2 is an executive organisation, which must be added in any realisation of this learning model to regulate the allocation of mental effort. The important feature of the construct is that each box is likely to contain goal-directed systems (or concepts) at various levels of abstraction. In the L^0 box we refer to the more abstract systems as 'plans' or as aptitudes. In the L^1 box we refer to them as 'learning sets'.

In this framework, teaching is conceived as a process whereby an external goal-directed system (which may also be more or less

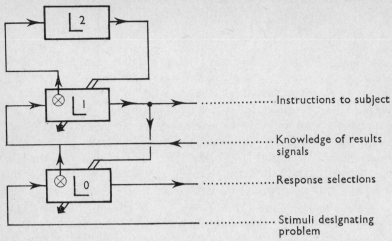

Conventions: ⊗ is the output from a comparator system; for example, the L^0 channel carries a signal indicating deficiencies in the L^0 repertoire.

⟋⟋ is a parameter input; for example, the L^1 output acts upon the goal-directed systems at L^0 and modifies them.

FIG. 2. The Hierarchy of Control Supposed to Exist in the Subject's Mind

abstract) usurps the function of the L^1 box or, at any rate, prescribes what the L^1 box will do. This idea is also illustrated in Fig. 2.

To express the notion in a more practically useful form, let us represent the goal-directed system as a canonical bit of flow-charting in a manner suggested by Miller, Galanter and Pribram (33). The flow-charted information structure of Fig. 3 is a TOTE or Test Operate Test Exit unit (familiar to computer programmers as an If Then Else loop). It may be concatenated into a string, and it may be abstracted (*one* special form of abstraction is shown in Fig. 4; this is by no means the *only* form, but it is one we need to use explicitly). Hence box L^0 or L^1 will contain structures representable in the manner of Fig. 3 and Fig. 4. In particular, we conceive the L^0 systems that are being used or modified (by L^1 operators) at any given moment as lodged or embodied in the student's intermediate (or working) memory and operating upon information held in short-term or immediate memory.

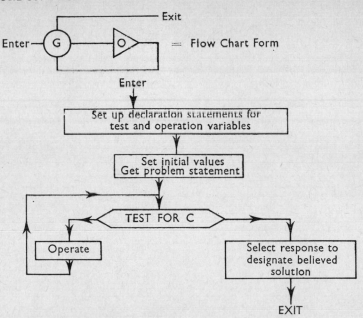

C = Test for T-goal C
O = Operation performed upon information in immediate memory to approximate C

FIG. 3. Shorthand and Flow Chart Forms for a Simple TOTE Unit

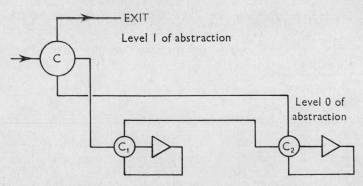

TOTE for C is more abstract than either of the subgoal TOTES for C_1 and C_2. Notice that all of the entities in this figure are at the *same* level of *control*, say at L^0.

FIG. 4. Shorthand Form of One Type of Abstraction

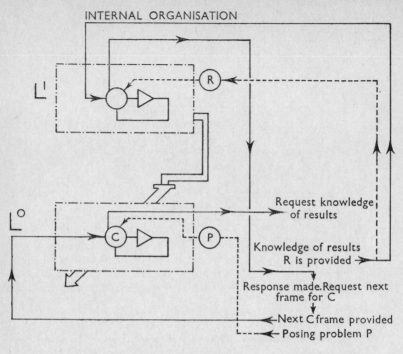

INTERNAL ORGANISATION

Request knowledge of results

Knowledge of results R is provided →

Response made. Request next frame for C

← Next C frame provided

← Posing problem P

→ Instruction or command statements.

⇒ Parametric operation. The domain upon which the L' TOTE unit operates is the L° TOTE unit .

---➤ Data transfer to memory location on which relevant unit operates.

Parametric operator upon the organisation embodied in a given memory location.

Encloses functionally distinct entity usually embodied in a distinct memory location.

The shorthand figure given above is equivalent to the flow chart in Fig. 5b.

Fig. 5a

Given this identification, and recalling the previous account of linear and branching programmes, it can be argued (1) that any *frame* of a linear programme acts upon a hierarchy of TOTES, probably in the manner suggested by Fig. 5; and (2) that any long sequence* of frames of a skip linear or branching programme

* In principle an indefinitely long sequence.

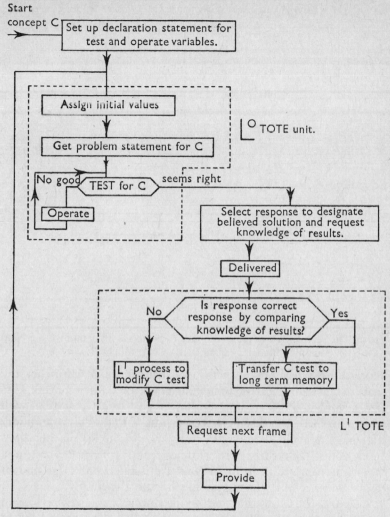

Start
concept C

Set up declaration statement for
test and operate variables.

Assign initial values

L⁰ TOTE unit.

Get problem statement for C

No good / TEST for C \ seems right

Operate

Select response to designate
believed solution and request
knowledge of results.

Delivered

No — Is response correct
response by comparing
knowledge of results? — Yes

L¹ process to
modify C test

Transfer C test to
long term memory

Request next frame

L¹ TOTE

Provide

When going from C_i to C_{i+1}, so that the frames contain explanatory material, there must be at least one other L¹ TOTE unit to generalise, discriminate, concatenate or define a further L⁰ TOTE unit.

Fig. 5b. The Simplest Type of Teaching Process

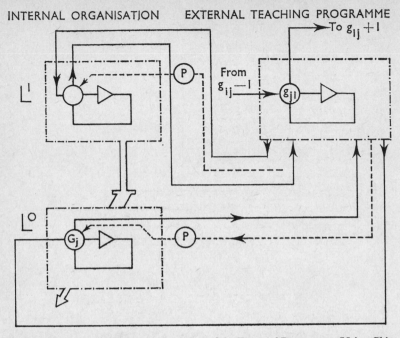

FIG. 6. The Sense in Which the Iteration of the External Programme Using Skip Linear or Branching Frames is a Coupled TOTE Unit

addressed to a *single* concept acts in the manner of Fig. 6. Further, the sequence of skip linear or branching frames teaching concept C is *representable* as a TOTE unit (and it *is* a goal-directed system) with the educational goal, G(C), of establishing C in the student's mind. Rather than labour the point, I refer back to the list of operations cited under 'Branching Programmes', and comment that in a 'branching' format these operations are iterated until the student shows evidence of having a system with the T-goal of C.

We are now in a position to describe a programme writing system based upon these broadly cybernetic ideas. It will be convenient, in the following discussion, to call any T-goal directed system in the student's mind a 'concept' and to use the term 'goal' in connection with the educational goals of actually teaching a concept. However, it is essential to keep the symmetry of the system in mind and to recall from Fig. 6 that the system with the educational goal of teaching C is itself an L^1 goal-directed system (on a par with the student's own L^1 systems).

A Simple Partially Adaptive Programming System*

The act of programme writing entails the following operations:
1. Specifying the main concept to be taught.
2. Reducing it to small concepts, hereafter referred to as 'concepts', which are to be instructed by programme segments of between 100 and 350 frames.†
3. Ascertaining the elementary subconcepts, relevant to these concepts, that are already available to all members of the population of students.
4. Choosing a programme format.
5. For each concept, determining a concept ordering.
6. Numbering the concept ordering, using a heuristic intended to minimise the deleterious effects of interference upon information structures embodied in intermediate memory.
7. Using the programme format and the numbered concept ordering to write a programme segment with the goal of instructing the concept.
8. Testing the programme on real students within a framework determined by the concept ordering.
9. Adapting the programme to approximate to certain desirable properties.
10. Repeating steps 7, 8 and 9 (and, if necessary, 5 and 6 also) until the testing gives a satisfactory result.
11. Repeating the process for each concept and assembling the programme segments into a programme.

The method is open to the serious criticism that (although it produces good programme segments) there is no assurance that the sum of these will constitute a good programme. In essence the reason why the programme might not be good is that it is based upon an assumption of some almost linear ordering of data in the mind (which we have already cast doubt upon). Some precautions can be taken to guard against the more glaring types of defect,

---

* I have used this system for industrial programing over several years. However, it was possible to think about it and develop it during a recent visit to UNAM, Mexico, whilst working on a programed instruction project for the university. As it stands, the scheme owes much of its merit but none of its defects to Professor Salazar Resines, who collaborated on this project.

† As later, most of these are skip linear frames. The programme segment is the material for one session in which the concept is consolidated in the student's mind.

though these are not described in the following account. (I can only
defend the method against the criticism by saying that it is better in
this respect than most other methods.)

1. The main concept to be taught is *given* by the subject matter
   to be taught; however, it must be made precise.
2. The main concept is reduced to constituent concepts in the
   following manner (which closely parallels the arguments of
   Gagne (34, 60)). We first observe that the main goal (sub-
   served by the main concept) could be achieved if (i) the
   student has a number of subsidiary concepts $C_1 \ldots C_r$, and
   (ii) if he was provided with an appropriate sequence of performance instructions; concisely a suitable algorithm, U, that
   refers to the $C_k, k = 1 \ldots r$. Our problem is to select a break-
   down of the main concept $R = C_1 \ldots C_r$ such that a U is
   available. In general this breakdown is not unique. There is a
   set R* of breakdowns R from which one must be chosen. To
   refine the choice we introduce a further condition, namely
   that for any $R \in R^*$ all of the C_k in R must be associated with
   a *legitimate* concept ordering in the sense of step 6. In practice,
   some R is chosen which satisfies conditions (i) and (ii) and is
   likely to satisfy the legitimacy condition. The legitimacy of the
   concept orderings for all C_k in R are tested at step 6 and, if
   necessary, R is revised. To quote one example, in Salazar
   Resines's elementary logic programme, the names of the
   concepts in R are as follows: propostions; truth tables; dis-
   junction and conjunction; negation; the conditional; the
   biconditional; arguments and truth tables; inference rules;
   predicate logic (general propositions and quantifiers);
   predicate logic (inference).
3. The elementary concepts available to the population are
   determined, in practice, by experience or intuition. In theory,
   they might be determined from student discourse, using the
   methods that social anthropologists address to discovering
   salient words in an alien language.
4. For the present puprose, we shall select the programme format shown in Fig. 7. Other branching formats with the properties cited below could be used, in particular the *structural
   communication* format described later in the chapter. The
   format of Fig. 7 is about the simplest compatible with the
   method. The main educational goal is designated G. the

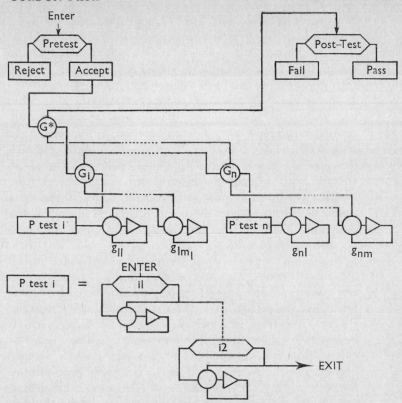

Where i1 ... i2 are precondition subconcepts for concept number i.

Fig. 7. Programme Format

educational goals are designated $G_1 \ldots G_n$ and the educational subgoals $(g_{11}, g_{1m_1}) \ldots (g_{n1} \ldots g_{nm_n})$. There is an obvious correspondence between concepts and goals; thus if the main concept is C^*, then $G^* = G(C^*)$; similarly for the concepts C_i and the subconcepts C_{ij} (so that for $i = 1 \ldots n$ and $j = 1 \ldots m_i$, $G_j = G(C)_i$ and $g_{ij} = G(C_{ij})$). Clearly, there is a rough correspondence between levels of *abstraction* in the programme and the levels of *abstraction* supposed to exist in the student's mind at the end of the instruction (if $>$ stands for 'more abstract', then $G^* > G \in \{G_i\} > g \in \{g_{ij}\}$ and similarly $C^* > C \in \{0_i\} > C \in \{C_{ij}\}$). However, the entire programme exists in a single level of control.* The

* Apart from cueing operators, which may be regarded as L^0 objects.

I

constituent TOTE units are L^1 operators that form L^0 structures in co-operation with L^1 systems in the subject. This, of course, is a weakness in the system that, to some extent, formalises the criticism voiced at the outset. Whereas the subject's mind can form definite learning sets* (structures at the level L^1 in the control hierarchy), our programme cannot do so. If it could, then there would be time variable relationships between the G_i and between g_{ij} (not merely an ordering 1 . . . n or ij . . . $^i m_i$). Further, any programme with this property would be real time and on-line adaptive, the adaptive process being formalised as an L^2 box in the teaching system. The adaptive process of steps 8, 9 and 10, below is isomorphic with such an L^2 box. But it does not act at the individual level, i.e. the programme is adapted only to a population of students.

5. Consider the first concept of the main concept stated in (1). Clearly it is made up of subconcepts. Some of these may be elementary concepts and others may be introduced by definitions. Form and ordering of these concepts, starting with the concept concerned, in which each subconcept is represented by a node in a directed graph and in which A is above B if, and only if, B must be attained before A is instructed (B is either part of A or the attainment of B is a necessary precondition for attaining A). To each directed edge of the graph and to each terminal node assign a type label according to the type of process used in reaching it. The list of type names will (for the present purpose) be restricted to generalisation, concatenation, discrimination and definition. A type label may be any 'type expression' where a 'type expression' consists in a type name or combination of type names using the connective *and*. (Thus 'definition *and* generalisation' is a 'type expression'.) The assignment of type labels is straightforward. If A is uniquely above B, then the edge connecting A to B is labelled by the process whereby A is obtained from B. If A is above B and C, then the edge AB is labelled by the process whereby B is used in building (part or all of) A and the edge AC by the process whereby C is used in building (part or all of) A. The concept ordering is closely related to an ordering of

---

* Using the box L^2 in the learning model of Fig. 2.

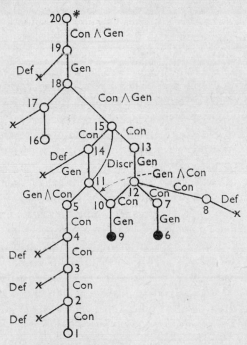

Type Names
Def = Definition
Con = Concatenation
Gen = Generalisation
Discr = Discrimination

Other Symbols
O = Subconcept node
● = Terminal node denoting initial subconcept
✱ = Concept at head of ordering
x = Terminal branch for introducing definition

FIG. 8. A Concept Ordering for a Logic Programme: The Numbers are Assigned by a
Heuristic to Indicate Sequence of Instruction

skills in Gagne's sense (34, 60).* To see this, we comment that if subconcept A is above subconcepts B and C in a concept ordering, then we can infer that a student having B and C could achieve the T-goal associated with A if he were given suitable instructions (this is Gagne's condition for a hierarchy of skills). Further, at first sight, the organisation of sub-concepts in a concept ordering is closely related to the organi-sation of the concepts of the main concept. But, on closer scrutiny, there are several important differences. The 'instructions' referred to in step 2 (the organisation of the concepts into a main concept) were parts of a performance algorithm. In contrast, in the present context, an 'instruc-tion' brings an L^1 operation into effect; this is an instruction to learn, not just an instruction to do. Next, because it has this status, an instruction may be of as many different types as there are type expressions. Finally, the instruction to learn can only be obeyed if it respects the limitations imposed by intermediate memory. Hence in (6) we shall say that a concept ordering is *legitimate* only if the instructions which it will give rise to are *likely* to prove consonant with these limitations.

6. Suppose it is necessary to deal with *one* concept at once. This is generally true of simple programme formats and is certainly true of the chosen format. If so, several different subconcepts must be kept in mind (and, by hypothesis, kept available in intermediate memory) whilst others are instructed. We can, however, choose a path (a sequence in which the subconcepts are to be instructed) that will minimise this loading; in case there is no unique path, a set of 'best' paths is determined. Several heuristics are available for numbering the subconcepts and thus defining a path; they differ according to the assump-tions made about interaction in intermediate memory. One of these heuristics is applied and the 'optimally' numbered concept ordering is tested to see whether a numerically valued property, μ, exceeds a critical limit interpreted as the estimated

---

* It is also closely related to a concept matrix in the Ruleg (35, 36, 37) programming system devised by Glaser and Homme. However, a rectangular matrix with concept names and its row and columns is unwieldy for dealing with a large programme. We do not necessarily want to compare all pairs of concept names.

capacity of intermediate memory.* If estimated capacity $> \mu$, then the numbered concept ordering is deemed *legitimate*. If *not*, then either (i) the choice of concepts in the main concept (the choice of R in R*) made at step 2 must be revised, or (ii) it is necessary to introduce repetitions in the instruction of a single concept. We regard the latter alternative as unacceptable (i.e. we wish to define a concept as having a legitimate concept ordering).

7. Suppose that the numbered concept ordering is legitimate. Consult the programme format of Fig. 7. (i) Write the test for elementary concepts. (ii) Write a concept statement (T-goal statement) for concept 1. This does not describe the concept (still less teach it). It must, however, allow the student to recognise whether or not he has mastered the concept after suitable instruction (whether or not he has achieved the T-goal). Further, it shows the student what he and the programme are aiming for. (iii) Write a precondition test, P-test 1, covering all the subconcepts other than definition concepts that are represented by terminal nodes in the numbered concept ordering. (The precondition test contains remedial loops, as indicated in Fig. 7. If the student does not have one of the subconcepts he is instructed, remedially, until he does have it.) (iv) Take subconcept 1 in concept 1. Using the type label, write eight or more sequentially cued skip linear frames (possibly interpolated with linear frames) on examples dealing with this subconcept, having stated the subconcept in the first frame.† Proceed to subconcept 2 and so on, until the last. (v) Write a test for concept 1 as a whole (by the definition of a concept ordering, this is a test for concept number m_i).‡

8. Select several groups of students from the target population. These are matched with respect to verbal abilities and with respect to speed of programme reading (using other programmed materials for this purpose). But they should

---

* A much more elegant scheme, based upon Atkinson's (61) memory model, is currently being developed.

† This is essentially the recommendation given in Glaser and Homme's Ruleg programming system amended by the more recent comments of Ivor Davies (38).

‡ If the student fails in this test, the present format returns him to the start of the programme segment for concept 1. It would be advantageous to return him to remedial material.

retain the variability anticipated in the target population (hence, choose equal numbers of students from each cell in the pre-test score scattergram for assignment to each group). Administer the concept 1 programme segment to group A. Record latency per subconcept and number of errors per subconcept and number of frames per subconcept. It is also useful to record student comments, such as 'I can't see where this is leading' or 'I'm bored', that can be ticked off on each frame. We now aim to achieve criteria of the following type: latency per *frame* should be uniform. Mean error should not exceed 15 per cent. Error per subconcept should not exceed 30 per cent for any subconcept. No student should fail to exit from the subconcept TOTES (that is, no student should go through *all* the available frames). Adverse comment scores should be less than the population mean for all concepts in the programme.* The test data are conveniently tabulated in the framework of Fig. 9, in which the programme format bears a direct relation to the numbered concept ordering. Several heuristics are available for searching backwards along the concept ordering or the tabulation shown in Fig. 9 to ascertain why the criteria cited above are not satisfied (on the assumption that some of them are not). An analysis according to one of these heuristics is returned, together with the gross data, to the programme writer. He is required to modify the programme so that the criteria *are* satisfied (the analysis giving him guidance in how to rewrite it).

9. The programme segment is rewritten (in rare cases the concept ordering may also have to be changed). The rewritten programme segment is now administered to group B of the students and (8) is repeated. The adaptive process goes on (in practice, not beyond group C or D) until the basic criteria *are* satisfied.

10. When the programme segment for concept 1 is complete, steps 6, 7, 8, 9 are repeated for concept 2, and so on, until all the concepts in the main concept have been exhausted. Finally, write the post-test covering the main concept as a whole. The only significant difference (as against concept 1) occurs in step 7. Here the precondition test for a concept i,

---

* These are not simply magical numbers. The parameters are chosen according to data of the type mentioned in the next section of this chapter.

Concept Name	CI																	
Subconcept name	←——— Cil ———→								←——— Ci 2 ———→									
Frame Number	70	71	72	73	74	75	76	77	78	79	80	81	82	83	84	85	86	87	88
Frame Type	B	A	A	A	A	A	A	A	A	D	C	A	A	B	A	A	A	A	A
Mean latency	2	4	4	7	4	6	3	2	0	1	2	3	5	4	5	2			0
Mean Correct Responses	8	5	7	6	4	2	2	1	0	8	7	5	6	1	2	4	2	0	0
Mean Mistakes	0	3	1	2	4	6	6	0	0	0	1	3	2	7	6	4	6	0	0
Mean omissions	0	0	0	2	4	4	7	7	8	0	0	0	0	0	5	7	7	8	8
Comment 1 frequency	0	1	2	0	1	0	0	1	0	0	8	0	0	0	1	0	0	0	0
Comment 2 frequency	0	2	0	0	0	0	0	1	0	0	2	0	0	0	1	0	0	0	0
Comment 3 frequency	0	5	7	0	0	1	0	0	0	0	3	2	0	0	1	0	1	0	0
Comment 4 frequency	0	7	8	0	1	0	0	0	0	0	5	4	0	5	0	1	0	0	0
Concept latency	4									3									
Concept mistakes	22									29									
Mean Frames concept	40									45									
Rate of increase of mistakes	0·43 — 0·57									0·55 — 0·44									
Comment 1 frequency	5									9									
Comment 2 frequency	3									3									
Comment 3 frequency	3									7									
Comment 4 frequency	16									15									

Fig. 9. Recording Sheet for Programme Data from Student Group

$i > 1$, includes tests for all those concepts established in previous programme segments what are terminal nodes of the ith concept ordering.

A few broad comments are in order. First of all, this adaptive technique is an L^2 box in the previous sense. Next, it is a heuristic. Certain features of the heuristic are readily mechanised (for example, the numbering of the concept ordering) and others *could* be (for example, the housekeeping details of programme writing could be handled by co-operative interaction with a computer). But some steps, notably writing the frames and possibly finding a good break-down into subconcepts, are in the human domain. Next, there is no reason why the student groups should not be used in an interlaced fashion, providing each group receives the programme segments in the right order. Thus the segment for concept 2 can be administered to group A whilst the segment for concept 1 is still being tested by groups B, C or D. Finally, the parameter μ is an estimate. It may be a bad estimate, and for lengthy programmes it has been possible to use information from testing to adjust the value of μ and improve its reliability.

SKILL INSTRUCTION

The following comment upon skill learning is a cursory overview of studies that have been reported, quite exhaustively, elsewhere. The interested reader is referred to the publications cited in this section. There are two reasons for introducing the topic at all, as part of the present paper: (1) to show that the principles of instruction, outlined earlier, apply equally well in the area of skill instruction where the learning process is no longer constrained by serial presentation; (2) to show how numbers such as μ and the various proficiency levels are derived from well-controlled laboratory experiments.

Skill instruction can run closely parallel to the educational techniques already outlined (39, 40, 41, 42, 43, 44, 45). For example, it is often possible to reduce the skill to subskills, to organise these in a structure somewhat analogous to the concept ordering and finally to instruct these subskills in a predetermined sequence.

Adaptive Machines

For the present purpose, however, I am anxious to make some points that stem from an adaptive teaching method that (in a sense) treats the task situation as a whole. We conceive the task as posing problems which are randomly selected by a problem source, for example the problems posed by the perturbation of a vehicle, the problems posed to a typist by the appearance of a character to type, etc. If the novice was presented with such a sequence of real life problems he would find them far too difficult to solve, and any teaching system whatever entails some co-operative agent which is able to simplify or partially solve the problems before they are presented to the student. Without this facility, the novice would simply never be able to learn.

Further, the simplifying facility must be controlled by the student's performance, so that the student is kept working in an operating region where problems are sufficiently coherent to be intelligible but sufficiently novel to warrant learning. Hence a paradigm system has the form shown in Fig. 10, where the teaching machine, in terms of

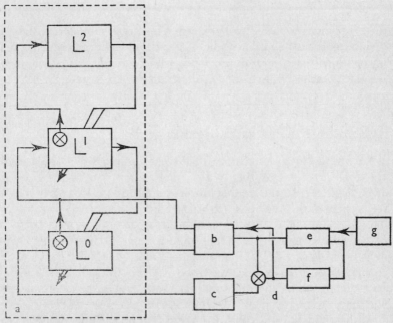

Channel b also conveys a knowledge of results signal as in Fig. 2. Instruction signals are not shown.

FIG. 10. A Simple Adaptive Training System

our previous formalism, corresponds to a *class* of *interacting* TOTE units. Here a is the subject, b is the problem display delivering stimuli and knowledge of results information, c is the response board, d is a comparator that finds a measure of the difference between what the subject did at a given trial and what he should have done, e is a simplification box, f is an averager that assesses performance and g is the random source of real life problems (46, 47, 48, 49, 50).

I 2

If, for example, the problems are typewriting problems (early in training), an unsimplified problem is posed by the appearance of an alphabetic character on an indicator tube display, a problem is simplified (to yield the current stimulus) by adjoining information about where and how to move the fingers, the degree of simplification is varied by changing the delay of the latter type of information. The performance measure is a mean, latency weighted, correct response. On the other hand, in a training system for vehicle control, the problems are posed by displacements of the simulated vehicle, a variable degree of simplification is introduced by changing *either* the mean displacement amplitude *or* the vehicle dynamics and the proficiency measure is inversely proportional to the student's R.M.S. error.

Models Employed for Adaptive Instruction

Such a teaching system can readily be designed on the basis of Harlow's error factor theory (learning entails the elimination of error factors).* In this connection it is appropriate to remark that a real system of this type has vectorial (multi-dimensional) proficiency measures and many types of simplification; broadly, one dimension of control is assigned to each relevant error factor. However, a cybernetic learning theory is also applicable, and from this point of view we conceive the skill as broken down into constituent subskills, one for each dimension of control, which are simultaneously† rehearsed to varying degrees and finally assembled into the entire skill.

To integrate several subskills the system must be modified, as in Fig. 11, to include a box, h, containing a teaching strategy that externally parallels the learning strategy which we have all along supposed to exist in the student's mind. Clearly, in this case, the teaching machine formally corresponds to a class of TOTE units controlled, at a higher level, by an adaptive TOTE unit.

Teaching systems of this sort have been extensively studied, especially in connection with simple and multiple rule application

---

* Error factor theory is a specific construct; see, for example, Harlow (51). Though pertinent, a knowledge of error factor theory is not essential for an understanding of the subsequent discussion.

† This is only a half-truth. For any sizeable skill the material must be reduced to constituents that are sequentially rehearsed. But the sequential control programme uses information from the teaching machines that execute it locally.

tasks (52, 53, 54, 55, 56). On the basis of this work it has been possible to estimate proficiencies, correct response rates and cueing parameters that lead to efficient teaching. For example, the numbers inserted in the 'partially adaptive programming system' described earlier in this chapter are all based upon this data.

Adaptive Metasystems in Skill Instruction

In Fig. 11 the interaction between the student and the teaching machine (a form of 'discourse') takes place at the lowest level of

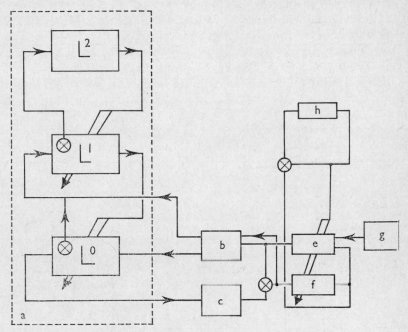

Channel b also conveys a knowledge of results signal as in Fig.2. Instruction signals are not shown.

FIG. 11. A Fully Adaptive Training System

control, L^0. The machine poses problems and the student solves them or tries to do so. But any tutorial conversation is richer than this. The tutor can make comments *about* the L^0 dialogue, and comments that modify the student's learning strategy. In contrast, the present machine can only impose its external teaching strategy by way of an outright edict that replaces the internal learning strategy. Again, in conversation the student can make suggestions with the same calibre as the comments of a tutor, and these (if the tutor weighs them up and thinks them helpful) lead to modifications in the teaching strategy. Obviously, this sort of discourse is at a higher level of control, namely L^1.

A teaching system that embodies the possibility of L^1 interaction is called an 'adaptive metasystem' (because the L^1 statements are metastatements *about* the lowest level discourse). It is a fairly elaborate system, and it is outlined in Fig. 12, b* and c* forming the L^1 channel for student–machine interaction.

Several adaptive metasystems have been built (57, 58), and their performance is impressive, in respect to both motivation and teaching efficiency. Motivation is high because the student engages in an enjoyable game. The increment in efficiency is largely due to the possibility of ironing out inept learning strategies which almost

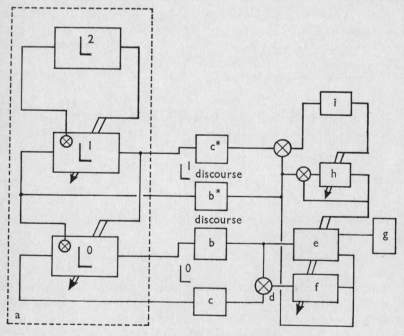

FIG. 12. Adaptive Metasystem

any student is prone to adopt and which he is loath to relinquish (not unnaturally, for he has invested effort in devising the strategy and using it). To effect this sort of control, box i of Fig. 12 must contain an arrangement for carrying out the operations cited below: (1) Discover the current student's learning strategy. (2) Find a set of logically efficient teaching strategies, given a specification of the skill and a learning *model* which is updated by information from this individual. (3) Compare the student's learning strategy (inferred from behaviour or from probability measurements, statements and the like) with the set of efficient teaching strategies. (4) Reach a compromise. (5) Impose the compromise strategy and give the student a (possibly specious) reason why it *is* imposed.

EDUCATION REVISITED

With these ideas from skill-learning in mind, we can return to education (1) disposed to employ individually adaptive systems, and (2) inclined to incorporate higher levels of control or of discourse which, amongst other things, reduce the stringent constraints imposed by a sequential presentation.

Computer Systems

The hardware required in pursuit of (1) has already been mentioned; it is the paraphernalia of a properly used C.A.I. facility. Of course (2) may be fostered in the same medium. For example, the PLATO system is equipped with an inquiry mode in which the student is encouraged to explore his symbolic environment. He can ask for facts and figures, he can obtain statements of more abstract concepts in the same field, and to a limited extent he can change the universe of discourse. In the same vein, Feurzeig and Papert (72), have employed the computer (equipped with a special programming language) as an instrument that children can use to explore mathematical concepts such as recursion. Here, the interface is a simple teletype terminal.

Structural Communication Teaching

But a computer is not strictly necessary. One of the more recent programming techniques, the *structural communication* method of Bennett and Hodgson (59, 68), appears to do all that is needed with paper and pencil (though special purpose teaching devices containing the necessary logical circuits are of great assistance and are widely used). Any study unit (corresponding roughly to a programme segment) consists in the following sections:

1. A *statement* of the author's intention; that is, the underlying concept* and goal.
2. A *viewpoint* which orients the student and leads him to explore the field.
3. A *presentation* of the background material relevant to the concept of the study unit.
4. An *investigation* in which the student is posed certain problems, say five of them.
5. A *solution* phase involving a response *indicator*. This is a page containing statements, say twenty of them, all of which refer to some of the problems. The student tackles each problem in turn and selects statements that he believes to be true.
6. A *discussion* guide. Contingent upon the student's selecting and not selecting certain combinations of statements in the response indicator, he is directed, through a number of stages of analysis, to study certain of the discussion comments which are described below.
7. Discussion *comments* which remedy obvious misconceptions, resolve ambiguities, make statements and encourage the student to justify his point of view. All the comments also direct the student to do something by going back to the problems, the viewpoint or the intention.

Progress through this system is logical and systematic enough. The student adopts some path which is recordable. But he is not held in the strait-jacket of sequential presentation and, broadly speaking, the wiser he is the less restricted he will be. The 'programming scheme', perhaps it would be more accurate to say 'organisation', is applicable to subject matters as diverse as history, art

* The term 'concept' is used in the sense of the present essay. This departs slightly from Bennett and Hodgson's usage.

appreciation, physics and biology. It turns out to be a very efficient teaching system, especially when open-ended thinking is involved.

Other Methods

In conclusion, two other mechanical teaching systems need to be mentioned, though they will not be discussed. The first of these is a system in which students are taught 'as a group'. Communicating through mechanised interfaces, the members of the group are impelled to teach one another (62, 63, 64). Hence the students are the adaptive controllers, and the mechanical part of the system acts as an overall controller that sets up requisite communication pathways.

The other system is a 'game-like' teaching system (65). A computer controls a simulation, for example of an economy. The student is invited to adopt a role and to take part in the simulation.

Motivation Effects

What makes the student stick at his job? Reinforcement and the like may have a local effect both in maintaining attention and in enhancing the learning rate, but the global influences are more subtle and less well understood.

Bruner (66) discusses the matter in a fairly recent paper. Clearly, people have a curiosity drive that impels them to explore their environment. Next, they are motivated by a desire to achieve competence at an *accepted* task (this is closely related to Bartlett's (67) 'search for meaning', and to a hypothesised need to learn how to control novel features of a real or symbolic environment). Finally, students aim to 'identify themselves' with their tutor or (in a group teaching system) another student.

Something is known about the properties required in a teaching situation in order that it shall foster and harness the curiosity and competence drives. Both the group situation and the teaching game just mentioned are very effective instruments, largely because they *do* have the requisite qualities. So far as the conversational systems are concerned, it is possible to go into the matter quite deeply and to winkle out those aspects of student participation that make a major contribution in this respect.

The other global influence, identification, is much more obscure but just as interesting. We have seen that a teaching programme need not be an arid question-and-answer sequence. It can contain broadly stated problem situations and it can be rehearsed quite freely, for example in the C.A.I. inquiry mode. We have also seen that programmes may engender several levels of discourse which reference one another. In this context, it makes sense to ask 'What would it be like to have something in the programme, some symbolic entity, with which the student may want to be identified?' I am not sure of the answer to this question, but it is clearly along the lines of writing some sympathetic 'character' into the programme, analogous to a character in a play. The administration of the programme is, in turn, analogous to the performance of a play, apart from the fact that the student can influence the character and his behaviour. Since identification is one of the strongest motives, this is an area which deserves considerable research.

Choice of a Teaching System

Even a simple linear programmed teaching machine can be expected to do as well as classroom instruction. For a homogeneous population (to which the programme is adapted) and for an inherently conditionable skill, the teaching machine will appreciably reduce learning time (retention being no worse). For heterogeneous populations, for more inquisitive students and more elaborately structured subject matter, a branching programme machine is clearly preferable. This comment applies, *a fortiori*, to C.A.I. systems, which can yield quite dramatic, though not unequivocal, results; maybe halving the learning time. There is some evidence that their main virtue lies in disentangling tangled-up individual learning strategies and, as a result, that they are likely to enjoy differential success. For C.A.I. systems that embody conversational interaction (in the full sense of this essay), it appears that significant learning enhancement demonstrable in the context of a skill sometimes carries over into the academic field, though there is little evidence on this score. In general, it is probably safe to say that teaching machines are *no less effective* than conventional instruction and that C.A.I. systems, almost by definition, are *no less effective* than simple teaching machines.

Of course the choice of a teaching system depends upon its cost, upon the availability of conventional instructors and upon the greater flexibility of operation that is possible (students are not necessarily bound by classrooms and timetables). The cost of simple teaching machines ranges from a few dollars (for trivial paper rolling devices) to $1200 or so. The cost of programming ranges from $3·50 per frame to $35 per frame, depending upon the subject matter, the programme format, the variability in the population and the amount of adaptation carried out before the programme is published. A figure of $7·50 per frame is probably a practical minimum for well-written material.* Since the distribution of a published programme is rather variable it is difficult to estimate the cost of using a teaching machine in terms of student hours. But the price is not horrendous, and the use of these devices can be adequately justified on the grounds of teacher availability (or lack of it) and, in universities or technical training centres, where the course of events is not so rigidly constrained by a timetable, on grounds of flexibility.

Current C.A.I. estimates, based upon expected hours of utilisation, hardware, software and programming costs, indicate that these systems are out of court as schoolroom teaching devices except for special applications. However, in the context of higher education or technical education, it is plausible at the moment to cite $2·61 per student hour (69), which is becoming a reasonably competitive price. Recent reductions in terminal cost and certain simplifications of the equipment lead to expected costs of between $0·80 (70) and $0·13 (71) per student hour, which are very competitive figures indeed.

* Taking account of the fact that many programmes are written in the format of mathetics, structural communication or the hybrid form described under 'A Simple Partially Adaptive Programming System' above.

Bibliography

CHAPTER 2

Glossary

Cerebral dominance	Where one cerebral hemisphere of the brain leads in certain functions such as the learning of language.
Cerebral palsy	Motor dysfunction as a result of brain damage.
Constitution	Biological make-up dependent upon inheritance.
Critical period	A period in an organism's life at which adequate external stimuli are necessary for further maturation.
Dizygotic	Pertaining to a twin pair produced by two eggs (non-identical twins).
Electroencephalogram	A record of electrical activity of the brain.
Kinaesthetic sense	The sensation of movement, the sense organs being in muscles and joints.
Mental defect	Impairment or lack of capacity for intellectual growth and development.
Monozygotic	Pertaining to a twin pair produced by one egg (identical twins).
Organicity	Having an organic origin.
Perceptual-motor function	A co-ordinated activity between sensory modalities and motor function.
Sociopathic	Usually refers to a personality who has persistent difficulties in adjusting to society.
Temporal	Related to time sense.

References and Suggested Reading

1. Thompson, L. J. *Reading Disability* (Illinois: Thomas, 1966).
2. Delacato, C. H. *The Diagnosis and Treatment of Speech and Reading Problems* (Illinois: Thomas, 1967).
3. Money, J. (ed.) *Reading Disability – Progress and Research Needs in Dyslexia* (Baltimore: Johns Hopkins Press, 1962).
4. Critchley, M. *Developmental Dyslexia* (London: Heinemann Medical Books, 1964).
5. Schonell, F. J. *Backwardness in the Basic Subjects* (Edinburgh: Oliver & Boyd, 1962).
6. Prechtl, H. F. R. 'Reading Difficulties as a Neurological Problem in

Childhood', in Money, J. (ed.) *Reading Disabilities* (Baltimore: Johns Hopkins Press, 1962).

7. Westman, J., Arthur, B. and Schiedler, E. 'Reading Retardation and Overview', *Amer. J. Dis. Child*, CIX (1965).

8. Kephart, N. *The Slow Learner in the Classroom* (Columbus: Merrill, 1961).

9. Barnes, D. 'The Poor Reader', in *The Difficult Child*, ed. Roucek, J. (London: Owen, 1966).

10. Jefferies, D. *Illiteracy* (London: Pall Mall Press, 1967).

11. Burt, C. *The Causes and Treatment of Backwardness* (University of London Press, 1952).

12. Monroe, M. *Children Who Cannot Read* (Chicago University Press, 1939).

13. Orton, S. *Reading, Writing and Speech Problems in Children* (New York: Norton, 1937).

14. Vernon, M. D. *Backwardness in Reading* (Cambridge University Press, 1957).

15. Kolson, C. J. and Kaluger, G. *Clinical Aspects of Remedial Reading* (Illinois: Thomas, 1963).

16. Pratt, R. T. C. *The Genetics of Neurological Disorder* (Oxford University Press, 1967).

17. DeKirsch, K., Jansky, J. J. and Langford, W. S. *Predicting Reading Failure* (New York: Harper & Row, 1966).

18. Barrett, T. C. 'Visual Discrimination Tasks as Predictors of First Grade Reading', *Reading Teacher*, XVIII (1965).

19. Castner, B. M. 'Predicting Reading Disability Prior to the First Grade Entrance'. *Amer. J. of Ortho.* V (1935).

20. Frostig, M., Maslow, P. and Leferre, D. W. 'The Marion Frostig Developmental Test of Visual Perception – 1963 Standardization', *Perception and Motor Skills*, XIX (1964).

21. Hermann K., *Reading Disability – Medical Study of Word Blindness and Related Handicaps* (Illinois: Thomas, 1959).

22. Steward, R. S. 'Personality Maladjustment and Reading Achievement', *Amer. J. of Ortho.* XX (1950).

23. Miller, D. R. and Westman, J. C. 'Reading Disability as a condition of Family Stability', *Family Proc.* III (1964).

24. Blanchard, P. 'Psychoanalytic Contributions to the Problem of Reading Disability', *Psychoanal. Study Child*, II (1946).

25. Jersild, A. T. *Meaning of Psychotherapy in a Teacher's Life* (Columbia University Press, 1962).

26. Weisbach, P. T. 'Ophthalmologist's Role in the Management of Dyslexia', *Amer. J. of Ophthal.* LIX (1965).

27. Eisenberg, L. 'Reading Retardation – Psychiatric and Social Aspects', *Pediatrics*, XXXVII (1966).

28. Eisenberg, L. 'Reading Retardation – Psychoeducational Aspects', *Pediatrics*, XXXVII (1966).

29. Benton, A. L. 'Dyslexia in Relation to Form Perception and Directional Sense', in *Reading Disability*, ed. Money, J. (Baltimore: Johns Hopkins Press, 1962).

30. Ilg, F. L. and Ames, L. B. *School Readiness – Behaviour Tests used at the Gesell Institute* (New York: Harper & Row, 1965).

31. McKerrecher, D. M. 'Alleviation of Reading Difficulties by a Simple Operant Conditioning Technique', *J. of Child Psychiat. Psychol. and Allied Sc.* VIII (1967).

32. Eames, T. H. 'The Relationship of Reading to Speech Difficulties', *J. of Educ. Psychol.* XLI (1950).

33. Cruikshank, W., Bentzen, F., Ratzeberg, F. and Tannhauser, M. *A Teaching Method for Brain Injured, and Hyperactive Children* (Syracuse University Press, 1967).

34. Stern, C. and Gould, J. *Children Discover Reading* (London: Harrap, 1966).

35. Strachey, J. 'Unconscious Factors in Reading', *Int. J. Psychoanal.* XI (1930).

36. Moxon, C. *A Remedial Reading Method* (London University Press, 1962).

37. Neale, M. C. *Neale Analysis of Reading Ability* (London University Press, 1958).

38. Schonell, F. J. *Diagnostic and Attainment Testing* (Edinburgh: Oliver & Boyd, 1956).

39. Gates, A. 'The Role of Personality Maladjustment in Reading Disability', *J. of Genetic Psychol.* LIX (1941).

40. Collins, J. L. *The Effects of Remedial Education* (University of Edinburgh Press, Educational Monograph 4, 1961).

41. Sobel, F. S. 'Remedial Teaching as Therapy', *Amer. J. of Psychoanal.* XII (1948).

42. Tuklin, S. H. 'Emotional Factors in Reading Disability in School Children', *J. of Educ. Psychol.* XXVI (1935).

43. Vorhaus, P. 'Rorschach Configurations Associated with Reading Disability', *J. Projective Techniques*, XVI (1952).

44. Belmont, L. 'Lateral Dominance, Lateral Awareness, and Reading Disability', *Child Development*, XXXIV (1965).

45. Benton, A. L., and Kemble, J. 'Right-handed Orientation and Reading Disability', *Psychiatria et Neurologia*, XCIV (1960).

46. Christine, D. and Christine, C. 'The Relation of Auditory Discrimination to Articulatory Defects and Reading Retardation', *Elementary School Journal*, LXV (1964).

47. Silver, A. A. and Hagin, R. A. 'Specific Reading Disability Follow-up Studies', *Amer. J. of Ortho.* XXXIV (1964).

48. Spalding, R. B. and Spalding, W. T. *The Writing Road to Reading* (New York: Whiteside and William Morrow, 1962).

49. Zangwill, O. L. 'Dyslexia in Relation to Cerebral Dominance', in Money, J. (ed.) *Reading Disability* (Baltimore: Johns Hopkins Press, 1962).

50. Orton, S. T. 'Neuropathology Lectures', *Archives Neurol. Psychiat.* (Chicago, 1926).

51. Hallgren, B. 'Specific Dyslexia', *Acta Psychiat. Scan.* Suppl. (1950).

52. Rabinovitch, R. 'Reading and Learning Disabilities', in '*American Handbook of Psychiatry*, ed. Arieta, S. (New York: Basic Books, 1959).

53. Bender, L. *Visual Motor Gestalt Test* (New York: Psychological Corporation, 1946).

54. Benton, A. L. *Benton Visual Retention Test* (New York: Psychological Corporation, 1955).

55. Money, J. (ed.) *The Disabled Reader* (Baltimore: Johns Hopkins Press, 1966).

CHAPTER 3

Suggested Reading

Association of Teachers of Mathematics, *Notes on Mathematics in Primary Schools* (Cambridge University Press, 1967).

Bloom, Benjamin S. (ed.) *Taxonomy of Educational Objectives, Handbook I: Cognitive Domain* (New York: David McKay, 1956).

Bruner, Jerome S. *The Process of Education* (Cambridge, Mass.: Harvard University Press, 1962).

Bruner, Jerome S. *Towards a Theory of Instruction* (Cambridge, Mass.: Harvard University Press, 1966).

Cambridge Conference on School Mathematics, *Goals for School Mathematics* (Boston: Houghton Mifflin, 1963).

Cambridge Conference on Teacher Training, *Goals for Mathematical Education of Elementary School Teachers* (Boston: Houghton Mifflin, 1967).

Central Advisory Council for Education (England), *Children and Their Primary Schools* (London: H.M.S.O. 1967).

Davis, Robert B. *The Changing Curriculum: Mathematics* (Washington: Association for Supervision and Curriculum Development, N.E.A.).

Davis, Robert B. *Discovery in Mathematics: A Text for Teachers* (Addison-Wesley, 1964).

Davis, Robert B. *Explorations in Mathematics: A Text for Teachers* (Addison-Wesley, 1967).

Dienes, Z. P. *Building Up Mathematics* (London: Hutchinson, 1960).

Dienes, Z. P. *Mathematics in the Primary School* (London: Macmillan, 1964).

Flavell, John H. *The Developmental Psychology of Jean Piaget* (Princeton: Van Nostrand, 1963).

Fletcher, T. J. (ed.) *Some Lessons in Mathematics by Members of the Association of Teachers of Mathematics* (Cambridge University Press, 1964).

Goutard, Madelaine, *Mathematics and Children* (Reading: Educational Explorers, 1964).

Holt, John, *How Children Fail* (Pitman, 1964).

International Study Group for Mathematics Learning, *Mathematics in Primary Education* (Hamburg: UNESCO Institute for Education, 1966).

Lockard, J. David (ed.) *Report of the International Clearinghouse on Science and Mathematics Curricular Developments* (American Association for the Advancement of Science and the Science Teaching Center, University of Maryland).

Lovell, K. *The Growth of Basic Mathematical and Scientific Concepts in Children* (University of London Press, 1961).

Schools Council, *Mathematics in Primary Schools. Curriculum Bulletin No. 1* (London: H.M.S.O. 1965).

Scott, Lloyd, *Trends in Elementary School Mathematics* (Chicago: Rand McNally, 1966).

Sealey, Leonard G. W. *The Creative Use of Mathematics in the Junior School* (Oxford: Blackwell, 1960).

Sharpe, Glyn H. *Some Behavioral Objectives for Elementary School Mathematics Programs* (Denver: Colorado State Department of Education, 1966).

Stern, Catherine, *Children Discover Arithmetic* (New York: Harper, 1949).

CHAPTER 4

References

1. Riessman, F. *The Culturally Deprived Child* (New York: Harper, 1962) p. 1.

2. Jensen, A. R. 'The Culturally Disadvantaged, Some Psychological and Educational Aspects', in *Educ. Res.* x 1 (Nov 1967) 5.

3. Vernon, P. E. *The Measurement of Abilities* (U.L.P. 1956).

4. Jensen, A. R. 'Learning Abilities in Retarded, Average and Gifted Children', *Merrill-Palmer Q.* IX (1963) 123-40.

5. Terman, L. M. and Merrill, M. A. *Measuring Intelligence* (Harrap, 1937) pp. 38 ff.

6. Ibid. pp. 29 ff.

7. Barber, W. B. 'Investigation and Diagnosis of the Needs of Educationally Retarded Chidren', in (N.S.S.E.) *The Educationally Retarded and Disadvantaged* (University of Chicago Press, 1967) p. 118.

8. Biesheuvel, S. *African Intelligence* (S.A.R.R. 1943) pp. 201 ff.

9. Rose, B. W. 'Some Educational Aspects of the Non-coping School Child', *S.A. Journal of Science*, LXIII 20 (Feb 1967) 62-7.

10. Haggard, E. A. 'Social Status and Intelligence', *Genetic Psychology Monographs*, XLIX (1954) 141-156.

11. Bossio, V. 'Intellectual, Emotional and Social Development of Deprived Children', in *Vita Humana*, I 2 (1958) 65-92.

12. Jensen, in *Educ. Res.* x 1 (Nov 1967) 8.

13. Riessman, *The Culturally Deprived Child*, p. 56.

14. Chauncey, H. *Report of the President, 1962-1963* (Princeton, N.J.: Educational Testing Service Annual Reports, 1962-3) p. 17.

15. Silberman, C. E. *Crisis in Black and White Cape* (London, 1964) pp. 278 ff.

16. Goldfarb, W. 'The Effect of Early Institutional Care on Adolescent Personality', *Child Development*, XIV (1943) 213-23.

17. French, E. L. *Psychological Factors in Cases of Reading Disability* (Devereux Reports, U.S.A., n/d) p. 2.

18. Douglas, J. W. B. *The Home and the School* (McGibbon & Kee, 1964).

19. Davis, A. *Social Class Influences upon Learning* (Harvard University Press, 1948).

20. Bernstein, B. 'Social Class and Linguistic Development', in *Education, Economy and Society*, ed. Hasley, A. H. *et al.* (New York: 1961) pp. 288-314.

21. Piaget, J. *The Language and Thought of the Child* (Kegan Paul, Trench Trubner, 1932) p. 184.

22. Riessman, *The Culturally Deprived Child*, p. 54.

23. *Children and their Primary Schools* (H.M.S.O. 1967) 1 23.

24. Haggard, E. A. in *Genetic Psychology Monographs*, XLIX.

25. Riessman, *The Culturally Deprived Child*, p. 84.

26. Bereiter, C. and Engelmann, S. *Teaching Disadvantaged Children in the Preschool* (Englewood Cliffs, N.J.: Prentice-Hall, 1966).

27. McCarthy, D. 'Language Development in Children', in Carmichael, L. (ed.) *Manual of Child Psychology* (New York: Wiley) pp. 467 ff.

28. Jensen, in *Educ. Res.* x 1 (Nov 1967) 14.

29. Bernstein, in *Education, Economy and Society*, ed. Hasley, p. 292.

30. Lawton, D. 'Social Class Differences in Language Development', *Language and Speech*, VI (July-Sept 1963) 120-43.

31. Bernstein, B. 'Social Class, Speech Systems and Psycho-Therapy', in *British J. of Sociology*, XV 1 (1964) 54-64.

32. Hess, D. and Shipman, V. 'Early Blocks to Children's Learning', *Children*, XII 189-94.

33. Flavell, J. H. *The Developmental Psychology of Jean Piaget* (New York: Van Nostrand, 1963) p. 242.

34. Mussen, P. H. *The Psychological Development of the Child* (Prentice-Hall, 1963) p. 12.

35. Kirk, S. A. *Early Education of the Retarded Child, An Experimental Study* (University of Illinois Press, 1958).

36. *Children and their Primary Schools* (H.M.S.O. 1967) par. 70.

37. Deutsch, M. 'The Disadvantaged Child and the Learning Process', in *Education in Disadvantaged Areas*, ed. Passow, A. H. (New York: Columbia Teachers College, 1963).

38. *Deprivation of Maternal Care* (Geneva: W.H.O. 1960).

39. Flavell, *The Developmental Psychology of Jean Piaget*, p. 84.

40. Deutsch, in *Education in Disadvantaged Areas*, ed. Passow, p. 170.

41. Flavell, *The Developmental Psychology of Jean Piaget*, pp. 164 ff.

42. Deutsch, in *Education in Disadvantaged Areas*, ed. Passow, p. 171.

43. Flavell, *The Developmental Psychology of Jean Piaget*, p. 367.

44. Bullock, H. A. 'A Comparison of the Academic Achievements of White and Negro High School Graduates', *J. Educ. Res.* XLIV (1950) 179-92.

45. Osborne, R. T. 'Racial Differences in Mental Growth and School Achievement', *Psych. Reps*, VII (1960) 233-9.

46. McBroom, E. 'The Importance of Social and Economic Conditions on Human Development', in *Headstart in Action* (Parker, 1967) p. 204.

47. Silberman, C. E. *Crisis in Black and White* (London: Cape, 1965).

48. Stallings, F. H. 'A Study of the Immediate Effects of Integration on

Scholastic Achievement in Louiseville Public Schools', *J. Negro Education*, XXVIII (1959) 439-44.

49. Lazarus, R. S. *Adjustment and Personality* (New York: McGraw-Hill, 1961).

50. Coles, R. *Desegregation in a Southern School, A Psychiatric Study* (New York: Anti-defamation League, 1963).

51. Lazarus, R. S. *et al.* 'The Effects of Psychological Strain upon Performance', *Psychol. Bull.* XLIV (1952) 293-317.

52. Roberts, S. O. 'Test Performance in Relation to Ethnic Group and Social Class' (Nashville: Fisk University, Report 1963, mimeo).

53. Silberman, *Crisis in Black and White*, p. 260.

54. *Children and their Primary Schools* (H.M.S.O. 1967) II app. 12.

55. Gordon, H. *Mental and Scholastic Tests among Retarded Children* (H.M.S.O. Educational Pamphlet No. 44, 1923).

56. Ashe, E. J. 'The Inadequacy of Current Intelligence Tests for Testing Kentucky Mountain Children', *J. Genetic Psychol.* XLVI (1935) 480-6.

57. Ausubel, D. P., p. 18.

58. Smilansky, M. 'Fighting Deprivation in the Promised Land', in *Jewish Affairs* (Johannesburg, May 1968) 9-14.

59. Ausubel, ibid.

60. Olsen, J. L. and Larson, R. G. 'An Experimental Curriculum for Culturally Deprived Kindergarten Children', in *Educational Leadership* (May 1963) 553-8.

61. Sears, P. S. and Dowley, E. M. 'Research on Teaching in the Nursery School', in Gage, N. L. (ed.) *Handbook of Research on Teaching* (Chicago: Rand McNally, 1963).

62. Fowler, W. 'Cognitive Learning in Infancy and Early Childhood', *Psychol. Bull.* LIX 116-52.

63. *Children and their Primary Schools* (1967) p. 63.

64. Smilansky, in *Jewish Affairs* (May 1968).

65. Fantini, M. D. and Weinstein, G. 'Taking Advantage of the Disadvantaged', *The Record*, LXIX 2 (Nov 1967) 103-14.

66. *Britain, an Official Handbook* (H.M.S.O. 1968); Horrell, H. *Survey of Race Relations in S.A., 1967* (S.A.I.R.R. 1968); *Survey of Commerce and Business* (U.S. Dept. of Commerce, 1968).

67. Gray, S. W. and Klaus, R. A. 'Interim Report of the Third Year of an Intervention Project (Peabody College) with Young, Culturally Deprived Children etc.', in *Child Development*, XXXVI (1965) 887-8.

68. Irwin, R. in McCandless, B. R. (ed.) *Children and Adolescents – Behaviour and Development* (Holt, Rinehart & Winston, 1961) p. 260.

69. Bloom, B. S., Davis, A. and Hess, R. *Compensatory Education for Cultural Deprivation* (Holt, Rinehart & Winston, 1965).

70. Riessman, *The Culturally Deprived Child*, p. 1.

71. Frost, J. E. and Hawkes, G. R. *The Disadvantaged Child* (Houghton Mifflin, 1966).

72. Deutsch, M. 'Nursery Education: The influence of Social Programming on Early Development', in *Journal of Nursery Education* (April 1963) 191-7.

CHAPTER 5

Suggested Reading

Rogers, E. M. *Physics for the Inquiring Mind* (Oxford University Press and Princeton University Press, 1960).
Nuffield Science Teaching Project: Some sixty volumes, published by Longmans/Penguins for their physics, chemistry and biology courses.
O.E.C.D. *Chemistry Today* (Paris: O.E.C.D. 1963).
O.E.C.D. *Teaching Physics Today* (Paris: O.E.C.D. 1965).
Physical Sciences Study Committee, *Physics* (Boston, Mass.: Heath).

CHAPTER 6

Suggested Reading

Allen, Harold B. *Teaching English as a Second Language: A Book of Readings* (New York: McGraw-Hill, 1965).
Brooks, Nelson, *Language and Language Learning: Theory and Practice*, 2nd ed. (New York: Harcourt, Brace & World, 1964).
Chomsky, N. *Syntactic Structures* (The Hague: Mouton, 1957).
Dacanay, Fe R. *Techniques and Procedures in Second Language Teaching* (Manila: Phoenix, 1963).
Fries, Charles C. *Teaching and Learning English as a Foreign Language* (Ann Arbor: University of Michigan Press, 1948).
Gleason, H. A., Jr, *An Introduction to Descriptive Linguistics*, 2nd rev. ed. (New York: Holt, 1961).
Gurrey, P. *Teaching English as a Foreign Language* (London: Longmans, 1955).
Halliday, M. A. K., McIntosh, A. and Strevens, P. *The Linguistic Sciences and Language Teaching* (London: Longmans, 1964).
Mackey, William F. *Language Teaching Analysis* (Indiana University Press, 1967).
Moulton, William G. *Linguistic Guide to Language Learning* (New York: Modern Language Association, 1966).
Prator, Clifford H. *Manual of American English Pronunciation*, rev. ed. (New York: Holt, Rinehart & Winston, 1957).
Rivers, Wilga, *The Psychologist and the Foreign Language Teacher* (University of Chicago Press, 1964).
Rivers, Wilga, *Teaching Foreign-Language Skills* (University of Chicago Press, 1968).
Rutherford, William E. *Modern English: A Textbook for Foreign Students* (New York: Harcourt, Brace & World, 1968).
Stevick, Earl W. *A Workbook in Language Teaching* (New York: Abingdon Press, 1963).
West, Michael, *Teaching English in Difficult Circumstances* (London: Longmans, 1960).

CHAPTER 7

Suggested Reading

Brethower, D. M., Markle, D. G. *et al. Programmed Learning: A Practicum* (Michigan: Ann Arbor Publishers, 1965).

Cavanagh, P. and Jones, C. *Programmes in Print* (London: Association for Programmed Learning, 1966) (Supplements appear in *New Education*).

Leith, G. O. M. *A Handbook of Programmed Learning*, 2nd ed. (University of Birmingham, Educational Review Occasional Publications No. 1, 1966).

Mager, R. *Preparing Objectives for Instruction* (San Francisco: Fearon, 1960).

Markle, Susan M. *Good Frames and Bad: A Grammar of Frame Writing* (London: Wiley, 1964).

National Centre for Programmed Learning *Programmed Learning – A Symposium* (London: National Committee for Audio Visual Aids in Education, 1966).

Taber, J. I., Glaser R. and Schaeffer, H. H. *Learning and Programmed Instruction* (Reading, Mass.: Addison-Wesley, 1965).

Tobin, M. J. (ed.) *Problems and Methods in Programmed Learning*, parts 1–5 (University of Birmingham, National Centre for Programmed Learning, 1967).

References

1. Amaria, Roda P., Biran, L. A. and Leith, G. O. M. 'Individual versus Cooperative Learning, I: Influence of Intelligence and Sex', *Educ. Res.* XI (1969) 95–103.

2. Angell, G. W. and Lumsdaine, A. A. *Prompted plus unprompted Trials versus Prompted Trials Alone* (Pittsburgh: American Institutes for Research, 1960).

3. Ausubel, D. *The Psychology of Meaningful Verbal Learning* (New York: Grune & Stratton, 1963).

4. Biran, L. A. Unpublished research, National Centre for Programmed Learning, University of Birmingham, 1966.

5. Biran, L. A., Gregory, P. and Leith, G. O. M. Unpublished research, National Centre for Programmed Learning, University of Birmingham, 1966.

6. Biran, L. A. and Pickering, E. 'Unscrambling a Herringbone: An Experimental Evaluation of Branching Programming', *Brit, J. Med. Educ.* II (1968) 213–19.

7. Bloom, Benjamin, *et al. Taxonomy of Educational Objectives, Handbook I: Cognitive Domain* (New York: Longmans, 1956).

8. Bruner, J. S. 'The Act of Discovery', *Harvard Educ. Rev.* XXXI (1961) 21–32.

9. Bryan, G. L. and Rigney, J. W. *An Evaluation of a Method for Shipboard Training in Operations Knowledge* (University of Southern California, Tech. Rep. No. 18, Electronics Personnel, 1956).

10. Carpenter, C. R. and Greenhill, L. P. *Comparative Research on Methods and Media for Presenting Programmed Courses in Mathematics and English* (Pennsylvania State University, 1963).

11. Dietze, D. 'The Facilitating Effect of Words on Discrimination and Generalization', *J. Exper. Psychol.* L (1955) 255-60.

12. Duncan, K. D. and Gilbert, T. 'Effects of Omitting Branches and Questions from a Scrambled Text', *Brit. J. Educ. Psychol.* XXXVII (1967) 314-19.

13. Elley, W. B. 'The Role of Errors in Learning with Feedback', *Brit. J. Educ. Psychol.* XXXVI (1966) 296-300.

14. Entwistle, G. and Entwistle, D. R. 'The Use of a Digital Computer as a Teaching Machine', *J. Medic. Educ.* XXXVIII (1963) 803-11.

15. Evans, J. L., Glaser, R. and Homme, L. E. 'The Ruleg System for the Construction of Programmed Verbal Learning Sequences', *J. Educ. Res.* LV (1962) 513-18.

16. Fleming, M. L. *Influence of Three Teaching Machine Factors – Feedback to Programmer, Participation by Learner and Feedback to Learner – on the Production and Utilization of Science Films* (Audio-Visual Centre, School of Education, Indiana University).

17. Gagné, R. M. and Bassler, O. C. 'Study of Retention of Some Topics of Elementary Non Metric Geometry', *J. Educ. Psychol.* LIV (1963) 123-31.

18. Galperin, P. Ya. and Talyzina, N. F. 'Formation of Elementary Geometrical Concepts and their Dependence on Directed Participation by the Pupils', in O'Connor, N. (ed.) *Recent Soviet Psychology* (Oxford: Pergamon Press, 1961).

19. Gilbert, T. F. 'Mathetics: The Technology of Education', *J. Mathetics,* I (1962) 7-73.

20. Grimes, J. W. and Allinsmith, W. 'Compulsivity, Anxiety and School Achievement', *Merrill-Palmer Quart.* VII (1961) 427-71.

21. Harlow, H. F. 'The Formation of Learning Sets', *Psychol. Rev.* LVI (1949) 51-65.

22. Hildreth, G. 'The Difficulty Reduction Tendency in Perception and Problem Solving', *J. Educ. Psychol.* XXXII (1942) 305-13.

23. Jones, C. H. and Leith, G. O. M. 'Programming an Aspect of Reading Readiness', *Remed. Educ.* I (1966) 5-8.

24. Kersh, B. Y. *Directed Discovery vs. Programed Instruction: A Test of a Theoretical Position involving Educational Technology* (Monmouth, Oregon: Teaching Research, Oregon State System of Higher Education).

25. Kimble, G. A. and Wulff, J. J. 'Response Guidance as a Factor in the Value of Audience Participation in Training Film Instruction', in Lumsdaine, A. A. (ed.) *Student Response in Programmed Instruction* (Washington, D.C.: National Academy of Sciences, 1961).

26. Kiss, G. and Biran, L. A. Unpublished data summarised in Leith, G. O. M. *Abstracts of Research* (National Centre for Programmed Learning, University of Birmingham).

27. Leith, G. O. M. 'An Evaluation of Programmed Learning in a College of Further Education' (unpublished research, 1966).

28. Leith, G. O. M. 'An Investigation of the Role of Stimulus and Response Meaningfulness in Verbal Learning', *Programmed Learning and Educational Technology,* IV (1967) 284-9.

29. Leith, G. O. M. 'Learning and Personality', in *Aspects of Educational Technology*, II (London: Methuen, 1969).

30. Leith, G. O. M. 'The Effects of Vicarious Practice and Feedback on Performance in a Kinaesthetic Learning task', *Atlantic Psychologist* (to appear).

31. Leith, G. O. M., Amaria, Roda P. and Williams, H. *Applications of Programmed Learning Principles to the Preparation of Television Lessons in Elementary Science and Mathematics* (Report to the Nuffield Foundation, Resources for Learning Projects, 1968).

32. Leith, G. O. M., Biran, L. A. and Oppollot, J. 'The Place of Review in Meaningful Verbal Learning Sequences', *Canad. J. Behav. Sc.* (in press).

33. Leith, G. O. M. and Burke, K. M. 'Mode of Responding and Redundancy', *Programmed Learning and Educ. Technol.* IV (1967) 10-15.

34. Leith, G. O. M. and Clarke, W. D. *Transfer of Learning as a Function of Task Variation* (National Centre for Programmed Learning, University of Birmingham, Research Reports No. 22 1967).

35. Leith, G. O. M. and Davies, D. F. 'Interference and Facilitation in a Programmed Learning Task', *Programmed Learning*, III (1966) 154-62.

36. Leith, G. O. M. and Eastment, D. E. *A Study of Prompting versus Confirmation in Machine and Text-Presented Programmed Learning under Two Conditions of Responding* (National Centre for Programmed Learning, University of Birmingham, Research Reports No. 15, 1967).

37. Leith, G. O. M. and Ghuman, A. S. 'The Effects of Prompting and Confirmation on Two Methods of Responding to a Self-Instructional Programme on Coordinate Geometry', *Programmed Learning and Educ. Technol.* IV (1967) 15-19.

38. Leith, G. O. M. and Gordon, M. *The Role of Overt Reinforced Practice in Classroom Learning* (National Centre for Programmed Learning, University of Birmingham, Research Reports No. 2, 1965).

39. Leith, G. O. M., Lister, A., Teall, C. and Bellingham, J. 'Teaching the New Decimal Currency by Programmed Instruction', *Industrial Training International*, III (1968) 424-7.

40. Leith, G. O. M. and McHugh, G. A. R. 'The Place of Theory in Consecutive Conceptual Learning', *Educ. Rev.* XIX (1967) 110-17.

41. Leith, G. O. M. and Webb, C. C. 'A Comparison of Four Methods of Programmed Instruction with and without Teacher Intervention', *Educ. Rev.* XXI (1968) 25-31.

42. Leith, G. O. M. and Wildbore, 'Schedules of Responding' (National Cen. for Programmed Learning, University of Birmingham, unpublished, 1967).

43. Ling, Chu Poh, 'Self-Instruction in Geography – An Approach in the Teaching of Geography with Reference to Malaysia' (B.Ed. dissertation, Education Faculty, University of Malaya, 1967).

44. May, M. A. and Lumsdaine, A. A. *Learning from Films* (New Haven: Yale University Press, 1958).

45. McMullen, F. Unpublished Dip. Ed. Dissertation, School of Education, University of Birmingham, 1967.

46. Meddleton, I. G. 'An Experimental Investigation into the Systematic Teaching of Number Concepts', *Brit. J. Educ. Psychol.* XXVI (1956) 117-27.

47. Middleton, R. G. 'The Effects of Size of Step on Programmed Learning Using a Spelling Programme', *Educ. Rev.* XVI 99-108.

48. National Centre for Programmed Learning, programmes prepared by teachers during courses on programming techniques given by N.C.P.L.

49. National Centre for Programmed Learning, *A Selection of Technical Reports on Teaching Machines* (London: National Committee for Audio-Visual Aids in Education, Working Paper No. 2, 1968).

50. National Society for the Study of Education, 'The Measurement of Understanding', *The Forty-Fifth Yearbook* part I (University of Chicago Press, 1946).

51. Newark, J. H. *Improved Quality Control at J. R. Freeman* (Oxford: Pergamon Press, Programmed Instruction in Industry, II 1, 1968).

52. Orlov, K. Contribution to UNESCO Seminar on Programmed Instruction, Varna, Bulgaria, August 1968.

53. Oldfield, W. J. *Individual versus Group Methods in Programmed Instruction* (National Centre for Programmed Learning, University of Birmingham, Research Reports No. 1, 1964).

54. Pressey, S. L. 'Development and Appraisal of Devices Providing Automatic Scoring of Objective Tests and Concomitant Self-Instruction', *J. Psychol.* XXIX (1950) 417-7.

55. Rowntree, D. *Basically Branching* (London: MacDonald, 1967).

56. Schuffenhauer, H. Oral report, Seminar on Programmed Instruction, Varna, Bulgaria, August 1968.

57. Seidel, R. J. and Rotberg, I. C. 'Effects of Written Verbalisation and Timing of Information on Problem-Solving in Programmed Learning', *J. Educ. Psychol.* LVII (1966) 151-8.

58. Skinner, B. F. *Science and Human Behavior* (New York: Macmillan, 1953).

59. Skinner, B. F. 'The Art of Teaching and the Science of Learning', *Harvard. Educ. Rev.* XXIV (1954) 86-96.

60. Spiker, C. C. 'Effects of Stimulus Similarity on Discrimination Learning', *J. Exper. Psychol.* LVII (1956) 393-5.

61. Szekely, L. 'Productive Processes in Learning and Thinking', *Acta Psychologica*, VII (1950) 388-407.

62. Taber, J. I. and Glaser, R. 'An Exploratory Evaluation of a Discrimination Transfer Learning Program Using Literal Prompts', *J. Educ. Res.* LV (1962) 508-12.

63. Thomas, C. A. *et al. Programmed Learning in Perspective* (London: City Publicity Services, 1963).

64. Tiemann, P. W., Paden, D. W. and McIntyre, C. J. *An Application of the Principles of Programmed Instruction to a Televised Course in College Economics* (Urbana: University of Illinois, 1966).

65. Tobin, M. J. 'Teaching Machines in Programmed Instruction', UNESCO Working Paper, Seminar on Programmed Instruction, Varna, Bulgaria, August 1968.

66. Tobin, M. J., Biran, L. A. and Waller, J. A. F. *A Study of Audio-Visual Programmed Learning in Primary Schools* (National Centre for Programmed Learning, University of Birmingham, Research Reports No. 29, 1968).

67. Torrance, E. P. and Gupta, R. *Programmed Experiences in Creative Thinking* (Bureau of Educational Research, University of Minnesota, 1964).

68. Tyler, R. W. 'The Functions of Measurement in Improving Instruction', in Lindquist, E. F. (ed.) *Educational Measurement* (Washington D.C.: American Council on Education, 1951).

69. Van Wagenen, R. K. and Travers, R. M. W. 'Learning under Conditions of Direct and Vicarious Reinforcement', *J. Educ. Psychol.* LIV (1963) 356-62.

70. Wallis, D., Duncan, K. D. and Knight, M. A. G. *Programmed Instruction in the British Armed Forces* (London: H.M.S.O. 1966).

71. Walther, R. E. and Crowder, N. *A Guide to Preparing Intrinsically Programmed Instructional Materials* (Springfield, Virginia: Clearinghouse for Federal Scientific and Technical Information, 1965).

CHAPTER 8

Suggested Reading

Anastasi, Anne, *Differential Psychology* (New York: Macmillan, 1958). An excellent introductory text to the nature and measurement of individual differences, and particularly good in the treatment of intellectual functioning.

Annual Review of Psychology (Palo Alto, Calif.: Annual Reviews, Inc.). An excellent yearly publication which regularly includes a section dealing with intellectual ability and other aspects of developmental psychology, as well as recent investigations in neurobiology and biochemistry.

Eysenck, H. J. 'Intelligence Assessment: A Theoretical and Experimental Approach', *British Journal of Educational Psychology*, XXXVII (1967). A concise summary of past research in intelligence as well as a critical look at some contemporary contributions; for example, Guilford's.

Flavell, J. H. *The Developmental Psychology of Jean Piaget* (Princeton: Van Nostrand, 1963). An excellent summary of Piaget's presentation of ideas concerning the development of understanding in the child. A good book for those interested in Piaget.

Guilford, J. P. 'Intelligence: 1965 Model', *American Psychologist*, XXI (1966) 20-6. Guilford presents his modification of the structure of the intellect model. Excellent for the student desiring more information concerning Guilford's model.

Haimowitz, Morris L. and Haimowitz, Natalie Reader (eds) *Human Development: Selected Readings* (New York: Crowell, 1966). This book of readings contains several reprints of key articles by such current thinkers as Guilford, Piaget and Bruner, as well as many other articles dealing with the development of intelligence.

Herrnstein, Richard J. and Boring, Edward G. *A Source Book in the History of Psychology* (Cambridge, Mass.: Harvard University Press, 1966) ch. XI, pp. 407-53. Another comprehensive source book which permits the examination of selected authors' original views concerning intelligence: ch. XI is particularly useful.

Jenkins, James J. and Paterson, Donald G. *Studies in Individual Differences: The Search for Intelligence* (New York: Appleton-Century-Crofts, 1961). A most comprehensive source book for examining the writings of many traditional authorities, early leaders, and contemporary theorists. Essential for the student desiring a further exposition of intelligence.

National Society for the Study of Education, *Intelligence: Its Nature and Nurture*, part I: 'Comparative and Critical Exposition' (Public School Publishing, 1940). Summarises in symposium style some of the early work in the investigation of intelligence from a more technical viewpoint. For the student interested in an in-depth study of intelligence.

References

1. Eysenck, H. J. 'Intelligence Assessment: A Theoretical and Experimental Approach', *British Journal of Educational Psychology*, XXXVII (1967) 81-98.

2. Terman, L. M. 'Intelligence and Its Measurement', *Journal of Educational Psychology*, XII (1921) 127-33.

3. Munn, Norman L. *The Evolution and Growth of Human Behavior* (Boston: Houghton Mifflin, 1965) p. 409.

4. Ibid.

5. Binet, Alfred and Simon, Theophile, 'The Development of Intelligence in Children', *Studies in Individual Differences*, ed. Jenkins, James J. and Paterson, Donald G. (New York: Appleton-Century-Crofts, 1961) pp. 81-111.

6. Baller, Warren and Charles, Don C. *The Psychology of Human Growth and Development* (New York: Holt, Rinehart & Winston, 1968) p. 246.

7. Terman, in *Journal of Educational Psychology*, XII.

8. Spearman, Charles, 'The Abilities of Man', *Studies in Individual Differences*, ed. Jenkins and Paterson, pp. 241-67.

9. Cattell, R. B. 'Theory of Fluid and Crystallized Intelligence: A Critical Experiment', *Journal of Educational Psychology*, LIV (1963) 1-22.

10. Thorndike, E. L. 'Intelligence and Its Measurement', *Journal of Educational Psychology*, XII (1921) 123-47.

11. Guilford, J. P. 'Intelligence: 1965 Model', *American Psychologist*, XXI (1966) 20-6.

12. Munn, *The Evolution and Growth of Human Behavior*, p. 35.

13. Burt, Cyril, 'The Inheritance of Mental Ability', *American Psychologist*, XIII (1958) 1-15.

14. Newman, H. H., Freeman, F. N. and Holzinger, K. J. *Twins: A Study of Heredity and Environment* (University of Chicago Press, 1937).

15. Skodak, M. and Skeels, H. M. 'A Final Follow-up Study of One Hundred Adopted Children', *Journal of Genetic Psychology*, LXXV (1949) 85-125.

16. Skeels, H. M. 'Adult Status of Children With Contrasting Early Life Styles', *Monograph of Social Research for Child Development* (University of Chicago Press, 1966).

17. Reymert, M. L. and Hinton, R. T. ('The Effect of Change to a Relatively Superior Environment upon the I.Q.'s of 1,000 Children', *The Thirty-Ninth Yearbook of the National Society for the Study of Education*, part II (University of Chicago Press, 1940) pp. 255-68.

18. Bayley, Nancy, 'Some Increasing Parent–Child Similarities during the Growth of Children', *Journal of Educational Psychology*, XLV (1954) 1-21.

19. Honzik, Marjorie, 'A Sex Difference in the Onset of the Parent–Child Resemblance in Intelligence', *Journal of Educational Psychology*, LIV (1963) 231-7.

20. Combs, Arthur W. 'Intelligence From a Perceptual Point of View', *Journal of Abnormal and Social Psychology*, XLVII (July 1952) 662-73.

21. Eells, K. *Intelligence and Cultural Differences* (University of Chicago Press, 1959).

22. Dreger, R. M. and Miller, K. S. 'Comparative Psychological Studies of Negroes and Whites in the United States', *Psychological Bulletin*, LVII (1960) 361-402.

23. Edwards, A. J. and Kirby, Elsie M. 'Predictive Efficiency of Intelligence Test Scores: Intelligence Quotients Obtained in Grade One and Achievement Test Scores Obtained in Grade Three', *Educational and Psychological Measurement*, XXIV (1964) 941-6.

24. Taft, Ronald, 'Predicting School Examination Results by Tests of Intelligence and Creativity', *Australian Journal of Education*, II (1967) 126-33.

25. Kunce, Joseph, Rankin, L. S. and Clement, Elaine, 'Maze Performance and Personal, Social, and Economic Adjustment of Alaskan Natives', *Journal of Social Psychology*, LXXIII (1967) 37-45.

26. Vernon, Philip E. 'Administration of Group Intelligence Tests to East African Pupils', *British Journal of Educational Psychology*, XXXVII (1967) 282-91.

27. Terman, L. M. and Merrill, Maud A. 'Measuring Intelligence', *Studies in Individual Differences*, ed. Jenkins and Paterson, pp. 449-67.

28. Honzik, Marjorie, Macfarlane, Jean W. and Allen, L. 'The Stability of Mental Test Performance Between Two and Eighteen Years', *Journal of Experimental Education*, XVII (1948) 309-24.

29. Ibid.

30. Owens, W. A. 'Age and Mental Abilities: A Second Look, *Journal of Educational Psychology*, LVII (1966) 311-25.

31. Bradway, Katherine, and Robinson, Nancy, 'Significant I.Q. Changes in Twenty-Five Years', *Journal of Educational Psychology*, LII (1961) 74-9

32. Bayley, Nancy, 'Mental Growth During the First Three Years', *Genetic Psychology Monographs*, XIV (1933) 1-92.

33. Wiener, G., Rider, R. and Oppel, W. 'Some Correlates of I.Q. Change in Children', *Child Development*, XXXIV (1963) 61-7.

34. Asher, E. U. 'The Inadequacy of Current Intelligence Tests for Testing Kentucky Mountain Children', *Journal of Genetic Psychology*, XLVI (1935) 480-6.

35. Terman, L. M. *Genetic Studies of Genius* (Stanford University Press, 1959) vols I–V.

36. Varma, R. M., Surya, N. C., Jindal, R. C. and Gupta, S. C. 'Investigation of Headache Cases', *Transactions of All India Institute of Mental Health*, V (1965) 6-21, as reported in *Psychological Abstracts*, XL (1966) 744.

37. Bloom, B. A. *Stability and Change in Human Characteristics* (New York: Wiley, 1964) p. 68.

38. Harms, Ernest, 'A Differential Consideration of the Problems of Adolescence', *International Mental Hygiene Research Newsletter*, III (1961) 3-6.

39. Gordon, Edward M. and Thomas, Alexander, 'Children's Behavioral Style and Teacher's Appraisal of Their Intelligence', *Journal of School Psychology*, V (1967) 292-300.

40. Haywood, H. Carl, 'Motivational Orientation of Overachieving and Underachieving Elementary School Children', *American Journal of Mental Deficiency*, LXXII (1968) 662-7.

41. Russell, D. H. *Children's Thinking* (Boston: Ginn, 1956).

42. Inhelder, Barbel, and Piaget, Jean, *The Growth of Logical Thinking from Childhood to Adolescence* (New York: Basic Books, 1958).

43. Ibid.

44. Ibid.

45. Ibid.

46. Hunt, J. McV. *Intelligence and Experience* (New York: Ronald Press, 1961).

47. Wallach, M. A. 'Research on Child Thinking', *The Sixty-Second Yearbook of the National Society for the Study of Education*, part I (University of Chicago Press, 1963) pp. 238-40.

48. Jean Piaget, as interpreted by Baldwin, Alfred L. 'Cognition in Childhood', *Human Development: Selected Readings*, ed. Haimowitz, Morris L. and Haimowitz, Natalie Reader (New York: Crowell, 1966) pp. 276-85.

49. Smedslund, J. 'The Acquisition of Conservation of Substance and Weight in Children: External Reinforcement of Conservation of Weight and of the Operations of Addition and Subtraction', *Scandanavian Journal of Psychology*, II (1961) 71-84.

50. Whowill, J. F. 'A Study of the Development of the Number Concept by Scalogram Analysis', *Journal of Genetic Psychology*, XCVI (1960) 348-77.

51. Elkind, David, 'Giant in the Nursery – Jean Piaget', *New York Times Magazine*, 26 May 1968, pp. 25-7, 50-62, 77-80.

52. Ibid.

53. Bruner, Jerome S. 'The Course of Cognitive Growth', *Human Development: Selected Readings*, ed. Haimowitz and Haimowitz, pp. 285-300.

54. Ibid.

55. Bruner, Jerome S. 'Learning and Thinking', *Harvard Educational Review*, XXIX (1958) 184-92.

56. Bruner, Jerome S. *On Knowing* (Cambridge: Harvard University Press, 1962).

57. Rosenzweig, Mark R. and Leiman, Arnold L. 'Brain Function', *Annual Review of Psychology*, XIX (1968) 55.

58. Flexner, J. B., Flexner, L. B. and Stellar, E. 'Memory in Mice as Affected by Intracerebral Puromycin', *Science*, CXLI (1963) 57-9.

59. IDEA Occasional Paper, 'The Chemistry of Learning', *Education Digest*, XXXIII (Nov 1967) 20-3.

60. Agranoff, B. W., Davis, R. E. and Brink, J. J. 'Memory Fixation in the Goldfish', *Brain Research*, I (1966) 303-10.

K

61. IDEA Occasional Paper, in *Education Digest*, XXXIII.
62. Ibid.
63. Ibid.
64. Gilgash, Curtis A. 'Glutamic Acid: Its Effect on the Mental Functioning of Adult Male Retardates', *Science Education*, LI (1967) 324-7.
65. McConnell, J. V. 'Memory Transfer Through Cannibalism in Planarium', *Journal of Neuropsychiatry*, III (1962) 542-8.
66. Perlman, David, 'The Search for the Memory Molecule', *New York Times Magazine*, 7 July 1968, pp. 8-9, 33-7.
67. Hartry, A. L., Lee, P. Keith, and Morton, W. D. 'Planaria: Memory Transfer Through Cannibalism Reexamined', *Science*, CXLVI (1964) 274-5.
68. IDEA Occasional Paper, in *Education Digest*, XXXIII 23.

CHAPTER 9

References

Bavelas, A. A. (1948): 'A Mathematical Model for Group Structures', *Applied Anthropology*, VII (1948) 3 16-30.
Bavelas, A. A. (1950): 'Communication Patterns in Task-Orientated Groups', in Cartwright, D. and Zander, A. *Group Dynamics* (London: Tavistock, 1950; 2nd ed. 1960).
Bion, W. R. (1961): *Experiences in Groups and Other Papers* (London: Tavistock, 1961).
Blau, P. M. and Scott, W. R. (1963): *Formal Organizations* (London: Routledge & Kegan Paul, 1963).
Borgatta, E. F. (1960): 'Small Group Research', *Current Sociology*, IX 3 (1960).
Cartwright, D. and Zander, A. (eds) (1960): *Group Dynamics*, 2nd ed. (London: Tavistock, 1960).
Deutsch, M. A. (1949): 'An Experimental Study of the Effects of Co-operation and Competition upon Group Process', *Human Relations*, II (1949) 199-232.
Deutsch, M. A. (1954): 'Field Theory in Social Psychology', in Lindzey, G. (ed.) *Handbook of Social Psychology* (Cambridge, Mass: Addison-Wesley, 1954).
Etzioni, A. (1961): *A Comparative Analysis of Complex Organisations* (Glencoe: Free Press, 1961).
Evans, K. M. (1962): *Sociometry and Education* (London: Routledge & Kegan Paul, 1962).
Festinger, L. (1949): 'The Analysis of Sociograms Using Matrix Algebra', *Human Relations*, II (1949) 153-8.
Fleming, C. M. (1955): 'The Child within the Group: The Bearings of Field Theory and Sociometry on Children's Classroom Behaviour', in *University of London Studies in Education, No. 7* (London: Evans, 1955).
Glanzer, M. and Glaser, R. (1959): 'Techniques for the Study of Group Structure and Behaviour, I: Analysis of Structure', *Psychol. Bull.* LVI (1959) 317-32.
Glanzer, M. and Glaser, R. (1961): 'Techniques for the Study of Group Struc-

ture and Bahaviour, II: Empirical Studies of the Effects of Structure in Small Groups', *Psychol. Bull.* LVIII (1961) 1-27.

Gronlund, N. E. (1959): *Sociometry in the Classroom* (New York: Harper, 1959).

Hallworth, H. J. (1952): 'A Study of Group Relationships among Grammar School Boys and Girls between the Ages of Eleven and Sixteen Years' (unpublished M.A. thesis, University of London, 1952).

Hargreaves, D. H. (1967): *Social Relations in a Secondary School* (London: Routledge & Kegan Paul, 1967).

Katz, L. (1947): 'On the Matrix Analysis of Sociometric Data', *Sociometry*, X (1947) 233-41.

Lewin, K. (1947): 'Frontiers in Group Dynamics: Concept, Method and Reality in Social Science; Social Equilibria and Social Change', *Human Relations*, I (1947) 5-41.

Maccoby, E. E., Newcomb, T. M. and Hartley, E. L. (1959): *Readings in Social Psychology* (London: Methuen, 1959).

McGrath, J. E. and Altman, I. (1966): *Small Group Research* (New York: Holt, 1966).

Moreno, J. L. (1953): *Who Shall Survive?* 2nd ed. (New York: Beacon House, 1953).

Muller, K. M. and Biggs, J. B. (1958): 'Attitude Change through Undirected Group Discussion', *J. Educ. Psychology*, XLIX (1958) 224-8.

Northway, M. L. (1953): *A Primer of Sociometry* (University of Toronto Press, 1953).

Oeser, O. E. (ed.) (1960): *Teacher, Pupil and Task: Elements of Social Psychology Applied to Education*, 2nd ed. (London: Tavistock, 1960).

Orth, C. D. (1963): *Social Structure and Learning Climate: The First Year at the Harvard Business School* (Division of Research, Graduate School of Business Administration, Harvard University, 1963).

Partridge, J. (1966): *Middle School* (London: Gollancz, 1966).

Phillips, B. N. and D'Amico, L. A. (1956): 'Effects of Co-operation and Competition on the Cohesiveness of Small Face-to-Face Groups', *J. Educ. Psychology*, XLVII (1956) 65-70.

Proctor, C. H. and Loomis, C. P. (1951): 'Analysis of Sociometric Data', in Jahoda, M., Deutsch, M. and Cook, S. W. *Research Methods in Social Relations*, part II (New York: Dryden Press, 1951).

Rasmussen, G. R. (1956): 'An Evaluation of a Student-Centred and Instructor-Centred Method of Conducting a Graduate Course in Education', *J. Educ. Psychology*, XLVII (1956) 449-61.

Richardson, J. E. (1948): 'An Investigation into Group Methods of Teaching English Composition, with some Consideration of their Effects on Attainment and Attitude and a Sociometric Study of the Two Groups of Children Involved' (unpublished M.A. thesis, University of London Library, 1948).

Shaw, M. E. (1954a): 'Some Effects of Problem Complexity upon Problem Solution Efficiency in Different Communication Nets', *Journal Exp. Psychol.* XLVIII (1954) 211-17.

Shaw, M. E. (1954b): 'Group Structure and the Behaviour of Individuals in Small Groups', *Journal Psychol.* XXXVIII (1954) 139-49.

Shaw, M. E. (1954c): 'Some Effects of Unequal Distribution of Information upon Group Performance in Various Communication Nets', *Journal Abn. and Soc. Psychol.* XLIX (1954) 547-53.

Shaw, M. E. (1956): 'Randon versus Systematic Distribution of Information in Communication Nets', *Journal of Personality*, XXV (1956) 59-69.

Shaw, M. E. (1958): 'Some Effects of Irrelevant Information upon Problem-Solving by Small Groups', *Journal Soc. Psychol.* XLVII (1958) 33-7.

Shaw, M. E. and Rothschild, G. H. (1956): 'Some Effects of Prolonged Experience in Communication Nets', *Journal Applied Psychol.* XL (1956) 281-6.

Smith, C. G. and Tannenbaum, A. S. (1965): 'Some Implications of Leadership and Control, for Effectiveness in a Voluntary Association', *Human Relations*, XVIII 3 (1965) 265-72.

Stogdill, R. M. (1948): 'Personal Factors Associated with Leadership: A Survey of the Literature', *Journal of Psychology*, XXV (1948) 35-71.

Tannenbaum, A. S. (1961): 'Control and Effectiveness in a Voluntary Organization', *Am. Journal Soc.* LXVII (1961) 33-46.

Thelen, H. A. (1954): *Dynamics of Groups at Work* (University of Chicago Press, 1954).

Thelen, H. A. (1960): *Education and the Human Quest* (New York: Harper & Row, 1960).

Webb, J. (1962): 'Sociology of a School', *British Journal of Sociology*, VIII 3 (1962) 264-72.

CHAPTER 10

References

1. Pask, G. 'Man as a System that Needs to Learn', in Stewart, D. (ed.) *Automaton Theory and Learning System* (London: Academic Press, 1967).

2. Pask G. *An Approach to Cybernetics* (London: Hutchinson, 1961).

3. Pressey, S. L. 'A Machine for Automatic Teaching of Drill Material', in *Teaching Machines and Programmed Learning*, I, ed. Lumsdaine, A. A. and Glaser, R. (National Education Association of the United States, 1960).

4. Skinner, B. F. 'Teaching Machines', in *Teaching Machines and Programmed Learning*, I, ed. Lumsdaine, A. A. and Glaser, R. (National Education Association of the United States, 1960).

5. Skinner, B. F. 'Reflections on a Decade of Teaching Machines', in *Teaching Machines and Programmed Learning*, II, ed. Glaser, R. (National Education Association of United States, 1965).

6. Holland, J. G. and Skinner, B. F. *The Analysis of Behaviour* (McGraw-Hill, 1961).

7. Glaser, R. 'Implications of Training Research', in *Theories of Learning and Instruction*, ed. Hilgard, E. R. (University of Chicago Press, 1964).

8. Markle, S. M. 'Programmed Instruction in English', in *Teaching Machines*

and Programmed Learning, I, ed. Lumsdaine, A. A. and Glaser, R. (National Education Association of the United States, 1960).

9. Gilbert, T. F. 'Mathetics, Technology of Education', *Journal of Mathetics*, I (1962).

10. Anderson, S. M. 'Whole versus Part Procedures for Teaching Children a Problem Solving Skill', *Journal of Educational Psychology* (in press).

11. Crowder, N. A. 'Automatic Tutoring by Intrinsic Programming', in *Teaching Machines and Programmed Learning*', I, ed. Lumsdaine, A. A. and Glaser, R. (National Education Association of the United States, 1960).

12. Galanter, E. (ed.) *Automatic Teaching. The State of the Art* (Wiley, 1959).

13. Lumsdaine, A. A. 'Assessing the Effectiveness of Instructional Programmes', in *Teaching Machines and Programmed Learning*, II, ed. Glaser, R. (National Education Association of the United States, 1965).

14. Stolhurow, L. M. 'Teaching by Machine', *O.E.* 34010, *Co-operative Research Monograph No 6* (Washington: U.S. Department of Health, Education, 1961).

15. Fry, E. *Teaching Machines and Programmed Instruction* (McGraw-Hill, 1963).

16. Atkinson, R. C. and Estes, W. K. 'Stimulus Sampling Theory', in *Handbook of Mathematical Psychology*, ed. Luce, R. D., Bush, R. R. and Galanter, E. (Wiley, 1963).

17. Matheson, J. E. 'Optimum Teaching Procedure Derived from Learning Models', *Report C.C.S. 2* (Stanford University, 1966).

18. Smallwood, R. D. *A Decision Structure for Teaching Machines* (M.I.T. Press, 1962).

19. Shuford, E. H., Albert, A. and Massigill, H. E. 'Admissible Probability Measurement Procedures', *Psychometrika*, XXXI 2 (July 1966).

20. Baker, J. 'The Uncertain Student and the Understanding Computer', in *Programmed Learning Research*, ed. Bressow, F., and Mowtmollin, M. (Paris, 1969).

21. Bitzer, D., Dichtenberger, W. and Bramfield, P. G. 'PLATO, an Automatic Teaching Device', *I.R.E. Transactions in Education*, vol. E-4 (Dec. 1961).

22. Rath, G. J. 'The Development of Computer Assisted Instruction', *I.E.E.E. Transactions on Human Factors in Electronics*, vol. H.F.E. 8, no. 2 (June 1967).

23. Coulson, J. E. 'A Computer Based Laboratory for Research in Education', in *Programmed Learning and Computer Based Instruction*, ed. Coulson, J. E. (Wiley, 1962).

24. Kay, H. and Sime, M. personal communications. (For a broad account of the viewpoint adopted, see also their book *Teaching Machines*, Penguin, 1968.)

25. Kopstein, F. 'The Amplified Teacher. The Guidance of Human Learning through Controlling Functional Automata', *Research Memorandum, RM-65-15* (Educational Testing Service, Oct 1965).

26. Seidel, R. J. and Kopstein, F. 'A General Systems Approach to the Development and Maintenance of Optimal Learning Conditions' (HumRRO, George Washington University, Professional Paper 1-68, Jan 1968).

27. Donnio, S. 'Les éléments du contrôle en enseignement programmé', in

Programmed Learning Research, ed. Bresson, M. and Montmollin, M. (Dunod, 1969).

28. Landa, L. *Diagnostique et enseignement programmé* (Paris: C.D.E.P. 1967).

29. Atkinson, R. C. and Dear, R. E. 'Optimal Allocation of Items in a Simple Two Concept Automated Teaching Model', in *Programmed Learning and Computer Based Instruction*, ed. Coulson, J. E. (Wiley, 1962).

30. Licklider, J. C. R. 'Preliminary Experiments in Computer Aided Teaching', in *Programmed Learning and Computer Based Instruction*, ed. Coulson, J. E. (Wiley, 1962).

31. Uttal, W. R. 'Conversational Interaction', in *Programmed Learning and Computer Based Instruction*, ed. Coulson, J. E. (Wiley, 1962).

32. Russian colleagues of Landa: One English translation, which also references much of the relevant work, is Lomov, B. F. *Man and Technology* (U.S. Department of Commerce, Office of Technical Services, O.T.S. 64 21030: Lenin State University, 1963).

33. Miller, G., Galanter, E., Pribram, K. H. *Plans and the Structure of Behaviour*.

34. Gagne, R. M. 'The Acquisition of Knowledge', *Psychological Review*, LXIX (1965).

35. Bird, J. B., Davies, I. K., Openshaw, D. and Thomas, C. A. *Programmed Learning in Perspective* (Lamson, 1963).

36. Glaser, R. 'Some Research Problems in Automated Instruction. Instructional Programming and Subject Matter Structure', in *Programmed Learning and Computer Based Instruction*, ed. Coulson, J. E. (Wiley, 1962).

37. Mann, P. 'A Survey of Programming Techniques', in *Mechanisation in the Classroom*, ed. Goldsmith, M. (Souvenir Press, 1963).

38. Davies, I. 'Mathetics' (Research Task 224, Technical Training Command).

39. Bilodeau, E. (ed.) *The Acquisition of Skill* (Academic Press, 1966).

40. Lewis, B. N. 'The Rationale of Adaptive Teaching Machines', in *Mechanisation in the Classroom*, ed. Goldsmith, M. (Souvenir Press, 1963).

41. Shoemake, H. A. and Holt, H. O. 'The Use of Programmed Instruction in Industry', in *Teaching Machines and Programmed Learning*, I, ed. Lumsdaine, A. A. and Glaser, R. (National Education Association of the United States, 1960).

42. Zopthkoff, E. Z. 'Heuristic Discussions of Psychological Bases for the Conduct of Training by Automatic Devices', in *Teaching Machines and Programmed Learning*, I, ed. Lumsdaine, A. A. and Glaser, R. (National Education Association of the United States, 1960).

43. Kelley C. R. 'Adaptive Performance Measurement' (Final Report, Dunlapp Associates, N.O.N.R. 498600, N.R. 196050).

44. Hudson, R. M. 'An Adaptive Tracking Simulator' (Otis Elevator Company Technical Report, 1965).

45. Gaines, B. 'Automated Feedback Trainers for Perceptual Motor Skills' (Final Report, Ministry of Defence, Sept 1967).

46. Pask, G. 'A Teaching Machine for Radar Training,' *Automation Progress* (April 1957).

47. Pask, G. 'Electronic Keyboard Teaching Machines,' *J. Nat. Assoc. Education and Commerce* (July 1958): reprinted in *Teaching Machines and Programmed Learning*, I, ed. Lumsdaine, A. A. and Glaser, R. (National Education Association of the United States, 1960).

48. Pask, G. 'The Teaching Machine as a Control Mechanism', *Trans. Soc. Instr. Technol.* (June 1960).

49. Pask, G. 'Interaction Betewen a Group of Subjects and an Adaptive Automaton to Produce a Self Organising System for Decision Making', in Yovits, M. C., Jacobi, G. T. and Goldstein, G. D. (eds.) *Self Organising Systems, 1962* (Washington: Spartan Press, 1962).

50. Pask, G. and Lewis, B. N. 'An Adaptive Automaton for Teaching Small Groups', *Perceptual and Motor Skills*, XIV (1962) 183.

51. Harlow, H. 'Learning Set and Error Factor Theory', in *Psychology, the Study of a Science*, ed. Koch, S. (McGraw-Hill, 1959).

52. Pask, G. 'Men, Machines and the Control of Learning', *Educational Technology*, VI 22 (Nov 1966).

53. Pask, G. and Lewis, B. N. 'The Adaptively Controlled Instruction of a Transformation Skill', *Programmed Learning* (Sweet & Maxwell, April 1967).

54. Pask, G. and Lewis, B. N. 'The Theory and Practice of Adaptive Teaching Systems', in Glaser, R. (ed.) *Teaching Machines and Programmed Learning* II: *Data and Directions* (Washington National Education Assoc. 1965) pp. 213-66.

55. Pask, G. 'Machines à Enseigner', *Cegos* (Paris, 1962).

56. Pask, G. and Lewis, B. N. 'Studies in the Acquisition of Simple and Complex Transformation Skills using a Null Point or Steady State Method', *British Journal of Math. and Stat. Psychology*, XXI i (May 1968) 61-84.

57. Pask, G. 'The Control of Learning in Small Subsystems of a Programmed Educational System', *I.E.E.E. Transactions on Human Factors in Electronics*, vol. H.F.E. 8, no. 2 (June 1967) 88-93.

58. Pask, G. 'Adaptive Teaching Machines', in Austwick, K. (ed.) *Teaching Machines* (London: Pergamon Press, 1964) pp. 79-112.

59. Pask, G. 'Adaptive Machines', in *Programmed Learning Research*, ed. Bressow, F., and Mowtmollin, M. (Paris, 1969).

60. Gagne, R. M. and Brown, L. T. 'Some Factors in the Programming of Conceptual Learning', *Journal of Experimental Psychology*, LXII 4 (Oct 1961).

61. Atkinson, R. E. and Shiffrin, R. M. 'Human Memory. A Proposed System and its Control Processes' (Institute for Mathematical Studies in the Social Sciences, Stanford University, Technical Report No. 110, March 1967).

62. Lewis, B. N. and Pask, G. 'The Development of Communication Skills under Adaptively Controlled Conditions', *Programmed Learning*, II 69-88.

63. Pask, G. and Lewis, B. N. 'An Adaptive Automaton for Teaching Small Groups', *Perceptual and Motor Skills*, XIV (1962) 183-8.

64. Pask, G. 'Interaction Between a Group of Subjects and an Adaptive Automaton to Produce a Self-organising System for Decision Making', in Yovits, M. C., Jacobi, G. T. and Goldstein, G. D. (eds) *Self Organising Systems, 1962* (Washington: Spartan Press, 1962).

65. Leonard, J. M. and Wing, R. L. 'Advantages of Using a Computer in Some Kinds of Educational Games', *I.E.E.E. Transactions on Human Factors in Electronics*, vol. H.F.E. 8, no. 2 (June 1967).

66. Bruner, J. S. 'The Will to Learn', *Commentary* (Feb 1966).

67. Bartlett, F. *Remembering* (Cambridge University Press, 1932).

68. Hodgson, A. 'A Communication Technique for the Future' (Goldsmiths' College, University of London, Ideas, Curriculum Laboratory, No. 7, April 1968).

69. Kopstein, F. and Seidel, R. J. 'Computer Administered Instruction versus Traditionally Administered Instruction. Economics' (HumRRO Professional Paper 31-67, June 1967).

70. Based on a consensus of opinion sampled at recent NATO Conference on Programmed Learning, Nice, 1968.

71. Cited in (69) as a figure based upon a software forecast by Dr D. E. Bitzer.

72. Feurzeig, W. and Papert, S. 'Programming Languages as a Conceptual Framework for Teaching Mathematics', in *Programmed Learning Research*, ed. Bressow, F., and Mowtmollin, M. (Paris, 1969).

Notes on the Contributors

J. DONALD BOWEN, b. Malad, Idaho, U.S.A., 1922; B.A. Brigham Young University, 1947; M.A. Columbia University, 1949; Ph.D. University of New Mexico, 1963. Consultant at various times to Bureau of Indian Affairs; Centre of Applied Linguistics, India, English Teaching Survey; Agency for International Development, SEAMES survey. Presently Professor of English, University of California, and Field Director of the Survey of Language Use and Language Teaching in Eastern Africa. Professor Bowen has been a delegate to the Inter-American Symposium on Linguistics and Language Teaching since 1963. His publications include: *The Grammatical Structures of English and Spanish* (1965); *The Sounds of English and Spanish* (1965); *Patterns of Spanish Pronunciation* (1960). He has edited many publications and contributed a large number of articles in his fields of interest.

JOHN F. LAVACH, b. Teaneck, New Jersey, 1936. B.A. Montclair State College, N.J., 1961; M.A. (*magna cum laude*) Fairleigh Dickinson University, 1965; D.Ed. Duke University, N.C., 1965. Assistant to the Vice President for Institutional Research at Duke University, presently Professor of Psychology at the College of William and Mary in Williamsburg, Virginia.

G. O. M. LEITH was (1968-9) Visiting Professor of Psychology at the Memorial University of Newfoundland. He was Director of the National Centre for Programmed Learning at Birmingham University, where he carried out a programme of research on educational technology for six years and with his colleagues built up an advanced course in programmed learning and educational technology. He is a member of the National Council for Educational Technology and a number of other committees, was organiser of the 1967 annual conference of the Association for Programmed Learning and Educational Technology (of which he is a Vice President and was, until 1968, assistant editor of its journal). His writings can be found in *A Handbook of Programmed Learning, What is Programmed Learning?* and in journals such as *Educational Research, Educational Review, Visual Education, Canadian Journal of Behavioural Sciences, Special Education, Impact of Science on Society.* Professor Leith has worked for B.B.C. television and radio and as a UNESCO consultant in educational technology and curriculum development. He is presently Director of the Reginald M. Phillips Research Centre at the University of Sussex.

JOHN L. LEWIS, formerly a scholar of Pembroke College, Cambridge, is at present the Senior Science Master at Malvern College. He was involved in the work of the Association for Science Education in curriculum development in the late 1950s as a member of the physics panel and later as chairman of the Modern Physics Committee. In 1962 he became Associate Organiser of the Nuffield Physics Project and is a member of the Joint Committee for the Nuffield

'A' level projects in physics, chemistry and physical science. He is chairman of the Apparatus Committee of the Association for Science Education. He is a member of the International Commission on Physics Education and has been a consultant to UNESCO and O.E.C.D. on science educational matters.

R. K. MUIR, b. 1932, South Africa; B.A. University of the Witwatersrand, 1951; B.Ed. first class honours, University of the Witwatersrand, 1961; Transvaal Teachers Diploma, 1952; Lecturer, Department of Education, University of the Witwatersrand; Secretary, New Education Fellowship. Publications include: 'Leadership in a Dual Cultural Setting: A Sociometric Study', *British Journal of Educational Psychology*, xxx 3 (1963); 'The African's Drive for Education in S. Africa', *Comparative Education Reveiw*, ix 3 (1965).

GORDON PASK is Director of Research, System Research Ltd, and Professor in the Institute of Cybernetics, Brunel University, and Professor in the I.E.T., The Open University. He was educated at Cambridge University (M.A. in physiology) and at London University (Ph.D. in psychology). Most of his work has been in the fields of teaching, especially with adaptively controlled teaching systems; the psychology of learning and the cybernetics of self-organising and evolutionary systems. He writes and paints pictures.

SIR JAMES PITMAN, K.B.E., b. London, 1901; M.A. Oxford, 1928; Hon. D.Hum.Litt. (Hofstra, U.S.A.) 1969; Hon. D.Litt. (Strathclyde) 1970; Hon. D.Litt. (Bath) 1970; Director of the Bank of England, 1941-5; first Director of Organisation and Methods at the Treasury, 1943-5; M.P. (Con.) for Bath, 1945-64; President of the Association of Technical Institutions, 1962-3; a former Chairman of the British and Foreign Schools Society, and of the family firm, Sir Isaac Pitman & Sons (founded by his grandfather in 1840). Currently a Director of Boots Pure Drug Co. Ltd, Bovril Ltd and the Equity and Law Life Assurance Society; Vice-Chairman of the Management Committee of London University Institute of Education; and Charter Pro-Chancellor of Bath University of Technology.

ERNEST W. RAYNER, b. Johannesburg, South Africa, 1920. M.B., B.Ch. University of Cape Town, 1944. Specialisation in neurology and psychiatry; University of the Witwatersrand 1956. Senior Psychiatrist, Tara Hospital, 1963-5. Principal Psychiatrist at the Johannesburg Hospital and Senior Professional Assistant, Department of Psychiatry in the University of the Witwatersrand. Head of the Child and Family Unit, Transvaal Memorial Hospital for Children.

BRIAN ROSE, b. London, 1915, educated at Trinity College, Dublin; Hons B.A. (*cum laude*), University of South Africa, 1948; M.A. University of the Witwatersrand, 1952; Ph.D. University of the Witwatersrand, 1963. After twenty years of experience as a teacher, he was appointed Senior Lecturer to the Johannesburg College of Education in 1957, and Head of the Department of Education in 1970. He lectures at the University of the Witwatersrand in communication studies. He was awarded a United States–South Africa Leader Exchange Grant in 1964, and lectured at Mount Holyoke College, Massachusetts, in the Department of Psychology and Education during 1968-9. Articles by him have been published in the *South African Journal of Science*, *Medical Proceedings* (*S. Africa*), *The Times* (London), *Audiovisual Education* (Washington, U.S.A.), *Mental Health* (London); books include: *Education in Southern Africa*, *Modern Narrative Verse* and *Commonwealth Short Stories*.

LEONARD SEALEY, b. London and educated in England; trained at Loughborough College of Technology, Peterborough College of Education and Leicester University, served with the Royal Navy as aeronautical engineer. He was for nine years Adviser to Junior Schools in Leicestershire, and played a key role in the reform of primary education in that county. More recently he was Principal of the North Buckinghamshire College of Education in Bletchley. He has worked with UNESCO in the field of mathematics teaching, has served as consultant to the *Encyclopaedia Britannica*, Rank-R.E.C., and has worked with the Schools Council in the United Kingdom and with the British Council in tropical Africa. He has published a variety of works relating to elementary education. During 1968 he was the Director of a regional educational laboratory programme in the United States and now works as a full-time writer and consultant.

Index

Abbots Laboratories, 194
Adams and Smith Report, 85
Adaptive instruction and machines, 250–5: models, 252; error factor theory, 252 and n.; metasystems, 253–5
Agranoff, B. W., 193
Alexander, Sir William, 7 n.
Allen, L., 187
Altman, I., 203–5
Approach to the Electron, An, Esso film, 115
As DIFFICULT as ABC (Pitman), 27 n.
Association, 154
Association for Science Education, 103, 105
Association of Teachers in Mathematics, 71
Atkinson, R. C., 234, 247 n.
Ausubel, D. P., 86–8

Baker, J., 231
Baller, 188
Bartlett, F., 257
Bavelas, A. A., 205
Bayley, Nancy, 183, 187
Behavioural learning theory, 99
Bender-Gestalt, 46
Bennett, 256 and n.
Benton Test, 46
Berkeley Growth Study, 187
Bernstein, B., 79–82: on formal and public language, 80–1; on the restricted code, 81-2
Biggs, Edith, 71
Biggs, J. B., 200
Bilingual education, 134
Binet, Alfred, and Binet intelligence scale, 180
Biochemical research, 183–5
Bion, W. F., 177, 208
Blau, P. M., 209
Bloom, B., 93–4, 189
Booth, Mrs Vera, 20
Borgatta, E. F., 201, 203–5

Bossio, V., 78, 79
Bowen, J. Donald, 99: 'Recent Development in Second Language Teaching', 122-37
Brain function and reading process, 34-7: defects in secondary sensory areas, 35-6
Branching technique and programmes, 143–6, 160: teaching machines, 224–8
Bruner, Jerome, 62, 70, 189, 257: theory of mental growth, 70; and problem-solving, 192–3
Burt, Cyril, 182

C.A.I. (computer-assisted instruction), 231–4, 255, 258–9
Cartwright, D., 198, 202
Cattell, R. B., 179, 181
Central vowel, 26
Cerebral dominance, 47, 260
Changing Curriculum, The: Mathematics (1967), 72
Charles, 188
Chauncey, H., 78–9
Coles, R., 85
Colorado State Department of Education, 64
Combs, Arthur W., 183–4
Communication studies, 205–6. *See also* Structural communication teaching
Complex organisations, study of groups by theorists in field of, 208–12: structure and effectiveness of voluntary organisations, 208–9; group structures and individual behaviour, 209; study of schools, 209–10, 212; concept of compliance, 210–11
Computers: and teaching of mathematics, 67–8, 75; and teaching machines, 231–4, 255, 257–9
Concepts: formation of, 155; integration, 156–7; conceptual learning, 163

287

Concrete materials and operations, 68–70, 73
Conditional reflex therapy, 57
Critical path analysis, 152
Critical periods concept, 6, 36, 79, 82–6, 260
Crowder, N. A., 144, 152, 227
Cuisenaire Rods, 69, 72, 163
Cultural deprivation, 5–6, 77–94: differentiated from dyslexia and mental subnormality, 77–8; intellectual capacity or potential, 78–9; standard intelligence tests, 79; lower standards of language ability, 80–2; formal and public language, 80–1; restricted code, 81–2; stimulus deprivation, 82–3; Negro children, 84–5, 88; prevention and therapy, 87; 'rescue work' in preschool stage, 87–8; special curricula, 88–9; primary and secondary prevention, 89; starting with the child, 90–1; research work, 92–3; training of teacher college staff, 93–4; large numbers involved, 94
Cultural factors and measurement of intelligence, 184–8: individual and group tests, 185; maze learning studies, 186, 194; stability of I.Q scores, 186–7; intelligence related to other characteristics, 187–8
Cultural factors and the reading process, 38
Cybernetics, viii, xiii, 144, 177, 216, 222

Dalton Plan, the, 169
D'Amico, L. A., 200
Davies, Ivor, 247 n.
Davis, Allison, 79
Davis, Professor Robert, 67, 72–3
Depressed intellectual functioning, 188–9
Deutsch, Martin, 94, 199–200, 202: on stimulus deprivation and the socially deprived, 82–3
Developmental psychology, 5, 6, 62, 68–70, 82–4, 86, 89, 92

Diaphones, 28 and n., 31
Dienes, Zoltan, 69, 73: Multibase Arithmetical Blocks, 72, 163
Dizygotic twins, 47, 260
Donnio, S., 234
Dowley, E. M., 89
Downing, John, 7–8 n., 9, 14, 17, 19
Dreger, R. M., 184–5
Drugs and brain function, 183–5
Dyslexia, 4, 39, 41, 43–8, 77–9: genetic, 47

Education in revolution, viii–x: human explosion, ix, x; explosion of knowledge, ix–x; youth as a world power, x; universal primary education demanded as basis for literacy, x
Educational factors and the reading process, 38
Educational Services Inc., 115 n.
Educational treatment of reading retardation, 54–6: state of the child, 54–5; physical setting, 55; milieu of programme, 55; frequency, 55–6; methods, 56
Edwards, A. J., 185
Eells, K., 184
Electroencephalograms, 47, 260
Electromagnetic Kit, The, Esso film, 115
Eliot, T. S., xi
Elvin, Lionel, 7–8 n.
Environmental explanations of intelligence, 175, 181–4
Erikson, Erik, 82
Error factor theory, 252 and n.
Esso Petroleum educational films, 115
Estes, W. K., 228 n.
Etzioni, A., 210–12
Evaluating the Initial Teaching Alphabet (Downing), 15 n.
Evans, K. M., 214
Eysenck, H. J., 179

Factor theories of intelligence, 180–1
Fantini, M. D., 91
Festinger, L., 202, 214
Feurzeig, W., 255
Films in science education, 114–16

Flavell, J. H., 82–4
Fleming, C. M., 207
Flexner, J. B. and L. B., 193
Fluid and crystallised intelligence theory, 181
Ford Foundation, 91
Fowler, W., 89
Freeman, F. N., 183
Friedman, Professor, 154
Froebel's 'First Building Box', ix
Frog Development – Fertilization to Hatching, teaching film, 115 n.
Frost, J. E., 94
Frostig Test, 16

Gagne, R. M., 242, 246
Galanter, E., 228, 236
Galton, Francis, 179
Gattegno, Caleb, 69
Genetic explanations of intelligence, 181–4
Geneva School, the, 190. *See also* Piaget, Jean
Germany and science education, 105
Gilbert, T. F., 221, 223
Gilgash, Curtis A., 194
Glanzer, M., 205, 214
Glaser, Robert, 67, 169 n., 205, 214, 221, 246 n., 247 n.
Goals for Mathematical Education of Elementary School Teachers, Cambridge Conference Report (1967), 63
Goals for School Mathematics, Cambridge Conference Report (1963), 62–3
Goldfarb, W., 79
Gordon, Edward M., 189
Gordon, H., 85
Gould, Sir Ronald, 7 n.
Gray, S. W., 92
Great Cities School Improvement Project, 91
Gronlund, N. E., 214
Group dynamics approach, 202–8: topology and field forces, 202–3; phase space, 203; variables and their classification, 203–6; communication studies, 205–6; T-groups, 207–8

Group intelligence tests, 185
Group research and educational practice, 177, 196–215: facts and value judgements, 197–8; Lippitt and White study, 198–9; studies of group work in classroom, 200–1; small groups and group dynamics approach, 202 8; study by theorists in complex organisations field, 208–12; sociometry, 212–14
Guilford, J. P., 181, 189

Haggard, E. A., 78, 80
Hallgren, B., 47
Hallworth, H. J., 200
Hargreaves, D. H., 212
Harley, Randall, 31
Harlow, H. F., 154: error factor theory, 252 and n.
Harms, Ernest, 189
Harvard Business School, 209–10
Harvard University Centre for Cognitive Studies, 62
Hawkes, G. R., 94
Hawthorne Effect, 18–19, 183
Hawthorne Works, Mayo study at, 208
Haywood, H. Carl, 189
Hess, D., 82
Higher Horizons program, New York, 91
Hinton, R. T., 183
Hodgson, A., 256 and n.
Holland, J. G., 221
Holzinger, K. J., 183
Homme, 246 n., 247 n.
Honzik, Marjorie, 183, 187
HumRRO C.A.I. system, 233
Hunt, 183
Hyden, 193, 195
Hypothetico-deductive inference, 157–8

I.B.M. 150 C.A.I. system, 233
I Do and I Understand, educational film, 71
Individually Prescribed Instruction system, 67

Initial Teaching Alphabet (i.t.a.), viii and n., xiii, 3, 7–31: support for trial, 9; beginning of teaching, 9; report (*i.t.a. Symposium*), 9–10, 15, 17; positive purpose, 7–21, 25–31; objective evaluations, 9–15; reading readiness, 10–13; first standard of achievement, 10; comparisons of facility in learning, 11–15; transition in reading, 15–17; transition in writing, 17; self-expression in writing, 17–18; Hawthorne Effect, 18–19; greater enthusiasm for reading, 19; more interest in books, 19; overseas success, 20; Schools Council report, 20–1; negative purpose, 7, 21–5; effect on spelling reform, 21–3; desire for new writing alphabet, 23–4; future of i.t.a., 24–31; permissiveness in spelling, 25–6; elimination of difficulties from T.O., 27–31

Initial Teaching Braille, 31
Institut des Sciences de l'Education, Geneva, 64
Institute of Development Studies, New York, 83
Institute of Physics Bulletin, 101
Intelligence in modern education, 176, 179–95: nature of intelligence, 179–81; divergent views, 179; early tests, 180; I.Q., 180, 182–9; factor theories, 180–1; primary mental abilities theory, 181; genetic, environmental and interactional explanations, 181–4; cultural factors and measurement of intelligence, 184–8; depressed intellectual functioning, 188–9; modern interpretations of intelligence and intellectual development, 189–93; Piaget's work, 190–2; problem-solving, 192–3; biological research, 193–5

Introduction to Radioactivity, Esso film, 115
I.Q. tests and standard intelligence tests, 78, 79, 86, 89, 90, 180, 182–9,

194; individual and group tests, 185; stability of I.Q. scores, 186–7
Irwin, Orvis, 93
i.t.a., *see* Initial Teaching Alphabet
i.t.a.: An Independent Evaluation (report of the Schools Council), 20 n.
i.t.a. Foundation, 21 and n.
i.t.a. Reading Experiment, The (Downing), 19
i.t.a. Symposium, The, 7–8 n., 9–10, 15, 17

James, Walter, 7–8 n.
Jensen, Arthur R., 80, 175

Katz, L., 214
Kay, H., 233
Kersh, B. Y., 168
Kinaesthetic sense, 56, 260
Kirby, Elsie M., 185
Klaus, R. A., 92
Koegler, 79
Kopstein, F., 233
Kunce, Joseph, 186

Landa, L., 234
Language inadequacy in culturally deprived children, 80–2
Language laboratories, 131–2
Language Teaching Analysis (Mackey), 125
Larson, R. G., 88–9
Lavach, John F., 176: 'The Meaning and Use of Intelligence in Modern Education', 179–95
Lazarus, R. S., 85
Lawton, D., 81
Learning-set formation, 154–5
Learning systems, design and evaluation, 168–71
Leiman, Arnold L., 193
Leith, G. O. M., 100: 'Programmed Instruction', 138–71
Lewin, Kurt, 198: and group dynamics, 202–3
Lewis, John L., 97–8: 'New Trends in Science Education', 101–21

Licklider, J. C. R., 234
Linear programming, 141–3, 146: teaching machines, 220–4
Linguistics, 126–30: descriptive or structural, 126–8; transformational analysis, 128–30
Lippitt and White study, 198, 199, 202
Lock-step teaching, 169
London University Institute of Education, 9, 21 n.
Loomis, C. P., 214
Lumsdaine, A. A., 228

McBroom, E., 84
Maccoby, E. F., 198
McConnell, J. V., 194
Macfarlane, Jean W., 187
McGaugh, 194
McGrath, J. E., 203–5
Mackey, William P., 125
Madison Project, the, 67
Markle, S. M., 221
Massachusetts Institute of Technology, 202
Mathematics in Primary Education (Dienes), 73
Mathematics, teaching of elementary, 5, 60–76, 97: use of terms 'new' and 'modern', 61–2; fresh content in curriculum, 61; upgrading and reformulation, 61–2; relevance to industry and commerce, 62; psychological considerations and new approaches, 62, 68–70; training and retraining of teachers, 63, 75; evaluation, 63; behavioural objectives, 64; change from 'arithmetic' to 'mathematics', 65; emphasis on structure, 65–6; rejection of rote learning, 66; process of abstraction, 66; creation of positive attitudes, 66–7; motivational aspects, 66–7; reform of mathematical language, 68; concrete materials and operations, 68–70, 73; work in schools, 70–4; Nuffield Project, 63, 64, 72, 74; classification of new approaches, 73; symbol-game-oriented approach,

73–4; looking ahead, 75–6; 'premathematics', 76
Matheson, J. E., 228
Mathetics, 154, 223, 259 n.
Mathews, Geoffrey, 72
Mayo study at Hawthorne Works, 208
Maze learning studies, 186, 194
Measurement of Understanding, *The* 148
Meddleton, I. G., 141
Medical treatment of reading retardation, 56–7
Memorial University, 170
Memory transfer, 193–4
Mental subnormality, 77–8
Michigan, University of, 202
Miles, Matthew, 176
Miller, G., 236
Miller, K. S., 184–5, 188
Models for teaching machines, 217, 234–40: optimality and choice of models, 228–9; stochastic learning models, 228; for adaptive instruction, 252
Models of programmed learning, 139–45: adjunctive programming, 139–40; reinforcement, 140; linear programming, 141–3; branching technique, 143–5
Modern English (Rutherford), 130
Momentum and Collision Processes, Esso film, 115
Monozygotic twins, 47, 260
More Effective Schools program, New York, 91
Moreno, J. L., 177, 213
Muir, R. K., 177: 'The Influence of Group Research on Educational Practice', 196–215
Muller, K. M., 200
Multilingualism, 98
Munn, Norman, L., 179
Mussen, P. II., 82

National Foundation for Educational Research, 21
National Science Foundation (U.S.A.), 63

National Training Laboratory in Group Development, Bethel, Maine, 208
Negro problem in America, 5: educational performance of children, 5, 84–5, 88
Network analysis, 152
Neurological research, 183–5
Neurotic children, 42
New York education programs, 91
Newman, H. H., 183
Normal and abnormal reading process, underlying factors, 34–43: brain function, 34–7: social, cultural and educational factors, 38; psychological factors, 38–43
Northway, M. L., 213, 214
Nourissier, François, x
Nuffield Foundation, 72, 105
Nuffield Mathematics Project, 63, 64, 72–4: publications, 72
Nuffield Physics Project, 97: content of programmes, 108–11; question-books, 113; Esso films, 115; examination questions, 117–20
Nuffield science teaching projects, 105–6, 112, 121

Object-game-oriented approach to mathematics, 73, 74
Objectives of education, notion of, 147–50
Oeser, O. E., 208
Olson, J. L., 88–9
Oppenheimer, Robert, ix
Organicity, 44, 260
Orth, C. D., 209–10

Papert, S., 255
Parent Teacher Associations, 53
Paromycin, injection of, 193
Partridge, J., 212
Pask, Gordon, vii, xiii, 177–8: 'Teaching Machines', 216–59
Peabody College Intervention Project, 92–3
Perceptual-motor function and difficulties, 44, 46–7, 260

PERT analysis, 152
Phase space, 203
Phillips, B. N., 200
Phonemes, 28 and n.
Physical Sciences Study Committee (P.S.S.C.), 104–6, 112, 120
Piaget, Jean, vii, 138, 163, 189–92: developmental psychology, 5, 6, 62, 68–70, 82–4, 86, 89, 92: critical periods concept, 6, 82–4, 86; and stages of development, 190–2
Pitman, Sir Isaac, 23
Pitman, Sir James, viii n., xiii, 3: 'The Purpose, Meaning and Future of i.t.a.', 7–31
PLATO C.A.I. system, University of Illinois, 232–3, 255
Plotnikoff, 194
Plowden Report (Report of the Central Advisory Council for Education (England) (1966)), 67, 80, 82, 85, 89
Polansky, 202
Population explosion, the, ix, 94
'Pre-mathematics', 76
Preschool children and prediction of reading failure, 47–8
Pressey, Sidney L., 99, 139, 146, 221
Pribram, K. H., 236
Primary mental abilities theory, 181
Problem-solving, 157–8, 192–3
Proctor, C. H., 214
Programmed instruction, viii, 99–100, 138–71: and language learning, 132–3; models of programmed learning, 139–45; teaching machines, 145–7; objectives of education, 147–50; sequence of steps, 150–2; Ruleg system, 150–1; task analysis, 152–8; taxonomy of learning processes, 158–68; design and evaluation of learning systems, 168–71
P.S.S.C., see Physical Sciences Study Committee
Psychological factors and the reading process, 38–43: kindly authoritarian homes, 38–9; overprotective homes, 39; overindulgent homes, 40–1;

Psychological factors (cont.)
inconsistent homes, 41–2; neurotic
children, 42; psychotic children, 42
Psychological treatment of reading
retardation, 57–8; the child, 57;
parents, 57 8; the teacher, 58
Psychologist and the Foreign Language
Teacher, The (Rivers), 130

Rasmussen, G. R., 200
Rawls, Mrs Rachel, 31
Rayner, Ernest W., 4–5: 'Reading
Retardation', 32–59
Razan, 99
Reading retardation, 4, 32–59: definition and frequency, 32–3; reading age (R.A.) and mental age
(M.A.), 32, 33; factors underlying
normal and abnormal reading process, 34–43; prognosis, 58–9
recognition of the disorder, 43–
50: the child at school, 43–7; act of
reading, 44–5; reading process disturbances, 45; associated problems,
45–7; preschool children and prediction of reading failure, 47–
8; differential diagnosis, 48–50
ripple effect, 50–4: the child
himself, 50–1; parents and siblings,
52; teachers, 52–3; friends and
social activities, 53 4
treatment, 54–8: educational 54–
6; medical, 56–7; psychological,
57–8
Relaxed vowel, 26
Response information, 230–1: scoring
and scoring schemes, 230–1
Responses: integration, 153–4: novel
responses, 153
Resines, Salazar, 241 n., 242
Restricted code, concept of, 81–2
Reymert, M. L., 183
Richardson, J. E., 200
Riessman, F., 77, 78, 80, 94
Ripple effect of reading retardation,
50–4
Rivers, Wilga, 130–1
RNA (ribonucleic acid), 193, 194

Roberts, S. O., 85
Rogers, Professor Eric, 107, 119–20
Rose, Brian: 'The Culturally De-
prived Child', 77–94
Rosenzweig, Mark R., 193
Rothschild, G. H., 205
Ruleg programming system, 150–1,
246 n.
Russell, D. H., 190
Rutherford, William E., 130

Schonell Graded Tests, 15–17, 141
Schouland, Sir Basil, 178
School Science Review, 103
Schools Council: report on i.t.a., 20–1;
Curriculum Bulletin No. 1, 'Mathematics in Primary Schools' (1965),
71, 72; and Nuffield Mathematics
Project, 72
Schwa vowel, 26
Science education: new trends in,
97–8, 101–21; dissatisfaction with
existing conditions, 101; study of
examination papers, 101–3; self-
perpetuating system, 103; history of
recent changes, 103–8; reform of
syllabus, 103–4; call for complete
new programme, 104–8; influence of
of U.S.A. and U.S.S.R., 104–5;
Nuffield projects, 105–6; international experience, 106; content of
Nuffield Physics programme, 108–
11; teachers' guides, 111–12; role of
textbooks, 112–13; experimental
work, 113–14; films and visual aids,
114–16; examination questions, 116–
20; applied science, 120; projects,
120–1; teacher training, 121
Scott, W. R., 209
S.D.C. CLASS C.A.I. system, 233 n.
Sealey, Leonard, 5: 'The Teaching of
Elementary Mathematics', 60–76
Sears, P. S., 89
Secondary sensory areas, defects in,
352–6: constitutional defects, 35;
damage due to disease, 35; stimulus
deprivation, 36

Second-language teaching, recent developments in, 98–9, 122–37: basic idea, 123–4; 'direct method', 124–5; linguistics, 126–30; transformational analysis, 128–30; programmed instruction, 132–3; bilingual education, 134; E.S.L. for native speakers of English, 134

Seidel, R. J., 233

Sequential teaching machines, 220–34: linear programme, 220–4; 'classical' technique, 222–3; mathetics, 223; branching programmes, 224–8; skip linear programme networks, 227; optimality and the choice of models, 228–9; response information, 230–1; computer-assisted instruction (C.A.I.), 231–4

Servan Schreiber, xi

Shaw, Bernard: desire for new writing alphabet, 24–5

Shaw, M. E., 205

Shuford, E. H., 230

Silberman, Charles E., 79, 85

Sime, M., 233

Skeels, H. M., 183–4

Skill instruction and teaching machines, 250–5: adaptive machines 250–3; models for adaptive instruction, 252; adaptive metasystems, 253–5

Skinner, B. F., vii, 99, 140–2, 152, 161: techniques of programming, 141–2, 144, 146; teaching machines, 146, 221

Skip linear programme networks, 227

Skodak, M., 183

Small group theory and research, viii, xii

Smallwood, R. D., 228 n.

Smedslund, J., 191

Smilansky, Moshe, 87–9, 92

Smith, C. G., 209

Social factors and the reading process, 38

Sociometry and study of groups, 213–14: definitions of sociometric test, 213; the sociomatrix, 214; application to school classes, 214

Sociopathic personality, 41, 260

Southgate, Vera, 20

Spearman, Charles, 180–1

Speech delay, 46

Spelling reform: effect of i.t.a., 24; permissiveness in spelling, 25–6

Stanford–Binet intelligence scale, 180, 185–7

Status-orientated code, 81–2 Stellar, E., 193

Stern, Catherine, 69

Stimulus deprivation, 36: and the socially deprived, 82–3

Stochastic learning models, 228

Stogdill, R. M., 205

Stolhurow, L. M., 228

Structural communication teaching, 256–7

Strychnine, injection of, 194

Sullivan, Arthur, 170 n.

Suppes, Professor Patrick, 68

Symbol-game-oriented approach to mathematics, 73–4

Syntax difficulties in speech, 46

Szekely, J., 167

Szold Institute, 87

T-groups, 207–8

Tannenbaum, A. S., 208, 209

Task analysis, 152–8: distinction between stimuli, 153; novel responses, 153; response integration, 153–4; mathetics, 154; association or 'hook-up', 154; trial-and-error learning, 154; learning-set formation, 154–5; forming concepts, 155–6; concept integration, 156–7; problem-solving, 157–8

Tavistock Institute, 208

Taxonomy of Educational Objectives (Bloom *et al.*), 148

Taxonomy of learning processes, 158–68: size of step, 160; overt constructed responses, 160; prevention of errors, 160; verbal learning, 160–1; self-pacing, 161–2; individual learning, 162–4; conceptual learn-

Taxonomy (cont.)
ing, 163–4; elimination of individual differences in achievement, 164–6; incompatibility between programming and discovery, 166–7; teacher's role, 167–8
Teacher college staff, training of, 93–4
Teachers. changing image, x–xi; the new teacher, x–xiii; and reading retardation, 52–3, 57–8; role in programmed learning, 167–8
Teachers' guides in science programmes, 111–12
Teaching machines, viii, 99, 216–59: teaching or training as control of learning, 216; mechanisation, 216–17; models, 217; form of teaching system, 217–18; subject matter, 218–19; skill and knowledge, 218; machines, 219–20; sequential machines, 220–34; computer systems, 231–4, 255, 257–9; programming operations, 234–52; outline of programming model, 234–40; goal-directed systems, 234–40; simple partially adaptive programming system, 241–50; skill instruction, 250–5; structural communication teaching, 256–7; motivation effects, 257–8; choice of teaching system, 258–9
Tel Aviv University, Department of Educational Sciences, 87
Terman, Lewis, 179, 180, 187–8
Textbooks in science programming, 112–13
Thelen, Herbert, 176, 208
Thorndike, Edward L., 181
Thurstone, Louis, 181
Times Educational Supplement, The, 7–9

TOTE (Test Operate Test Exit) units, 236–40, 244, 248, 251, 252
Traditional orthography (T.O.), 8, 10–17, 21, 23, 24–8
Training: of teachers in mathematics, 63, 75; of teacher college staff, 93–4; of science teachers, 121
Transformational analysis, 128–30
Trial-and-error learning, 154
Tyler, Ralph, 147

U.S.S.R. and science education, 104–5
Uttal, W. R., 234

Varma, R. M., 188
Verbal and non-verbal ability, 46
Vernon, Philip, E., 186
Visual aids in science education, 114–16; overhead projectors, 115; transparencies, 115

Wall, William, 7 n., 9–10
Warburton, Professor F. W., 20
Webb, J., 212
Wechsler and Wechsler–Bellvue intelligence scales and tests, 185, 187, 194
Weinstein, G., 91
Western Electric Company, 208
W.H.O. Report on Deprivation of Maternal Care (1962), 82
Who Shall Survive? (Moreno), 213
Whowill, J. F., 191
Worcester Circuit Board, The, Esso film, 115
Word blindness, 4

Yamamoto, 188

Zacharias, Professor, 104
Zander, A., 198, 202

DATE DUE

DEMCO 38-297